ANIMALS IN THE
MIDDLE AGES

ANIMALS IN THE
MIDDLE AGES

EDITED BY
NONA C. FLORES

ROUTLEDGE
NEW YORK AND LONDON

First paperback edition published in 2000 by
Routledge
29 West 35th Street
New York, NY 10001

Published in Great Britain by
Routledge
11 New Fetter Lane
London EC4P 4EE

Routledge is an imprint of the Taylor & Francis Group

Copyright © 1996 by Nona C. Flores
Previously published in hardback as vol.1716 in the Garland Reference Library of the Humanities.

Library of Congress Cataloging-in-Publication Data

Animalsin the Middle Ages / edited by Nona C. Flores.
     p.   cm.
   Includes index.
   ISBN 0-8153-1315-2 (alk. paper)
   ISBN 0-415-92893-1(pbk.)
     1. Animals — Folklore. 2. Animals, Mythical. 3. Art, Medieval.
   4. Bestiaries in art. 5. Bestiaries in literature. I. Flores, Nona C.
GR705.A54   1996
39802'094'045—dc20   95-30586
                                                             CIP

Printed on acid-free, 250-year-life paper
Manufactured in the United States of America

10 9 8 7 6 5 4 3 2 1

CONTENTS

ACKNOWLEDGMENTS

A collection of essays such as this represents the scholarly labor of many individuals. I would like to thank the authors of these essays for sharing their work with me, for being so accommodating to my comments and requests about their articles, and for their patience and rapid replies to queries during the long process of editing and publication. I've enjoyed working with all of them.

As series editor, Joyce Salisbury has been a pleasure to work with: discerning in her criticism, prompt with her comments and help, and always encouraging toward a hesitant editor.

I would like to acknowledge Janetta Rebold Benton, with whom I organized several sessions on animals in medieval literature and art (formally titled "The Medieval Menagerie" but known more jocularly as "The Zoo at Ka'zoo") at the International Congress on Medieval Studies meetings held at Western Michigan University in 1988–1991 and 1994. Her friendship and support have been much appreciated.

Finally, special thanks go to my mentor John Block Friedman of the University of Illinois at Urbana-Champaign, who was the first to encourage me in the scholarly pursuit of such medieval creatures as the barnacle goose, the vegetable lamb, and the woman-headed snake. Whatever iconographic acumen I have developed is the result of his rigorous tutelage.

This collection is dedicated in memoriam to Homer, a dachshund "of infinite jest, of most excellent fancy."

INTRODUCTION

Omnis mundi creatura
Quasi liber et pictura
Nobis est et speculum.[1]

In the twelfth century, Alan of Lille explained, "Every creature of the world / Is like a book and a picture / To us, and a mirror." The essays in this collection focus on animals not as literal living organisms—food, prey, possessions, or companions to man—but as symbols, ideas, or images during the Middle Ages.[2]

The association of animals with symbolism during this period is largely due to the influence of the *Physiologus* and its later development, the bestiary. The origins, relationships between, and contributing sources of these works are better covered elsewhere,[3] but a brief summary might be in order here for readers less familiar with them. The *Physiologus*, or *The Naturalist*, was a Greek text originating in Alexandria, possibly as early as the second century A.D. It is a compilation of the supposed natural characteristics of some forty animals, birds, reptiles, fish, and mystic stones, which are then allegorized in terms of Christian dogma. The *Physiologus* interpreted the world in a moral and metaphysical sense in order to introduce its readers to the Christian mysteries, and was never intended, as Michael Curley has pointed out, to be read as a work of natural history.[4] Its author drew on the compilations and descriptions of classical naturalists such as Aristotle, Pliny, Oppian, Aelian, and Solinus and on folklore and oral tradition, rather than on direct observations of living creatures. He then reshaped his materials to conform with preconceived allegories related to specific biblical texts. Although these allegories were not accepted as canonical by later writers, the popularity of the *Physiologus* as a school text and handbook persisted. The work was widely disseminated in many forms as attested by its translation into such diverse vernaculars as Syriac, Ethiopian, Russian, Flemish, Provençal, Old English, and Icelandic. "Perhaps no book except the

Bible," according to E.P. Evans, "has ever been so widely distributed among so many people and for so many centuries as the *Physiologus*."[5] The *Physiologus* is ultimately responsible for many familiar symbols of Christianity, including the pelican, the phoenix, the unicorn, the lion, and the whale. In Michael Curley's words, the *Physiologus* ranks among the "books which have made a difference in the way we think."[6] Even today, when we refer to "licking someone into shape" or something "rising like a phoenix from the ashes," we refer to animal allegories that originated in the *Physiologus*.

Let us examine how the allegory works in the *Physiologus* by looking at the very short chapter on the mythical[7] ant-lion, which the author derives from Job 4:11. Here Eliphaz, King of the Temanites, said of the ant-lion, "He perished because he had no food." The *Physiologus* then gives us the natural characteristics of this creature: its father has a lion's face and eats flesh, while its mother has an ant's face and eats vegetation. Their offspring has a lion's face, and the fore and rear parts of an ant. It dies because of its conflicting dual natures: it cannot eat meat because of its mother nor can it eat plants because of its father, and therefore it starves. Finally, the *Physiologus* shows the reader the spiritual moral of the ant-lion's dual physical nature:

> So it is with each person: "The man of deceitful heart is confused in all his ways" [Jas. 1:8]. It is not proper, therefore, to follow two paths, O man of double mind, even in prayer to be a sinner following two paths. It is written wisely, "Let it be with you *yes* or *no*" [Matt. 5:37].[8]

The bestiary, or "book of beasts," was the generic title for a popular nature book that developed around the end of the twelfth century and flourished through the fourteenth century.[9] Some of the finest extant versions are Latin manuscripts produced in England, many of them beautifully illustrated. Like the *Physiologus*, the bestiary was a compilation of accumulated folklore, legend, pseudoscience, and rudimentary scientific observation of an assortment of real and imaginary animals. The bestiary included the *Physiologus*, but was greatly expanded by the incorporation of many additional sources, the original 40 chapters increasing to as many as 150 in some versions. These chapters were often organized into zoological categories: beasts, birds, serpents, and fish. There was less emphasis on allegory, and many animals that had not appeared in the *Physiologus* were given no moral interpretation at all.

Nevertheless, it is the *sensus moralis*, the interpretation of animals as symbols of moral and metaphysical truths, that lies at the very heart of the *Physiologus* and bestiary tradition. Given this cultural acclimation, it is understandable that Jan Ziolkowski has referred to animals as "the vocabulary in the language of creation by which God communicates in material form what exists immaterially"[10] during the Middle Ages.

The essays in this collection do not all deal with the moral allegorical significance of animals, but they do show how animals were used to convey meaning—whether religious or profane—in medieval culture.

MORE THAN AN ANIMAL

For the opening section, I have selected essays that demonstrate how animal images in medieval art and literature were used as—in the words of Alan of Lille—books or pictures to teach man some truth about his cosmos, or as mirrors to reflect the values of contemporary human society.

The collection begins with Stephen O. Glosecki's essay "Movable Beasts: The Manifold Implications of Early Germanic Animal Imagery," which poses the key questions about visual images of animals during the Middle Ages: does the image *mean* something, or is it "just for pretty"? Furthermore, if we believe the image does signify something beyond its obvious literal representation, which of the many possible meanings do we choose? And finally, how does the meaning change—that is, "move," in the author's own words—as its cultural context shifts? Illustrated with the author's own line drawings of early Germanic artifacts, the essay draws us beyond the fascinatingly intricate decorative surface of these pieces to suggest the symbolic power these images may have held for tribal people invested with an animistic outlook. Glosecki looks at several animals in the course of his essay, but his most extended discussion relates to the boar as a cultural symbol from Beowulf to Bercilak.

In "The Truculent Toad in the Middle Ages," Mary E. Robbins traces the use of the toad as a symbol of death and as an agent of evil in literature and art from the classical period to the end of the Middle Ages. This essay focuses on the use of an animal as a moral or symbolic image, an association we commonly make with animals during the medieval period because of the influence of the *Physiologus* and the bestiary. Robbins demonstrates how a moral interpretation gradually became attached to the toad, and how that association becomes increasingly complex over time. The toad's association with death and evil is well established by the twelfth century, when didactic and homiletic literature such as sermons and penitential literature often described the toad as one of the horrific punishments awaiting sinners after their death. Robbins includes contemporary visual representations of the toad's evil associations; these representations underline her many literary examples. The toad—which was thought to literally eat sinners in purgatory or hell, or to feed off their decomposing bodies in the grave—ironically provided medieval man with food for thought in regard to his eventual spiritual end.

Joyce E. Salisbury discusses examples of one of the major literary genres to use animals extensively: the fable. Since the time of Aesop, Phaedrus, and Avianus, authors have used the beast fable to reveal truths—as they understood them—about their own society. In "Human Animals of Medieval Fables," Salisbury examines the fables of Marie de France and Odo of Cheriton, to show how these tales are really about human society, specifically Marie's court and Odo's church. The animals in these tales serve as metaphors of contemporary human behavior, and through them we come to understand the social concerns of the fabulists, their political bias, and their general view of society.

This section concludes with David A. Sprunger's "Parodic Animal Physicians from the Margins of Medieval Manuscripts," an iconographic study in which animals are again used to reflect and expose the values of human society, this time in a largely satiric light. Sprunger examines how the age-old battle between doctor and patient is fought with humor in the marginal *drôleries* of medieval manuscripts using animal protagonists. The illustrations accompanying the essay clearly reflect how artists transferred the iconographic traits of human physicians to animal counterparts, showing so-called dumb beasts engaging in one of the most complex of human arts with apparent skill. Furthermore, the animal patient treated is often a traditional enemy of the animal physician, and the role reversal in the parody not only reflects the traditional mistrust of physician by patient but is also a reflection of the *inversus mundi* theme often found in marginal illustrations.

ANOTHER LOOK AT THE *PHYSIOLOGUS*

As I discussed earlier, the hermeneutic use of animal imagery during the Middle Ages is due primarily to the *Physiologus* and the bestiaries. Thus, studies examining these works are a necessary part of this collection. I have tried to select essays that bring fresh perspectives to this literary genre— hence, the section title.

Many previous studies have examined the sources of the *Physiologus*, its transmission and influence on later literary works, and its influence on contemporary art.[11] What Lesley Kordecki does in "Making Animals Mean: Speciest Hermeneutics in the *Physiologus* of Theobaldus" is to examine the *Physiologus* text itself utilizing semiotic methodology. Using the eleventh-century metrical Latin poem by Theobaldus as a typical exemplar of this genre, Kordecki considers the two texts of the bestiary—the *naturas* (the animal's physical characteristics) and the *figuras* (their symbolic approximation)—as base text and gloss, as signifier and signified. As Kordecki explains, "The 'world' of the descriptive sections of the bestiary becomes subverted under the 'word' of its allegorical passages." Thus Nature is appropriated by Discourse when human writers interpret the animal world to their own ends.

While Kordecki looks back to evaluate the Theobaldus *Physiologus* with a new critical perspective, Dietmar Peil brings the *Physiologus* forward in time several centuries to evaluate its use as a source for sixteenth-century emblem books in "On the Question of a *Physiologus* Tradition in Emblematic Art and Writing." A widely held critical opinion has been that medieval hermeneutical literature such as bestiaries and the *Physiologus* served as direct sources for emblem literature. Peil examines the accessibility of the *Physiologus* in the sixteenth century, as well as overt quotations and unidentified *Physiologus* motifs in a number of emblem books. He then suggests how motifs from the *Physiologus* may have been transmitted to Renaissance emblem literature using the chapter on the eagle's rejuvenation as his example. His closely reasoned conclusion contradicts the mainstream opinion: "The theory that the *Physiologus* widely influenced the emblematic tradition cannot be maintained."

NEITHER MAN NOR BEAST

The essays in this final section all deal with composite creatures, especially combined animal-human forms. So prevalent were these figures in medieval art that they came under specific attack from Bernard of Clairvaux for their appearance in church decoration:

> in the cloisters, before the eyes of the brothers while they read— what is that ridiculous monstrosity doing, an amazing kind of deformed beauty and yet a beautiful deformity? What are the filthy apes doing there? . . . The monstrous centaurs? The creatures, part man and part beast? . . . You may see many bodies under one head, and conversely many heads on one body. On one side the tail of a serpent is seen on a quadruped, on the other side the head of a quadruped is on the body of a fish. Over there an animal has a horse for the front half and a goat for the back; here a creature which is horned in front is equine behind. In short, everywhere so plentiful and astonishing a variety of contradictory forms is seen that one would rather read in the marble than in books, and spend the whole day wondering at every single one of them than in meditating on the law of God.

Perhaps fearing that his detailed catalogue inspired more interest than disdain of such ornament, St. Bernard concludes the chapter with a "bottom line" assessment: "If one is not ashamed of the absurdity, why is one not at least troubled at the expense?"[12]

The werewolf is not properly a composite creature, being either all animal or all human at a given point in time (except, of course, during Hollywood B-movie transformation scenes). However, it is a fabulous creature, especially when cast as a *comic* figure as discussed in Norman Hinton's "The Werewolf as *Eiron*: Freedom and Comedy in *William of Palerne*." Several critics have pointed out that the most interesting character in this fourteenth-century Middle English romance is the enchanted prince Alphouns of Spain, who appears throughout much of the poem as an unnamed werewolf. Hinton argues that the werewolf's role in the plot is akin to that of the "tricky servant" of Roman comedy, and that without his constant activity, the main characters would probably freeze in their conventional romantic tracks. Moreover, the werewolf's "wittiness"— though primarily manifested by natural animal behavior—is constantly played against human dullness, humorously raising some potentially embarrassing questions: Who really is the master? and, Which is more intelligent, man or animal?

Janetta Rebold Benton brings an art historian's perspective to a specific group of medieval architectural drolleries in "Gargoyles: Animal Imagery and Artistic Individuality in Medieval Art." Although real animals are sometimes used as models for gargoyles, the majority "are in the form of completely bizarre beasts—unknown, unnamed, unspecified species." Benton classifies the kinds of composite animal images used by sculptors (providing several of her own photographs as illustrations) and suggests what these figures may have meant to medieval people. Furthermore, she looks at gargoyles in relation to the modern theory of "marginal art." She suggests that gargoyles are one of the few areas of medieval art in which the artist's "artistic license" was not severely restricted, and that such figures may constitute a kind of individual signature for an otherwise anonymous artist.

I conclude the collection with my own essay "'Effigies amicitiae . . . veritas inimicitiae': Antifeminism in the Iconography of the Woman-Headed Serpent in Medieval and Renaissance Art and Literature." I feel the essay incorporates many ideas raised in earlier essays, and thus provides a kind of summary of the collection as a whole. The woman-headed serpent, or dracontopede, is part human and part animal. Both authors and, especially, artists were able to imply certain relationships between Adam, Eve, and the human-headed serpent by varying the visual depiction of the figures' gestures and appearances. According to patristic tradition, the human face of the tempter serpent is so beguiling that it causes Eve to ignore the telltale reptilian tail, and she Falls in the Garden of Eden, bringing the rest of mankind with her. Hence, the image of the dracontopede has a religious moral allegorical meaning, as do such kindred forms as the siren, the human-headed scorpion, and the viper. This symbolic interpretation is influenced by medieval hermeneutic literature such as the bestiary. Moreover, this meaning "moves" with the cultural context, so that a profane allegorical interpretation also becomes possible during the Renaissance.

In Job 12:7 we read, "But ask now the beasts, and they shall teach thee; and the fowls of the air, and they shall tell thee." My hope is that the animals discussed in each of these essays will provide the reader of today—as they once did for our medieval counterparts—with lessons that are both valuable and interesting.

Notes

1. Alan of Lille, *De Incarnatione Christi*, PL CCX, 579A.

2. To look at animals as food, prey, possession, or companion to man as well as symbolic figures during the Middle Ages, a good starting point would be Francis Klingender's *Animals in Art and Thought to the End of the Middle Ages* (Cambridge, Mass.: M.I.T. Press, 1971), the indispensable reference for those working in the field because of the breath of the material surveyed, the many illustrations, and the extensive bibliography. A more recent general study is Joyce E. Salisbury, *The Beast Within: Animals in the Middle Ages* (New York: Routledge, 1994).

3. Only a few select book-length studies with extensive bibliographies are given here: see Florence McCulloch, *Medieval Latin and French Bestiaries* (Chapel Hill, N.C.: University of North Carolina Press, 1960); *Beasts and Birds of the Middle Ages: The Bestiary and its Legacy*, ed. Willene B. Clark and Meradith T. McMunn (Philadelphia: University of Pennsylvania Press, 1989), continues McCulloch's bibliography; and *Physiologus*, trans. Michael Curley (Austin, Tex.: University of Texas Press, 1979), especially Curley's excellent introduction.

4. Curley, xv.

5. E.P. Evans, *Animal Symbolism in Ecclesiastical Art* (New York: Harry Holt, 1896), 62.

6. Curley, xxviii.

7. Wilma George and Brunsdon Yapp tentatively identify the ant-lion or mirmecoleon as the honey badger (*Mellivora capensis*) based on the description by Herodotus, in their book *The Naming of the Beasts: Natural History in the Medieval Bestiary* (London: Duckworth, 1991), 64.

8. Curley, 49.

9. The most accessible modern translation of the bestiary still remains that of T.H. White, *The Bestiary: A Book of Beasts, being a translation from the Latin Bestiary [Cambridge Univ. Library MS Ii4.26] of the Twelfth Century* (New York: G.P. Putnam's Sons, 1954); however, Richard Barber has recently translated Oxford M.S. Bodley 764 in an edition that also reproduces all the original miniatures in facsimile in *Bestiary* (Woodbridge: Boydell, 1993).

10. Jan Ziolkowski, *Talking Animals: Medieval Latin Beast Poetry, 750–1150* (Philadelphia: University of Pennsylvania Press, 1993), 34.

11. For literary sources, transmission, and influences, see note 3 above. Those books and that of Francis Klingender provide references for the influence of the *Physiologus* and bestiary on medieval art, but also see the following: Ann Payne, *Medieval Beasts* (London: New Amsterdam, 1990); Janetta Rebold Benton, *The Medieval Menagerie: Animals in the Art of the Middle Ages* (New York: Abbeville Press, 1992); J.P. Harthan, "Animals in Art. IX. Medieval Bestiaries," *Geographical Magazine* (22), 1949, 182–90; G.C. Druce, "The Medieval Bestiaries, and their Influence on Ecclesiastical Decorative Art," *J. Brit. Archeological Assoc.* 25 (1919), 41–82; Xenia Muratova, "Problemes de l'origine et des sources des cycles d'illustrations des manuscrits des bestiares," in *Épopée Animale Fable Fabliau Actes du IVe Colloque de la Société Internationale Renardienne (Evreux, 1981),* ed. Gabriel Bianciotto and Michel Salvat (Paris: Publications de l'Université de Rouen, 1984), 383–408; Brunsdon Yapp, "Birds in Bestiaries: Medieval Knowledge of Nature," *The Cambridge Review* (Nov. 20, 1984), 183–190); and Françoise Bibolet, "Portraits d'oiseaux illustrant le 'De avibus' d'Hugues de Fouilloy (Manuscrit de Clairvaux, Troyes 177)," *Mélanges à la mémoire du Père Anselme Dimier*, pt. II, vol. 4, ed. Benoît Chauvin (Beernem: De Windroos, 1984), 409–447.

12. Bernard of Clairvaux, Apologia XII.29, as translated by Conrad Rudolph in *The "Things of Greater Importance": Bernard of Clairvaux's Apologia and the Medieval Attitude Toward Art* (Philadelphia: University of Pennsylvania Press, 1990), 283.

ABBREVIATIONS

ANF   *The Ante-Nicene Fathers: Translations of the Writings of the Fathers down to* A.D. *325.* Eds. Alexander Roberts and James Donaldson. 10 vols. 1826–1901; rpt. Grand Rapids, Mich., 1969–1971. Cited by volume and page.

ASPR The Anglo-Saxon Poetic Records

CCSL *Corpus Christianorum, Series Latina.* Eds. D.E. Dekkers and I. Fraipont. Turnhout, 1966–. Cited by volume and page.

CSEL *Corpus Scriptorum Ecclesiasticorum Latinorum.* Consilio et impensis Academiae litterarum caesareae vindobonensis. Vienna, 1866–. Cited by volume and page.

EETS The Early English Text Society

PG   *Patrologiae Cursus Completus, Series Graeca.* Ed. J.-P. Migne. 161 vols. Paris, 1857–1903. Cited by volume and column.

PL   *Patrologiae Cursus Completus, Series Latina.* Ed. J.-P. Migne. 221 vols. Paris, 1844–1903. Cited by volume and column.

SATF Société des Anciens Textes Français

PART 1
MORE THAN AN ANIMAL

Movable Beasts

The Manifold Implications of
Early Germanic Animal Imagery

Stephen O. Glosecki

Early Germanic art—strange, fanciful, mysterious—tantalizes the mind with zoomorphic design. Graphic and literary sources alike confront us with convoluted images of energetic animals. Sometimes the media coalesce: boar figures on Beowulf's helmet appear in precisely the same place, *ofer hleorbergan* "above the cheekguards," as does the boar's head on the Sutton Hoo helmet (see figure 1).[1]

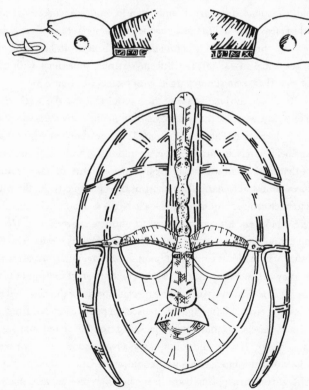

Figure 1. The Sutton Hoo helmet, front view. Detail, above: boar's head eyebrows terminals. (After Bruce-Mitford, Sutton Hoo *[n. 1 below], 35. The British Museum, London. This drawing first appeared as figure 7 in Glosecki,* Shamanism and Old English Poetry *[n. 6 below].)*

Similarly, architectural ornament looms up before us in these famous lines from the Old English *Wanderer* (97–98), which could be describing wall panels on the stave church at Urnes in the Sognefjord (see figure 2):

Stondeð nu on laste   leofre duguþe
weal wundrum heah,   wyrmlicum fah.[2]

[Stands now in the track   of the troop we loved
a wall wondrous high   writhing with snake-shapes.]

Serpentines on this high wall suggest the surface ornament so typical of Germanic art around the end of the first millennium, when stylized beasts explode into streamers of limbs, tendrils, and tangles that render the subject species unrecognizable and apparently inconsequential. Elsewhere, though, the species of beast is quite clear. Incised on stone, cast in bronze, filigreed in gold, cloisonnéed in garnet, embossed in repoussé, carved in oak, envisioned in elegy, invoked in epic, petrified in personal names—an entourage of the same animals unfolds before us—boar, bear, wolf, hart, horse, raven, eagle, serpent, fish—silent, fanciful, mysterious, sometimes with glittering garnet eyes that seem supercharged with secrets (see figure 3).

Returning the blank gaze of these obsolete icons, the height of human art in their day, we sense the symbolism of strength, many murky implications, including the notion that those who made such elaborate designs must have done so deliberately, in honor of ancient traditions. And yet there can be little doubt that as the centuries wore away, artist and artisan alike crafted these creatures almost automatically, as part of their patrimony. As the Migration Age interlace evolved through the so-called Style II of Sutton Hoo and on past Jellinge, Mammen, Ringerike toward its ultimate expression at Urnes,[3] one artisan undoubtedly imitated another, who mimicked his master, who followed his father, who had just carried on unquestioningly with conventional motifs initiated by the ancestors. Maybe by the end of the first millennium any clear meaning had melted away from the expected images of the same old animals. If we could revive a Viking Age artisan (see the palms calloused from smooth-hafted steel chisels, the thumbnails blackened from silver and stinging sulphur inlaid as niello), if we could ask a Norse silver-, stone-, iron-, or tree-smith why the workmanship crawled with contorted creatures, then perhaps, like a Pennsylvania farmer posing beneath the hex sign on the barn, this revenant would respond *jafn for fagr* "just for pretty."[4]

Thus, toward the end of the first millennium, as the graphic tradition followed the outmoded Germanic gods off into obscurity, when busy

Figure 2. Urnes stave church, Sogn, Norway: carved portal panel. (After Walther Roggenkamp in Lindholm, Stave Churches *[n. 5 below], pls. 26, 28.)*

surface ornament seems to have become an end unto itself, perhaps there lingered in the minds of those who made it no clear concept of this animal art's arcane origins. Imitation tarnishes inspiration. Maybe any mythic content had evaporated from the indeterminate quadruped all wrapped in snakes at Urnes, shown in figure 4. Perhaps by 1060 such sinuous beasts had become nothing more than wood shaped well to catch an idle eye.[5]

Yet such was not the case a century later, when carving on the Hylestad and Vegusdal churches delineated scenes that indisputably illustrate the Sigurð and Fáfnir story. For these woodsmiths, there was obviously meaning behind the medium. And for those who know the Volsunga cycle, the referent of a hero roasting a dragon heart by a sleeping smith beneath singing birds is immediately apparent: this warrior can be none other than the archetypal dragonslayer of Germanic myth, whether we call him Sigurð (ON), Sigemund (OE), or Siegfried (MHG).[6] Patently, these pictures such as figure 5 are not *efne for fæger,* "just for pretty." No, this anthropomorphic

Figure 3. Sutton Hoo purse-top plaque (Woden with wolf companions?) ("Man-between-monsters" motif, after Evans, Sutton Hoo Ship Burial [n. 1 below], pl. VIII. The British Museum, London. This drawing first appeared as figure 3 in Glosecki, "Men among Monsters" [n. 6 below]; subsequently it appeared as figure 17 in Glosecki, Shamanism.)

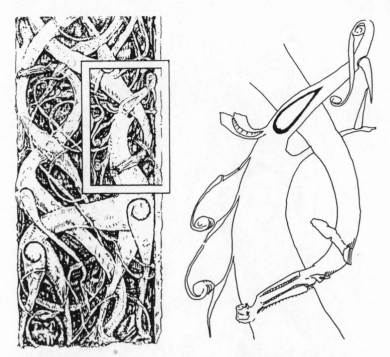

Figure. 4. Urnes carving, portal panel, detail. (After Roggenkamp in Lindholm, Stave Churches, pl. 29.)

art preserves the beleaguered mythos of a proud people whose artists saw no sacrilege in adorning Christian churches with the exploits of heathen heroes. Thus the narrative panels from Hylestad—in which literature and representational art again coalesce, this time to give us graphic *Heldensagen*—have glaring mythic content, quite particular implications.

Why should the situation be different for the recurrent animal motifs, even though—to us, at least—they seem so much less referential than the Hylestad illustrations? I suspect that at least in the earlier phases of this tradition, the more familiar beasts were equally referential. Although their mythic implications must have steadily eroded as the influence of Rome advanced, nonetheless these beasts originally conveyed socioreligious significance to those who made them and to those who admired them. As Foote and Wilson write, "There was apparently a need for art in everyday life."[7] And as I have argued elsewhere,[8] this mysterious animal art that originated in the Iron Age and persisted through the Viking Age was only coincidentally aesthetic. Originally, the icons on weaponry were not at all "for pretty": they were for protection from ethereal as well as corporeal adversaries. So the contemporary signifi-

Figure 5. Sigurð and Regin, carved portal panel, stave church at Hylestad, Norway. (After Roggenkamp in Lindholm, pl. 47. Universitets Oldsaksamling, Oslo.)

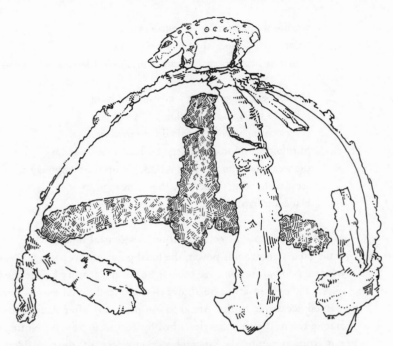

Figure 6. The Benty Grange boar helmet. (After Bruce-Mitford, Aspects [n. 1 below], pl. 63. The Sheffield City Museum, West Park, Sheffield. This drawing first appeared as figure 6 in Glosecki, Shamanism.)

cance of much of this animal art was broadly mythic, narrowly apotropaic. Such art—boars and bears on armor; wolves, stags, steeds, eagles on royal regalia—was *effective*, not *affective*. It was meant to acknowledge and probably propitiate the inscrutable cosmic forces whose powers ordinary people found impossible to resist. Moreover, among quasi-tribal societies still dependent upon the hunt, the natural embodiment of these animistic impulses regularly takes the shape of significant beasts, whose image, according to the principles of sympathetic magic, equals the object represented. "Watch out for the wolf when you see a wolf's ears!" (*Fáfnismál*, l. 35).

This is just one of the more crucial implications of the early animal art. The apotropaic power of the battle emblem is most obvious in representations of a sacral beast that bulled its way into the center of my studies fifteen years ago and still refuses to budge:

> Ac se hwita helm   hafelan werede,
> se þe meregrundas   mengan scolde,
> secan sundgebland   since geweorðad,
> befongen freawrasnum,   swa hine fyrndagum

worhte wæpna smið, wundrum teode,
besette swinlicum, þæt hine syðþan no
brond ne beadomecas bitan ne meahton. (*Beowulf*, ll. 1448–54)

[But the glittering helmet guarded his head;
it had to stir up the sea floor,
enter ocean currents exalted with treasure,
fit round with lordly bands; far back in the old days
the weapon-smith wrought it thus, worked it with magic,
set it with swine shapes so that thereafter no
blade nor battle sword might bite through.]

Manifold implications emanate from this central image. Most striking
is the boar's apotropaic power, the focal point of this passage. Whether
we date *Beowulf* to the "age of Bede" or to the century before the Con-
quest, the epic in any case shows that the traditional associations remained accessible to this Anglo-Saxon poet long after their dim origin
among the northern tribes described by Tacitus in 98 A.D.[9] Noting their
superstitious nature, the Roman historian writes that they considered the

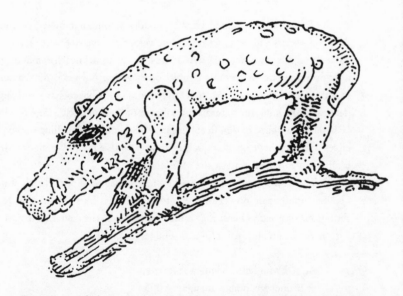

Figure 7. Detail, the Benty Grange helmet: boar crest. (After Webster and Backhouse,
Making of England, [n. 3 below], pl. 46. The Sheffield City Museum, West Park,
Sheffield.)

boar's effigy their best protection in battle (*Germania*, 45).[10] So, for this animal image at least, the ancient implications lived on tenaciously, despite drastic changes in the culture that preserved boar figures in its art (see figure 6).

The preeminence of the boar reflects this animal's importance as a food species in Iron Age Europe when, at 700 pounds, it snarled out of the brush to attack hunting parties, who thus knew the beast's formidable strength firsthand. People with an animistic outlook—tribal people who invest their universe with endless busy spirits—tend to equate physical force with spirit power. Thus, still today a symbol of tenacity, the boar quite naturally becomes the particular guardian of the armed man ringed by enemies, fighting for his life in times that must have been still more terrible than epic and saga show.

This boar crest (see figure 7) is thus a "movable beast": some of these talismans were literally removable, since *Njáls saga* says that, with hostility imminent, warriors put battle emblems on their helmets (ch. 142). Presumably, they removed these emblems after the fight, perhaps as a gesture of respect to the creature of power.

More importantly, though, the boar as an English symbol—a movable beast—survived cultural changes to reappear in a Middle English romance, where it retains an echo of its old value in the much earlier epic. It moved from one symbol system to another, its image fully intact, although its content shifted drastically. In *Gawain and the Green Knight*, where the boar's symbolic association with the tempted hero is well known, we still see remnants of ritual in the procession following the second hunt, when the boar's head is borne triumphantly back to Bercilak's castle (ll. 1615–18):

> Now with þis ilk swyn þay swengen to home;
> Þe bores hed watz borne bifore þe burnes seluen
> Þat him forferde in þe forþe þurg forse of his honde
>   so stronge.[11]

> [Now with this same swine homeward they sway,
> The boar's head borne before the baron himself
> Who killed it in the creek through craft of his hand
>   so strong.]

A few lines earlier, the romance describes the proverbial ferocity of this quarry, big game only marginally less dangerous than the aurochs or the bear (ll. 1571–80):

He gete þe bonk at his bak, bigynez to scrape,
Þe froþe femed at his mouth vnfayre bi þe wykez,
Whettez his whyte tuschez; with hym þen irked
Alle þe burnez so bolde þat hym by stoden
To nye hym on-ferum, bot nege hym non durst
for woþe;
He hade hurt so mony byforne
Þat al þugt þenne ful loþe
Be more wyth his tusches torne,
Þat breme watz and braynwod bothe.

[He gets the bank at his back, starts to gouge ground;
Froth foamed from his mouth, foul around jowls
While he whets his white tusks, filling with fear
All the hunters so hearty who crowd in around.
They attack from afar—but approach him?
No way!
He had hurt so many before
That everyone edged away
From the tusk that slashed and tore
Where the mad boar turned at bay.]

Thus the boar moves from epic to romance: although it cuts the same strong profile, the apotropaic sign of spirit power fades into a conventional literary symbol. Still, these lines reflect the overwhelming power of this beast in the wild—wounded, surrounded, doomed, yet fighting on alone against a small army of hunters. Iron Age warriors identified with this formidable strength, which they themselves needed to survive, and so claimed their most tenacious quarry as a noble spirit guardian. Though guardian no longer, the boar in *Gawain* remains a symbol of strength.

More than that, though, this boar symbolizes social status as it did on Germanic helmets, where its function was thus protoheraldic as well as talismanic.[12] In the romance, ordinary huntsmen hold back when the boar turns at bay, i.e., when it is, proverbially, danger incarnate. But the ranking nobleman, Bercilak, towers above his retainers as he rides in on his charger (in itself a status symbol), dismounts, draws his sword, wades into white water, and when the boar charges, calmly sights like a bullfighter along his blade to slaughter the beast his men pointedly avoid.[13] Horns blare, hounds bay, and the field dressing begins with the boar's decapitation. This grisly trophy—aside from its oblique connection with Gawain—embodies lordship, prowess, the high status of Hautdesert. Further, as he parades homeward in triumph, the head of the beast held up high before him, Bercilak presides over merry yuletide pageantry that retains a trace of the ancient animal powers, a ghost of hunting rituals which often emphasize the head of the quarry.

Subtly, although it keeps a quasi-heraldic significance, the boar shifts from talisman to trope, from effective to affective impact. Noted by Tacitus, prominent in Celtic as well as Germanic lore,[14] crucial as meat but spiritually important too—the boar moves across a spectrum of possible implications. Scholars in general have been too eager to narrow this spectrum. We should rather be expanding the possibilities for likely referents of these animal signs that have been left over from the Iron Age. In general, this boar figure is shackled to the god Frey.[15] But why invoke the fertility god on battle gear? Emblems of Tyr, Thor, or Odin would be much more appropriate. It makes sense to connect Frey with Sæhrímnir, Valhalla's recurrent main course, but not with the boar on armor. And should Frey be linked with the boar traditionally cast overboard by Helgi the Lean, who followed it along to found his Icelandic farmstead? Or with the unetymologizable nautical term

Figure 8. Torslunda die D: horned man with wolf dancer. (After Bruce Mitford, Aspects, pl. 59a. Statens Historiska Museum, Stockholm.)

(as in the Boars of Duncansby) that denotes a tide race in a channel or a tidal surge up an estuary?[16]

We need to give these beasts wider range to roam. We need to acknowledge Frey's boar Gollinbursti without seeing Frey as the referent for every early Germanic image of the boar. The situation is considerably more complex: as the symbol moved from one context to another, even within the same society, it probably had different implications. The name Eofor from *Beowulf* suggests totemism. Its Icelandic cognate *jofurr* "prince" suggests sacral kingship; Gollinbursti, fertility; the helmet crest, shamanic guardianship; the nautical term, some arcane link between boars and dangerous tides.

Thus the animal symbols of early Germanic art probably had multiple referents, with particularity determined by context. Therefore, Hatto overstates his case when he writes that "the wolf . . . was negatively accentuated as portending savage destruction and revenge among the Germani."[17] Surely this implication holds true for the poetic beast of battle, for that doomsday machine Fenrir, for the lupine *fylgja* of the sagas, and possibly for the shape shifter, the *úlfheðinn* mentioned in sagas and depicted on the Torslunda die in figure 8.[18] But concurrent and contradictory implications probably existed, too. Perhaps, in a migratory millennium many sons were named after the wolf because of its tireless traveling, a connection that may equally account for Odin's shamanistic wolf companions, Geri and Freki, whose ramblings would have brought good gossip to the know-it-all god. More likely still, the wolf could have been a totem in proto-Germanic Europe, its name given to offspring associated with a certain agnatic sib. Various possibilities, not all negative, should be articulated and explored in our effort to see the full spectrum of symbolic associations lurking behind this early animal art.

Figure 9. Petroglyph from Alskog, Sweden: horse-fight (Hestavíg, after Davidson, Mythology (n. 24 below), 87. Statens Historiska Museum, Stockholm.

The same is true for other recurrent animals in the Germanic entourage. Like Bercilak's mount in the boar hunt, the horse stands out as a status symbol in the sagas, in *Beowulf*, *The Wanderer*, and in these lines from *The Rune Poem* (55–58):

M(eh) byþ for eorlum   æþelinga wyn,
hors hofum wlanc,   ðær him hæleþ ymbe,
welege on wicgum,   wrixlaþ spræce,
and biþ unstyllum   æfre frofur.[19]

[The charger before champions   is cherished by princes,
the horse hoof-proud   where heroes around him,
the rich on their steeds,   wrangle with words;
and always the restless   can ride to find peace.]

And yet the horse meant more than wealth and rank. Various sources suggest ritual: eating horseflesh, overtly proscribed after the Icelandic conversion,[20] may have been connected with Frey-worship, as apparently was Hrafnkels's sacral steed, Freyfaxi.[21] Horses were sacrificed during ship burials and during other rites as well.[22] Egil spits a severed horse head on a rune-stick to cast an evil spell.[23] Odin's *Sleipnir* "Slippery One" carries the shaman god between upper world and underworld. Manifold implications confront us, among them the likelihood that the *Beowulf* horse race and the saga *hestavíg* "horsefight" (see figure 9) may reflect obsequies, seasonal festivals, or formalized rites of interaction between potentially hostile groups.[24]

Early Germanic animal art thus implies many possibilities, the least likely being that the product was purely ornamental. Striking creatures stare across the centuries at us, blankly indifferent to our urge to understand. We see livestock, food, and draft species (*nietencynn*) as well as feral beasts (*deorcynn*) whose associations seem largely martial. Like the Sigurð panels from Hylestad or the boar figures on Beowulf's helmet, these animal motifs have mythic resonance, however faintly their echoes may ring for us today. Aside from acknowledging the simple economic importance of animals in an ancient agrarian culture,[25] we need to see the manifold implications of myth, magic, shamanism, totemism, protoheraldry, warrior cults, and rites of propitiation, of passage, of fertility, of diplomacy, and of warfare.

The most uncanny creatures—the fantastic—will probably remain inscrutable. They defy interpretation, these were-beasts in both graphic and literary sources,[26] these dragons whose lithe forms writhe through lines of *The Wanderer* and coil in oak at Urnes. Clearly the dragon implies gold, greed, destruction, perhaps heroic initiation. Sigur<, after all, gains the shamanic gift of interspecies communication from the bare taste of dragon blood: prodding Fáfnir's sizzling heart, he sears his thumb, plunges it into his mouth, and suddenly understands the language of the birds. So the dragon stands for wisdom, as in *Fáfnismál*, where, seerlike, it instructs the initiate; as, too, in *Beowulf*, where the wary old king and the wicked old worm are both called *frod* "wise, experienced."

As a movable beast, the dragon shifts easily to a Christian context, where, emptied of earlier meaning, it signifies Satan, ultimate evil. So too for the horned man, whose autochthonous North European avatar had something to do with fertility but, originally, had no Satanic associations at all (see figure 10).

This horned man—reflecting a divinity, however barbaric—underlies ceremonial headgear seen on helmet plaques and in small talismanic figurines (see figure 11).[27] Like the were-creatures, he unites human and animal at-

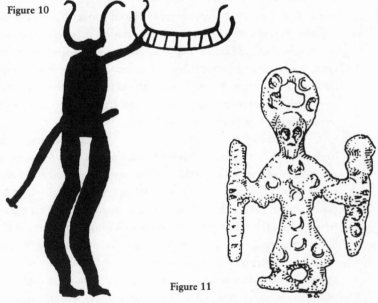

Figure 10

Figure 11

Figure 10. Horned man petroglyph, Bohuslän, Sweden. (After Gelling and Davidson, Chariot of the Sun, *[n. 27 below], fig. 29a. This drawing first appeared as figure 2a in Glosecki, "Wolf Dancers and Whispering Beasts" [n. 9 below].)*

Figure 11. Horned man pendant, silver, from Birka, Uppland. (After Graham-Campbell, Viking Artefacts *[n. 27 below], pl. 516. Statens Historiska Museum, Stockholm.)*

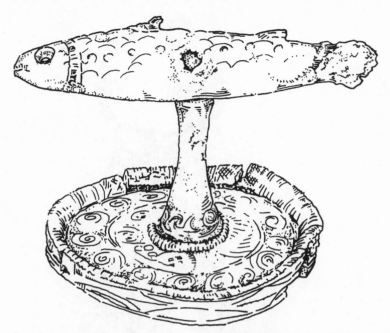

Figure 12. Detail, fish and pedestal mount from the large hanging bowl, Sutton Hoo. (After Evans, Sutton Hoo Ship Burial, pl. 58. The British Museum, London.)

tributes. Like his zoomorphic counterparts, his image implies a range of possibilities.

The manifold implications of early Germanic animal art enrich the movable beasts that have reached us from an era when they made sense to their makers, however mysterious they may seem to us today. Literally, many were movable goods back then; figuratively, they cross historical boundaries, too, with whispers of ways forgotten. A final figure looms in from the large hanging bowl found at Sutton Hoo and shown in figure 12. This whimsical fish rides its ornate pedestal, set to spin freely when touched by an idle king. Perhaps it was a plaything and nothing more. Yet the fish appears elsewhere, too—on the Kentish buckle in figure 13, for instance, which is hollow and hence seen by some as a reliquary.[28] But locketlike receptacles also held pre-Christian talismans.[29] Further, I cannot concur with those who see this Saxon fish as an unequivocally Christian icon. Surely it swam into the Roman sea but, before the conversion, lurked in the native Germanic mythos, too, as shown by this excerpt from a proto-Viking runic inscription:

> In what form comes Héráss to the land of the Goths?
> As a fish swimming out of . . . the river of the body . . .[30]

17

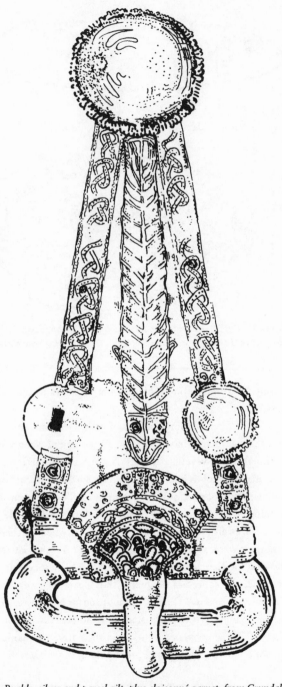

Figure 13. Buckle, silver and parcel gilt, plus cloisonné garnet; from Crundale, Kent. (After Wilson, Anglo-Saxon Art, [n. 28 below], pl. 16. The British Museum, London.)

Presumably Heráss "Army God" means Odin, whose wolves and ravens are joined by a fish companion. Along with the other animal images, this last movable beast, slipping from one symbol system to another, thus remains ambiguous. Ultimately, Germanic animal art itself—strange, fanciful, mysterious—will continue to enchant us with its multifarious ambiguities.

NOTES

Some research underlying this paper was funded in 1990 by the National Endowment for the Humanities and by the Graduate School of the University of Alabama at Birmingham. For valuable support I remain grateful to these agencies and also to the Fulbright Scholar Program for my 1991–92 grant funding a year's teaching and research in Norway, where the Institute for Language and Literature at the University of Tromsø also provided generous financial assistance.

    1. For placement of the *eoforlic* "boar likeness" on the Sutton Hoo helmet, see figure 1 (the line drawings in this essay are mine: for sources, see captions). Talismanic animal design, sometimes but not always porcine, regularly appears on the eyebrow terminals of Germanic *grimhelmas* "helmets with face masks," which were designed to terrify the beholder as well as defend the wearer. Cf. the Ægishjálmr "terror helm" that figures in the booty Sigurð takes after killing Fáfnir (*Volsunga saga* 18, *Reginsmál, Fáfnismál*; I assume no etymological link with the Greek *aegis* of Athena, although the similarities are striking). Also cf. the famous and formidable helms from Vendel and Valsgärde, which are closely related to their Sutton Hoo analog. This Upplandish connection is discussed in Rupert Bruce-Mitford's *Aspects of Anglo-Saxon Archaeology* (New York: Harper's, 1974), 208 et passim; plate 55 depicts the Vendel 14 helmet. Also see Bruce-Mitford's *The Sutton Hoo Ship Burial: A Handbook* (London: British Museum, 1979), 116–19. Magnus Magnusson's *Viking: Hammer of the North* (New York: Galahad, 1980) illustrates Vendel helms as well. In her current British Museum handbook, *The Sutton Hoo Ship Burial* (London: British Museum, 1986), A.C. Evans also acknowledges the close link between this Anglian find and its Swedish counterparts (49).

    Of the three extant Anglo-Saxon helmets, only the Benty Grange (this essay's centerpiece) lacks the eyebrow-terminal effigies. The Coppergate helmet has draconic beasts in the expected spot; these are more stylized and, as postconversion anachronisms, perhaps less overtly apotropaic than corresponding images on the much earlier, pre-Christian Sutton Hoo and Upplandish helmets.

    Still, I believe that the eyebrow-terminal animal crests applied sympathetic magic—*smiðcræft, searoþonc, searowundor* (see Paul Beekman Taylor, "*Searoniðas*: Old Norse Magic and Old English Verse," *Studies in Philology* 80 (1983), 109–25)— to protect the eyes as well as the weakest point of the wearer's skull, the temples, quite vulnerable to concussion even if the force of the blow were not powerful enough to deform the frame or plates of the *grimhelm*. Although the Benty Grange helmet lacks the ornamented mask, it has a cross on its nasal as well as the apex boar crest also depicted on Torslunda die C (Bruce-Mitford, *Aspects*, pl. 59b).

    2. G.P. Krapp and E.V.K. Dobbie, eds., *The Exeter Book*, Anglo-Saxon Poetic Records (ASPR) 3 (New York: Columbia University Press, 1936), 136. Although I also consult Dobbie's *Beowulf and Judith*, ASPR 4 (New York: Columbia University Press, 1953), my primary text for the epic remains Friedrich Klaeber's *Beowulf and the Fight at Finnsburg*, 3rd ed. (Boston: D.C. Heath, 1950). Modernizations of Old and Middle English are mine. For Urnes illustrations see figures 2 and 4.

    3. Originating in Bernhard Salin's *Die altgermanische Thierornamentik* (Stockholm: Kl. Beckmans Buchdruckerei, 1904), 214–90, the terms Style I, Style II, and Style III denote early, middle, and late phases of Vendelesque animal interlace, covering the

centuries that roughly correspond with the Early and Middle Saxon periods in England, i.e., from the migration period (c. 450–600) to Alfred's birth (849) in the midst of the Early Viking Age. Thereafter, successive stylistic developments are named after showcase exemplars found in Norway and Denmark: Borre style (840–980), Jellinge (870–1000), Mammen (960–1020), Ringerike (980–1090), and Urnes (1050–1170). P.G. Foote and D. Wilson call Urnes style "the last truly barbarian art" in *The Viking Achievement* (London: Sidgwick and Jackson, 1970), 311; chapter 9 of this book—my source for the preceding parenthetical dates—provides a concise summary of the later styles. My own impression is that Germanic animal art represents more of a continuum than the labels may imply, with "earlier" motifs still apparent in classificatorily "later" styles. In the definitive work on this subject, *Anglo-Saxon Animal Art and Its Germanic Background* (Oxford: Oxford University Press, 1980), George Speake engages the issue of style: "it remains, in spite of any definition, one of the most elusive and ambiguous concepts in the history of culture" (5). Speake's ensuing chapters treat the earlier styles in detail (esp. see ch. 3). Also see Leslie Webster and Janet Backhouse, *The Making of England: Anglo-Saxon Art and Culture 600–900* (Toronto: University of Toronto Press, 1991), glossary et passim. The heyday of the Urnes style overlaps the rise of Romanesque influence in Scandinavia. Norwegian place-names should not mislead the reader: the Ringerike style—named after a fertile region north of Oslo—was, for instance, "particularly popular and particularly successful in the British Isles" (Foote and Wilson, 309). The pervasive distribution of Germanic animal art suggests that during the first millennium, the extent of Viking settlement marks what amounts to a common culture area (cf. "Northwest Coast" Native American culture, which extends from California to Alaska, across thousands of miles, through dozens of languages, and scores of tribes). Regarding linguistic support for this cultural integrity see William G. Moulton, "Mutual Intelligibility among Speakers of Early Germanic Dialects," in *Germania: Comparative Studies in the Old Germanic Languages and Literatures*, ed. D.G. Calder and T.C. Christy (Wolfeboro, N.H.: D.S. Brewer, 1988), 9–28.

4. The compounds in this sentence anglicize ON terms for the respective artisans: *silfrsmiðr, steinsmið, járnsmiðr, trésmiðr*. See Foote and Wilson, 316.

5. For dating of the Urnes, Hylestad, and Vegusdal structures I rely upon *Stave Churches in Norway* by Dan Lindholm, trans. Stella and Adam Bittleston (London: Rudolf Steiner Press, 1969, 206–07.

6. Figure 5 depicts Sigurð roasting Fáfnir's heart for his dwarfish foster-father Regin. The entire episode is illustrated on adjacent panels from the Hylestad church portal. It is also represented in toto on an eleventh-century petroglyph from Ramsund, Jäder, Södermanland, Sweden (in Marijane Osborn's *Beowulf: A Verse Translation* [Berkeley: University of California Press, 1983], 32–33). On the shamanic overtones of Sigurð's initiation, see Glosecki, *Shamanism and Old English Poetry* (New York: Garland Publishing, 1989), ch. 5. Apparently Sigurð was considered a fit threshold guardian by syncretic Norse Christians (with Fáfnir allegorically Satan?), since his exploits appear carved on portals of several of the few remaining stave churches. I have elsewhere interpreted such patently referential figures as "graphic texts" that imply concomitant albeit unrecorded "verbal illustrations" ("Men among Monsters: Germanic Animal Art as Evidence of Oral Literature," *The Mankind Quarterly* 27.2 [1986], 207–14).

7. Foote and Wilson, 286. Cited in full above, n. 3.

8. In *Shamanism* (above, n. 6), 104–6 et passim.

9. This persistence of material culture traits from Classical antiquity through the Anglo-Saxon period—for seven or more centuries—is among the most cogent evidence for the concomitant persistence of intangible culture traits, e.g., animism, totemism, shamanism, the belief in animal guardians like the boar. Tacitus mentions boars on helmets in 98 A.D.; similarly, more than a century before Tacitus, Caesar describes the Germanic esteem for aurochs horns, decorated with gold, displayed at regal feasts. Seven hundred years later, a set of aurochs horns, ornamented with silver-gilt mounts, "all work of very high quality," was buried with an English king at Sutton

Hoo (Bruce-Mitford, *Ship Burial*, 57; cited in full above, n. 1). Also see Glosecki, "Wolf Dancers and Whispering Beasts: Shamanic Motifs from Sutton Hoo?" *Mankind Quarterly* 26.3&4 (1986), 305–19.

10. The boar's protective power is well established in Anglo-Saxon studies; see, e.g., A. Margaret Arent, "The Heroic Pattern: Old Germanic Helmets, *Beowulf*, and *Grettis saga*," in *Old Norse Literature and Mythology*, ed. E.C. Polomé (Austin, Tex.: University of Texas Press, 1969), 136; R.W. Chambers, *Beowulf: An Introduction* (Cambridge: Cambridge University Press, 1959), 359; H.R.E. Davidson, *Pagan Scandinavia* (New York: Praeger, 1967), 97; Glosecki, *Shamanism*, 193; A.T. Hatto, "Snake-Swords and Boar-Helms in *Beowulf*," *English Studies* 38 (1957), 155; Allan Metcalf, "Ten Natural Animals in *Beowulf*," *Neuphilologische Mitteilungen* 64 (1963), 382; Haakon Shetelig and Hjalmar Falk, *Scandinavian Archaeology*, trans. E.V. Gordon (Oxford: Oxford University Press, 1937), 402; and Speake 78–81 (cited in full above, n. 3). Of these, Arent, Chambers, Glosecki, Hatto, and Speake refer to Tacitus, as does Shetelig, who quotes the pertinent Latin.

11. J.R.R. Tolkien and E.V. Gordon, eds., *Sir Gawain and the Green Knight* (Oxford: Oxford University Press, 1967), 2nd ed., rev. Norman Davis, 45. The next *Gawain* excerpt appears on p. 44 of this edition. My text silently modernizes the yogh. Translations are mine, the second freer than the first.

12. The intriguing cognates OE *eofor* "boar" and ON *jofurr* "prince, king" shed light upon early Germanic sacral kingship. For the traditional associations of *eofor* see *Beowulf*, where the term describes helmet crests (303b, 1112a) and a battle standard (2152b), appears as a nobleman's name (2486b, 2964a, 2993a, 2997a), and figures as metonymy for warriors (1328a). For *jofurr* see, e.g., (jó<ólfr's *Sexstefja* 9.1–2 in R.G. Poole, *Viking Poems on War and Peace* (Toronto: University of Toronto Press, 1991), 62. Keyed by the boar figure, this aristocratic image cluster (helmet, standard, nobleman, warrior, prince) suggests that the helmet-wearer was of extremely high social status—virtually royal—in part because of the sheer value of such ornate craftsmanship in the early Germanic world, and in part because of the scarcity of iron (Tacitus, *Germania*, ch. 6), the forging of which involved magic (Glosecki, *Shamanism*, ch. 4).

13. Bercilak's brave deed is the stuff of romance, a superhuman hunting tactic, since a single sword could hardly halt a charging boar, whose momentum alone could prove lethal even after the heart-thrust. Standard procedure was to plant a stout boar-spear (*eoferspreot, Beowulf* 1437b) in the ground, to absorb the shock of the charge; as several men held on, a crosspiece below the blade kept the animal from storming up the shaft, impaling itself to get at its attackers.

14. Pork seems to have been the favorite meat of Celtic and Germanic peoples; for instance, Ibn Fadlan says that the Rus "are very fond of pork and many of them who have assumed the garb of Muslimism miss it very much" (H.M. Smyser, "Ibn Fadlan's Account of the Rus," *Franciplegius*, ed. J.B. Bessinger and R.P. Creed [New York: New York University Press, 1965], 96). The boar-feast has semisacral implications (cf. Sæhrímnir, the marvelous boar of Valhalla). Besides other porcine effigies of Celtic origin, the boar-crested helmet appears in relief on the Gundestrup cauldron, which is usually considered of Celtic workmanship, although it was recovered in a Danish bog. The best-known boar in Celtic tradition is Arthur's mythic quarry, Twrch Trwyth, in the Welsh folktale *Culhwch and Olwen*, regarding which see Gwyn Jones, *Kings, Beasts and Heroes* (London: Oxford University Press, 1972), esp. ch. 3.4, "Hunters with Beasts."

15. Cf. Chambers, 359; H.R.E. Davidson, *Gods and Myths of Northern Europe* (Harmondsworth: Penguin, 1964), 98; Shetelig, 402. Speake's interpretation is exceptionally astute (81): "There is some evidence to associate the boar motif with kingship, protection, and fertility. When it appears on brooches, bracelets, and ornaments from women's graves, its probable role is as a symbol of fertility . . . above all else the boar was a symbol of protection, whose protective power may be associated with Woden / Odin."

16. The OED cites *bare, boar,* and *boer* as orthographic variants of *bore, sb.*3: "A tidal wave of extraordinary height, caused by the meeting of two tides, or by the rushing of the tide up a narrowing estuary." A synonym cited is *eagre*—especially for tidal surges up the Severn and Humber—under which entry the connection with the Norse sea god Ægir is unconvincingly discounted. These rivers were avenues of entry throughout the Viking Age. A North Germanic source seems likely for both of these mysterious terms.

17. A.T. Hatto, "Germanic and Kirgiz Heroic Poetry," *Deutung und Bedeutung: Studies in German and Comparative Literature,* ed. B. Schludermann et al. (The Hague: Mouton, 1973), 25.

18. Torslunda die D (fig. 8) depicts a horned spear dancer consorting with a werewolf (or with a partner wearing a wolf skin); see Bruce-Mitford, *Aspects,* pl. 59a. The *fylgja* (possibly derived from *fulga* "skin, covering, cloak") "fetch" is a familiar attribute of saga characters, sort of a doppelganger or "shadow self" with bansheelike impact on plot lines. Esp. cf. *Njáls saga,* chs. 12, 23, 62, 69. ON * úlfheðinn* "wolf jacket" denotes an ecstatic warrior with lupine propensities, as in *Grettis saga,* ch. 2, where the comparable *berserkir* "bear shirt" also appears. See Glosecki, *Shamanism,* ch. 6. Since that chapter also treats bear lore in some detail, ursine imagery is not discussed in this essay.

19. E.V.K. Dobbie, *The Anglo-Saxon Minor Poems,* ASPR 6 (New York: Columbia University Press, 1942), 29.

20. See *Njáls saga,* ch. 105.

21. See *Hrafnkels saga Freysgoða,* ch. 3 and esp. ch. 6, where the stallion is sacrificed in a manner evocative of prehistoric bog deposits, with precautions taken against its evil eye.

22. Mounds 3 and 4 at the Sutton Hoo site yielded the remains of cremated horses (Evans, 16, 18). Horses were also sacrificed during the funeral rites of Norse nobility (Davidson, *Scandinavia,* 112, 114–18, 130). In 922, on the eastern fringe of the Germanic common-culture area, Ibn Fadlan witnessed the ritualistic "sweating" and dismemberment of two horses, followed by their cremation with the dead aristocrat in the midst of his rich grave goods (Smyser, 99; full citation above, n. 14). Animal bone is quite common among pre-Christian Anglo-Saxon grave goods; see J.D. Richards, "Anglo-Saxon Symbolism" in *The Age of Sutton Hoo,* ed. Martin Carver (Woodbridge: Boydell, 1992), 137–41. Often, fragments alone were deposited; sympathetically—*totum ex parte*—a single tooth may represent the entire beast.

23. *Egils saga Skalla-Grímssonar,* ch. 57.

24. A sixth-century petroglyph from Hägeby, Uppland, depicts a horse fight (fig. 9); Shetelig suggests that the stone was a grave-memorial (246). He also implies a long prehistory for this motif, if not for the rite it represents (146, 246). Some of the Gotland symbol stones bear striking equine ornament as well. One of these, from Alskog (see Davidson, *Scandinavian Mythology* [London: Paul Hamlyn, 1969], 45), depicts a rider on Sleipnir, an image that evokes Odin in his role as psychopomp, leading the fearsome cavalcade of the dead (*den ville jakt, Odens jakt, das wutende Heer, das Totenheer,* etc.)

25. Certainly the hunt remained crucial throughout the Middle Ages, especially in winter, as Bercilak demonstrates above. Efforts to pigeonhole animistic applications of animal powers, e.g., shamanism, in convenient pre-agrarian (i.e., palaeolithic and hence "other") periods are foredoomed, human societies being palimpsests of passing cultures. Here I have in mind Joseph Campbell's neat but unreal categories—each a Procrustean bed—in his Frazerian compendium, *The Masks of God* (Harmondsworth: Penguin, 1976).

26. Cf., e.g., Torslunda die D (fig. 8) alongside the *ulfheðnar* and *berserkir* (above, n. 18); in *Hrólf's Saga Kraka* recounts the exploits of Germania's best-known were-bear, Boðvarr Bjarki, often cited as a Beowulf analog.

27. For copious examples of the petroglyphic horned men, Bronze Age, probably incised by the Battleax People and their descendants, see Peter Gelling and H.R.E.

Davidson, *The Chariot of the Sun* (New York: Praeger, 1969). This tradition probably influenced the later Germanic horned figures, usually linked to Odin, illustrated, e.g., in James Graham-Campbell, *Viking Artefacts* (London: British Museum, 1980), pl. 516 (see fig. 11). Cf. Shetelig, 246: "Traditions from the older Scandinavian rockcarvings may well have entered into the conception of such pictures in the migration period; the rock carvings themselves were perhaps not yet a dead art at that time." For interpretation of the Germanic horned man see H.R.E. Davidson, "The Finglesham Man: The Significance of the Man in the Horned Helmet," *Antiquity* 39 (1965), 23–27; and Glosecki, "Wolf Dancers and Whispering Beasts" (above, n. 9).

28. E.g., Webster and Backhouse (above, n. 3), 25; also D.M. Wilson, *Anglo-Saxon Art* (Woodstock: Overlook Press, 1984), 24. Further, in Webster and Backhouse, the fish symbol is overconfidently labeled a Christian icon: "the fish is an early Christian symbol denoting Christ: its prominent use here . . . illustrates the replacement of pagan images . . . by the new Christian iconography." So too Wilson, 12, 24. It is nonetheless equally likely that the symbol illustrates the continuity of a native Germanic tradition all but lost to us today. I find it intriguing that although she carefully describes the Sutton Hoo fish, Evans does not jump to the conclusion that it is a Christian icon (*Sutton Hoo*, 73–75). Nor for that matter, does she suggest that the great gold buckle, also hollow, was a reliquary (89–91).

29. Magnusson (above, n. 1) illustrates a "small copper locket containing the coiled skeleton of a snake, found in Gotland" (113). While he is probably correct in calling the amulet "magical," its wearer may have considered the talisman *sacred*.

30. Gerd Høst's translation, quoted by Davidson (*Scandinavia*, 131), who reads these cryptic lines as a reference to Odin "travelling in the spirit world in the shape of a fish." Aside from figuring in Viking sobriquets like Ketil "Trout" and Thorstein "Cod Biter," the fish appears in myths retold by Snorri. After Baldr's demise, for instance, Loki assumes salmon shape to hide from the angry Æsir, but Thor snatches the shape-shifter and his strong grip gives the salmon its characteristically tapered tail. Further, in *Volsunga saga* as in Snorri, the river-dwarf Andvari swims round his gold in the shape of a fish. Hence a native Germanic source for this symbol on an early Middle Saxon artifact cannot be discounted.

The Truculent Toad in the Middle Ages

Mary E. Robbins *

The figure of the toad appears as a symbol of either death or the pain of divine punishment, or both, in the literature and visual art of the Middle Ages. It is consistently associated with an array of strident images on the medieval moral bandwagon, images designed to encourage the sinner to repent. Its image reminds the Christian of the Day of Judgement and the certainty of either heaven or hell by its continued association with both purgatory for the conditionally saved and hell for the damned. It is a minister of punishment to those in purgatory and inhabits the regions of hell as a familiar of the devil. The toad was not always distinguished from its cousin the frog, and although the two images have been confused for centuries, they have not always been used interchangeably. The toad was generally considered evil and the frog benign. A classical precedent exists for attributing wicked characteristics to the toad, and a biblical one assigns equally menacing qualities to the frog. Even though the creatures look nearly identical in visual art, the context of the work often determines the identity. The distinction authors intend between the two animals is generally apparent in written texts during the Middle Ages where the words themselves differ.

The frog's association with death began as early as Aristophanes and his play of that name, which contains a benign frog chorus in the underworld.[1] Aristotle distinguishes between toad and frog in his essays on natural history, giving greater attention to the frog. A hint of unpleasantness occurs in *Parts of Animals* when he states that the toad's liver is bad-looking and comments on the bad mixture of substances in its body.[2] Yet his other references to both animals are descriptive only.

The Romans considered the toad to be a type of frog and, like the Greeks, thought that both animals had the potential for evil. A poetic reference in Horace's fifth epode, the grizzly tale of a young boy about to be sacrificed by three witches in order to enhance a love potion, suggests the

Romans' tacit understanding of the animal's reputation. Canidia, the chief witch in the poem, calls for the other ingredients necessary to her mixture: "wild fig-trees uprooted from the tombs, funereal cypresses, eggs and feathers of a night-roving screech-owl smeared with the blood of a hideous toad."[3] Horace uses the word *rana* here, the Latin term for frog. Because the toad's connection with evil was a part of Roman folk culture, Horace's audience understood his reference to the poisonous type of frog, the toad.

In the first book of the *Georgics*, Virgil describes the proper way to fashion a threshing floor and writes that it must be "made solid with binding clay, lest weeds spring up, or, crumbling into dust, it gape open, and then divers plagues make mock of you . . . in holes may be found the toad, and all the countless pests born of the earth."[4] In this passage, when Virgil refers to the toad, he uses the word *bufo*: "inventusque cavis bufo et quae plurima terrae / monstra ferunt" (ll. 18–45). This description represents the first written occurrence of the word *bufo*, and according to R.A.B. Mynors, "all later literary usage could derive from this passage, though it [*bufo*] is thought to be an old Italian word."[5] It is not a term used in classical Latin, and the only other times the word appears are in commentaries on the *Georgics*. *Bufo*, however, was used during the medieval period and remains today the common word for toad, and thus Virgil's passage has had a lasting influence not only on the animal's reputation but on its name as well. Virgil's description of the animal as a type of plague and a pest born of the earth remained part of toad lore through the end of the Middle Ages.

Perhaps the directly evil connotation begins in the first century A.D. with Pliny, who refers to both toad and frog numerous times in his *Natural History*, a compendium of popular and learned material. This work was widely disseminated during the Middle Ages, and accounts for at least a portion of the prevailing sentiment regarding toads. He discusses the transmission of poison and states that "water or wine when a salamander has died in it is fatal, and so is even drinking from a vessel out of which one has drunk; and similarly with the kind of frog called a toad! so full of traps is life!"[6] Pliny sometimes uses the terms frog and toad, *rana* and *rubeta* (a type of bramble toad), interchangeably according to ancient custom. In Book XXXII he explains that some frogs, because they live in brambles, are called bramble toads and states that "these are the largest of all frogs, have as it were a pair of horns, and are full of poison."[7] He writes that authorities tell fantastic tales about the magical powers of the toad, *rubeta*: it can silence a crowd by its presence; and a bone in its right side (here he changes to the term *rana*) can cool boiling water, but a bone in its left side can repel the attack of a dog or function as an aphrodisiac (ll. 50–2). Roman folk beliefs that attributed magical powers to the frog / toad remained current in medieval witchcraft rituals.

Juvenal uses the term *rubeta* to signify not the animal but the poison itself. In his first satire, a characteristic indictment of the morally corrupt, he inveighs against a "matrona potens" [powerful lady] who poisons her husband's wine with *rubetam*, or toad's blood, teaches her neighbors to do the same, and then tells them "nigros efferre maritos" [to bury their blackened spouses].[8] Here Juvenal assumes his audience's familiarity with the folklore tradition of poisonous toad's blood. Following this passage, Juvenal wonders at the prevalence of avarice and the deification of wealth, and he concludes the work with the warning, "Turn these things over in your mind before the trumpet sounds; the helmet once donned, it is too late to repent you of the battle."[9] Juvenal's urbanity notwithstanding, elements of this satire, as it inclines toward moral correction, could have been written by a medieval churchman. The connection with avarice and the final warning about the wages of sin provide a classical authority tailored to the needs of the Middle Ages. In his second satire Juvenal proves himself less credulous than his countrymen when he writes that not even a child would believe in "such things as Manes, and kingdoms below the ground, and punt-poles, and Stygian pools black with frogs, and all those thousands crossing over in a single bark."[10]

The toad is also guilty by association with the frogs that feature prominently in the biblical account of the second plague visited upon the Egyptians, described in the Book of Exodus. God warns Pharaoh to free the Jews or accept punishment:

> I will smite all thy borders with frogs: And the river shall bring forth frogs abundantly, which shall go up and come into thine house, and into thy bedchamber, and upon thy bed, and into the house of thy servants, and upon thy people, and into thine ovens, and into thy kneading troughs: And the frogs shall come up both on thee, and upon thy people, and upon all thy servants. (Exod. 8:2–4)

This episode provides a scriptural precedent for divine retribution toward man in the form of bestial invasion. Throughout the Middle Ages the frog/toad image was popular in visual representations of pestilence in general. For example, figure 1, an illustration from a 1497 Lubeck edition of Sebastian Brant's *Ship of Fools*, refers to a section of the work describing the punishment that will be directed against fools who do not hear God's command.

The vision described in the Book of Revelations complements the Old Testament account, and by rights the two together should have established an evil connotation to the frog. When the sixth seal was opened, John saw issue "from the mouth of the dragon, and the mouth of the beast, and from the mouth of the false prophet, three unclean spirits like frogs. For they are the spirits of devils, working signs" (16:13–14). Representations of the Revelations episode appear frequently in the visual art of the period, and in such instances, when the artist is clearly working from this well-known source, the creatures are meant to be frogs rather than toads. Yet these powerful biblical images contributed significantly to the toad's reputation for evil because of the conflation of the frog and toad identities. The episode from Exodus describes the way in which man is punished for his disobedience to God

Figure 1. Woodcut from a 1497 Lubeck edition of Sebastian Brant's Ship of Fools. Brant's piece, along with the very popular illustrations, was widely disseminated and added to the toad's sinister reputation. (By permission of the Houghton Library, Harvard University.)

by means of a frog invasion, just as numerous medieval descriptions of purgatory and hell describe the sinner punished by means of vicious toads. The Revelations account describes the frogs as spirits of devils at the Last Judgement, and in medieval accounts toads play prominent roles as ministers of punishment in the underworld.

The image of the toad as an agent of evil is established in literary texts by the twelfth century, or at least it begins to appear frequently in the literature during that time. It is unlikely that the image became suddenly popular. Because a greater number and variety of texts are extant from that time period and those following than still exist from the years between the third and eleventh centuries, naturally a greater number of examples can be found now. The toad's reputation as established in classical tradition, a reputation associated as much with witchcraft as with folklore, was incorporated into written literature by medieval authors wanting to appeal in a practical way to their audiences.

The evil toad image appears in sermons and penitential literature, in descriptions of the evils that man will experience after death should his life be ruled by one of the seven deadly sins, and in visions of purgatory and hell. It appears almost casually in the *Anglo-Saxon Chronicle* for the year 1137. During the reign of King Stephen the evil bishops tortured men and women who had any type of goods, and "they put them into prisons that contained adders, snakes, and toads, and thereby killed them."[11] Here the danger present in these animals is taken for granted by an author who assumes his audience will understand the reference. The toad is sometimes an element used in witchcraft rituals. The origin of this use lies at least with the Romans and their poisonous toad's blood, but it appears in this context throughout the Middle Ages. Many of the witchcraft rites reverse the customary order of things, and the toad is used as an antidote rather than as the element for which an antidote is sought. The idea of poison is, perhaps, the one constant component of the toad's image over the centuries. A twelfth-century Latin bestiary simply calls the animal "venomous,"[12] and this label, perhaps a legacy from the past rather than a result of personal observation, was confirmed by Albertus Magnus in the thirteenth century. In describing the feeding habits of the stork, Albert states unequivocally that "it does not eat truly venomous animals, such as toads."[13] Although Albert says nothing new, he is a medieval Pliny, recording the knowledge of his time. Some toads do indeed produce a poison.[14] This natural virulence, along with the fact that most toads have somewhat less pleasing aspects than do most frogs, helps to account for the toad's greater reputation for evil.

Figure 2. Illustration, designed by Master A.F., from the Book of Relics, *Vienna, 1502. The motto reads, "Everybody afterwards." Here the toads are in the familiar company of snakes and a skeleton.*

Because it was generally thought that the toad had teeth, it is found in both literature and visual art literally feeding on those in purgatory and in hell, or feeding on their decomposing bodies, depending upon the emphasis of the piece. When the image appears in visual art, it functions as a reminder not only of death's eventuality but also of its hideousness, and is thus an immediately recognizable representation of the *memento mori* theme. For example, figure 2, an emblem of death from Vienna, dated 1502 and bearing the inscription "Everybody afterwards," contains toads along with other standard death symbols: the grave, skeletal remains, snakes.

The toad fits comfortably with the earthy language and direct message of the literature in which it appears, and the image was so useful during the Middle Ages precisely because it was so commonplace and thus could upend the deceptive remoteness of death. Literature of this type is essentially practical, geared toward altering human behavior by appealing to the very basic fear of bodily harm. When that harm can be readily pictured, the threat increases. A fire-breathing demon that may fly through the air, snatch up the sinner, and punch him down into the burning pit is a disturbing prospect, and this type of image occurs throughout the Middle Ages. Yet the infernal grandeur of it ensures a certain distance. A toad that can leap from under the next rock is an immediate and tangible reality, something with which most people could identify, that could encourage the sinner to recognize death close at hand.

The theme of animals torturing sinners in purgatory and hell is as old as the gospels. The chastising animal appears in the Apocrypha, Pseudo-apocrypha, and numerous other types of literature throughout the Middle Ages. The Book of Isaiah, for example, ends with the warning to transgressors that "their worm shall not die, neither shall their fire be quenched" (66:24). This verse was popular with preachers well into the Renaissance, and in literature having to do with the infernal regions, worms regularly appear along with toads, adders, vipers, spiders, and serpents. Novatian, in a discussion of Jewish foods, describes the way in which the early Church used animals to represent abstract qualities. He also makes clear the way in which animals represent human vices.[15] Gregory the Great in Book Four of his *Cura Pastoralis* describes a dragon who thrusts his head into the mouth of a sinner, draws out all of his breath, and prepares to devour him. The toad's sinister reputation ensured its inclusion in the tradition of these infernal devourers.

A particularly detailed representation of the truculent toad occurs in the late twelfth-century *St. Patrick's Purgatory*, a popular story of an Irish knight who descends into the other world through a cave entrance in the north of Ireland. The hero of the earliest version, in Latin, must sample some of the punishments of purgatory. The following passage, in which the author depicts the third torment sinners must endure, illustrates the kind of violent background that almost always accompanies the toad:

Similarly, this plain was packed with human beings of both sexes and all ages, pinned to the ground . . . . [T]hese were held fast on their backs. Flaming dragons were sitting on some of them, lacerating them with their burning teeth in a pitiful way as if they were eating them. Fiery snakes encircled other people's necks, arms or entire bodies and, pressing their heads against the chests of the poor wretches, they sank the burning fangs of their mouths into their hearts. One could also see toads of wonderful size and as if made of fire sitting on the chests of some and burying their hideous muzzles there as if trying to pull out their hearts. And those who were thus pinned and tormented never ceased crying and moaning. Also, the devils ran between them and above them and tortured them by beating them violently with whips. . . . The devils said: "You will suffer the tortures you see unless you agree with us to turn back." And as he was scorning them they tried as previously to pin him with nails but they were not able to do so when they heard the name of Jesus.[16]

Although the toad is always poisonous and always associated with death, this passage contains several specific motifs that form a backdrop to the creature in other pieces: it is in the company of other homiletic vermin, typically (as in this case) with snakes; and it gnaws at the body after death, often specifically at the face or the heart. The images here are designed to provoke an immediate, physical alarm in the listener. The type of literature in which the toad appears during the Middle Ages has little to do with courtly refinement or the subtleties of theological disquisition. The graphic and earthy language of this passage, representative of other literature of this type, is directed toward a popular audience. Just as the walls and windows of a Gothic cathedral provided a textbook for the unlettered, passages of this sort gave a sensory reference to Christian didacticism.

Predictably, as in most literature intended to reform the sinner, the way to avoid the punishments described is stated explicitly. Of course the avoidance of sin is always the surest way, and the idea is always implicit. In many passages of this sort, however, the idea of immediate respite is close by. In this instance, the knight, although threatened with torture by the devils, is freed at once when he invokes the name of Jesus. The extent and violence of the activity here contrasts sharply with the single utterance that immediately quells the disturbance. The author has demonstrated the power of the devil and the infinitely greater power of God. He also offers the twofold lesson that an ounce of sin must be paid for with a pound of repentance, and that an ounce of true repentance may compensate for a pound of sin.

In 1187 Giraldus Cambrensis, in *The Topography of Ireland*, observed that Ireland did not contain any poisonous reptiles, "neither snakes nor adders, toads nor frogs."[17] He goes on to explain that a potion made from thongs, "which are the real produce of the island, and made of the skins of animals born there, being grated in waters which is drunk . . . is an efficacious remedy against the bites of toads and serpents" (49). Here the notion that toads bite is an assumption of the author and, presumably, also of his readers.

In his *Itinerary Through Wales* (c. 1207) Giraldus talks again about the animal, this time relating the story of a young Welshman who was persecuted by toads

> as if the reptiles of the whole province had come to him by agreement; and though destroyed by his nurses and friends, they increased again on all sides in infinite numbers, like hydras' heads. His attendants, both friends and strangers, being wearied out, he was drawn up in a kind of bag, into a high tree, stripped of its leaves, and shred; nor was he there secure from his venomous enemies, for they crept up the tree in great numbers, and consumed him even to the very bones.[18]

This passage is noteworthy because of the anthropomorphism described. The toads pursue and destroy a live human rather than punish one already dead, and they outwit his friends and relatives in the bargain. Here they are not simply instruments of evil, but become the thinking, plotting evil force itself. This toad image is in the folklore tradition and not used as a vehicle for an exemplum or other type of moral commentary.

Caesarius of Heisterbach, in *The Dialogue on Miracles* from the early thirteenth century, combines both religious and folklore traditions in a story of the persistant zombie toad. Caesarius says in his introduction to the *Dialogue* that he has written it "propter inopes, non gratia, sed literatura" [for the sake of the needy, not for their pleasure but for their education]. In consequence, his images are plain, if unusual by current standards. He tells the story of a monk named Theodoric who lifted a harrow and found a toad underneath. As "it rose on its hind legs as if to fight, he killed it with a piece of wood."[19] However, the dead toad immediately arose and began to pursue the monk. He attacked the animal a second time and then burned it up, but to no avail. It followed him again and again. One day while out riding with a friend he discovered the toad creeping up the tail of his horse and ready to attack. His companion, seeing what was about to happen, exclaimed, "Take care, see, the devil is climbing your horse" (225). Theodoric jumped down from his horse and killed the toad. "'Look,' said he, 'where that devil is. Never shall I be free from him, unless he gets his revenge'" (225). He allowed the toad to bite him, and eventually was freed from the devil. Caesarius spells out the lesson to be learned here: "God often punishes sinners by monsters like this, that they may know how great a punishment is prepared in the future, where their worm shall not die nor their fire be extinguished" (226).

The elements of the story, if not the story itself, would have been familiar to the audience of Caesarius. Lifting a harrow, or any object, and discovering a toad underneath is a common occurrence in a rural setting, and most of the medieval European population was rural. A regular posture for a real toad is to sit with its forelegs raised. Caesarius begins his story with this image in order to prompt immediate recognition of the situation in his audience. He has made the ordinary ominous here. The mingling of the doctrinal with the familiar, the worm of Isaiah with the toad of witchcraft, reflects the integration of Catholicism with pagan superstition.

Here the toad acts as a familiar of the devil. Its relentless pursuit of the monk mirrors the ongoing struggle between good and evil. It represents satanic tenacity and resilience, as well as the fact that evil can lurk around any corner or hide under any stone. Good triumphs because, like Christ, the monk becomes a willing sacrifice. Yet Caesarius also demonstrates the fact that evil in this life cannot be avoided but must be confronted and dealt with just as the monk must confront the toad.

The narrative in the thirteenth-century "Sawles Warde" describes the cause and desired effect of the toad image to instill fear in the sinner's heart and to portend death. The piece is an allegory likening the Christian's inner self to a house that must be protected by Wit from the thieving devil who will attempt to steal the treasure, the soul. Prudence, guardian of the house, sends a messenger, "his appearance deathly, black, and livid"[20] to warn the inhabitants: "I am called Fear, and am death's messenger and death's reminder and am come before her to warn of her coming."[21] When Prudence asks Fear from whence he comes, he answers, "I come . . . from hell,"[22] and then goes on to ennumerate its tortures. To increase the pains of the damned, "the loathly hell worms, toads, and frogs eat out their eyes and nostrils. And adders and water-lizards—not like those we have here, but a hundred times more gruesome—sneak in and out at the mouth, ears, eyes, navel and at the breast-hollow."[23] The heart image is suggested by the "breoste holke" [breast-hollow], and the toad is in company with other demonic feeders: hell-worms, adders, and frogs.

The description of the body devoured by vermin is purposely extreme here and in the other places where it occurs, because it was meant to inspire not simply fear but also repugnance in the listener. The image of a toad's eating one's eyes and nostrils, in all of its tangible unpleasantness, can be immediately conceived by a listener. The fact that the elements of the vision are all common ones—eyes, nose, toad—makes it more threatening because it becomes more real and more clearly possible. A particularly vivid illustration of this type of vision can be found on the *transi* tomb of François de la Sarra, which dates from late fourteenth-century Switzerland. It is the figure of a nude reclining male, his head lying on a pillow and his hands across his chest; four toads are placed on his face and a fifth covers his genitals.[24]

A poem describing "The Visions of Seynt Poul Wan He Was Rapt Into Paradys," also from the thirteenth century, contains a list of the afflictions of hell. St. Paul sees a terrible flood and the "devil's beasts"[25] therein as "toads, adders, snakes, and many more; / And they eat and gnaw the sinful souls" (ll. 60–2). This passage is representative of many others of its type. The toad has become a useful literary image and a creature as at home in hell for medieval authors as it was for the ancients. Here they are specifically termed the devil's beasts, and all three of these animals become representations of the devil himself.

In the same vein, in his fourteenth-century meditation on the passion of Christ, Richard Rolle sternly warns the sinner,

> [T]hink, thou wretched caitiff, how it shall be for thee when thou shalt be cast into a pit under the earth, when toads, worms, snakes and other venomous beasts shall eat thy eyes, thy nose, thy mouth, thy lips, thy tongue, thy head, thy hands, thy feet, and all thy body. Then who shall be thy help, thy comfort, and thy refuge? . . . Therefore, thou wretched caitiff, now, when time still remains for mercy and pity, run to that dear lord Jesus and say "Mercy, dear Jesus."[26]

This passage fits the general pattern of the others. The toad is in the company of snakes, worms, and other venomous creatures; they feed on the corpse, and the idea of respite follows immediately with the admonishment to the reader to ask for divine mercy now while time permits. In the true spirit of meditation, Rolle calls attention to each specific body part. His process of description suggests the gradual progress of decomposition.

Caxton's Mirrour of the World briefly instructs that "a man or a woman bitten by the toad, frog, or spider will be in danger of dying; it has often been seen. The spittle of a man fasting commonly slays the spider and the toad if it should touch them."[27] Here the toad is accompanied by the spider. As always, it bites and is poisonous, and in this instance the sacred balm that acts as antidote is the "spttle of a man fastyng." The scarcity of this antidote betokens the difficult road the Christian must travel in order to avoid subjecting his soul to the venom of sin. The fact that each sinner has control over his own salvation gives hope. Fasting, the activity of a repenting sinner, can prevent both physical and spiritual death.

Many of the toad's environments in both literary and visual art include the motif of the seven deadly sins. A Middle English sermon from around 1400 includes a lesson on envy, saying that

> [H]e who bears envy in his heart does not consider men's welfare, and he is glad and joyful over man's evil-fare. And thus he may be likened to the fiend of hell. . . . It would be painful to such men to fail to get to heaven. . . . Yet, they will never arrive there unless they amend their ways. And therefore they are like a foul toad that may not see the bright sun without being greatly pained.[28]

Here the heart appears as the host of envy in the sinner, who is portrayed as a foul toad deprived of the bright light of salvation, not having repented. Deguileville's *Pilgrimage*, in a section on ire, cautions:

> When ire pains my heart,
> I am so venomous, in truth,
> That I swell as any toad does.[29]

Here the venom of ire fills the sinner's heart and makes him like the evil toad.

Many treatments of the deadly sins are much more elaborate than this. For example, a twelfth-century cleric, preaching on the topic "Of the Prophet Jeremiah" [Hic Dicendum Est De Propheta], connects the toad with both gluttony and avarice, and the creature is associated with these two sins throughout the Middle Ages. An immoderate concern with the pleasures of this world suggests that inadequate attention is being paid to those of the next. This Lambeth Homily describes the pit of sin into which the unwary may fall. Its inhabitants are, in part, "black toads, and have venom in their hearts."[30] The homilist explains further that

> those black toads that have venom in their hearts betoken the rich men that have many worldly goods and yet may neither eat nor drink in moderation, nor do anything for the love of God almighty

who has given it all to them. But they lie thereupon as the toad does in the earth, that never can eat her fill with moderation because she is afraid lest the earth fail her.

Here the imagery is milder than that found in other accounts, such as *St. Patrick's Purgatory*, yet the heart and eating images are both present. The toad was consistently represented as living underground, just as hell was thought to be somewhere underneath, in the middle of the earth. This concept is a natural one, since real toads characteristically burrow beneath ground. Here the demonic companions are adders, yellow frogs, and crabs; although the toad does not gnaw at a human heart, the creatures have venom in their hearts, and thus the passage utilizes the common motifs. As this preacher indicates, the wealth that man gathers will turn to "black venom" (53), and that blackness reflects the state of his soul. Of particular note in this passage is the representation of the toad as female. A twelfth-century relief of a toad with a woman's face from the cloister at Notre-Dame, Le Puy, France, visually demonstrates this theme. As Janetta Benton observes, "In an era when women were viewed as a source of temptation, this frog [or toad], symbol of sin, was given a woman's head."[31]

The *Fasciculus Morum*, a fourteenth-century preacher's handbook, also favors both avarice and gluttony as companions to the toad. The author provides two lessons on avarice and one on gluttony. He begins by describing a wealthy usurer who

> made his wife swear that after his death she would tie thirty marks from his profits on his body. . . . Shortly after he had been buried with the money, a legate came from the Curia and, hearing all this, ordered the priest who had buried him to take him out of the cemetery of the faithful and throw him in the open field and burn him. Now, when the priest and his assistants came to him, they found in the place where the money had been tied ugly toads that gnawed at his miserable decomposing body and countless worms instead of an armband of money. When they saw this, they burned him, and many died of the stench.[32]

Here the toads that gnaw the body are in the company of worms. The money, which the man had consumed during his lifetime and having changed to toads, literally consumes him after death. The theme of toads sharing a man's tomb is given grisly representation on the early sixteenth-century German *transi* figures of Peter Niderwirt, in the Pfarrkirche in

Figure 3. The gluttonous forced by demons to eat toads. Illustration from Le Grant Kalendrier et Compost des Bergiers, *printed by Nicolas Le Rouge, Troyes, 1496. This piece is one of a series illustrating the seven deadly sins.*

Eggenfelden, and Bernhard Beham, in the Pfarrkirche in Halle-in-Tyrol. Here the decomposing bodies are clearly inhabited by toads and snakes that writhe in and out of the skeletons, and in both instances the vermin center around the chest cavity and the face.[33]

The *Fasciculus Morum* continues with a story about a usurer who was disinterred, and when the stone was removed from his tomb, those present "saw his black and stinking body and a toad sitting on it, who, like a nurse, held burning coins to the dead man's mouth and fed him these. When they saw that, they fled in horror, and then demons came and carried the corpse with its coffin away, and he was nowhere seen again."[34] Here, the familiar pattern is reversed and the toad forces the sinner to eat. The man who had collected wealth during his lifetime is choked with it after death. This image suggests the punishments often depicted for the sin of gluttony, wherein the offender is force-fed by demons past the point of surfeit. Figure 3, a woodcut from the year 1496, shows gluttons being force-fed on toads. The piece is one in a series entitled *Le Grant Kalendrier et Compost des Bergiers* from Le Rouge, Troyes, depicting punishments for the seven deadly sins.

In a fifteenth-century sermon on gluttony ("De Dominica in Quinquagesima") the author, John Mirk, tells about the son of a rich man who visits his father's tomb. The father had eaten lavishly during his lifetime. When the son had the tomb slab removed, "then he saw a passing great toad, as black as pitch, with eyes burning like fire, that had embraced his father's throat with her four feet, and gnawed firmly thereon. Then, when the son saw this sight he said: 'O father, much sweet meat and drink has gone down that throat; and now thou art strangled with a foule hell-beast!'"[35] The son then had the slab replaced; left his home, wife, and family; and went to Jerusalem to live out his life as a beggar. When he died, he enjoyed heavenly bliss. This exemplum is also found in the *Fasciculus Morum*, which contains the additional warning: "They say that after death three kinds of vermin are literally born of a human body: a toad from his head and throat, a scorpion from his spine, and a weevil from his body and stomach."[36] Just as sin breeds death of the spirit, the residue left in the body of a sinner after death engenders vermin. Sin eats away at the soul during a person's lifetime, and it breeds vermin that eat away at the body after death.

A fifteenth-century female mystic, in *A Revelation of Purgatory*, describes the punishment for sinful nuns guilty of lechery and slander. She begins by explaining that they are being punished for improperly kissing men and goes on to describe the punishment: "Then," she writes, "I thought the devils took out their tongues and set adders and toads upon them, and then the devils said, 'Take this for your false lechery and foul words and foul dissemblance and backbiting and slandering.'"[37] Here the toads are again paired with adders, and both are fed to sinners. Slander and backbiting, of course, are sins of the mouth, and thus the nature of the punishment suggests the scene of the crime.

This section is followed by one describing the pains of single men and women who "were put on spits and roasted, and as many adders and snakes and toads, and also much foul venom as might swarm about them,

Figure 4. Danse Macabre illustration showing Death and a young man; engraving by the Master of the Housebook, Germany, 1490. The toad here suggests the innocent aspect that sin—and its companion, death—can assume in the world.

were set on them to suck and to gnaw them. And then they were taken off of these spits, and the devils drew them throughout the fire with hard, sharp hooks. . . . And they all drew out their hearts and their most privy members. Then the devils said to them, 'Take these pains because you abused yourself in the foul lust of lechery'" (75–76). Here the toads and snakes again gnaw the bodies, and although they do not center on the heart, the devils in the following lines do so by pulling out the hearts of the damned with sharp hooks.

In the fifteenth-century "Lazarus" pageant from the Towneley Corpus Christi Cycle, the main character, having just risen from the dead, describes to his listeners the experience awaiting each of them. He explains that worldly goods are worthless in the grave and advises immediate repentance. The toad assumes its traditional role as Lazarus cautions, "A sheet shall be your royal robe / Toads shall be your brooch; / Toads shall harm you, / Fiends will terrify you."[38] Here the animals sit upon the chests of the dead, and whereas fiends only terrify, toads actually harm. Lazarus goes on to tell the audience "Worms shall breed in you / As bees do in the hive, / And the eyes out of your head / Thusly shall toads pick."[39] The toad here is in the familiar company of worms, picking out the eyes of the dead rather than eating them.

In both literary and visual art during the Middle Ages, the toad functions as one of a group of images employed to remind the Christian of the four last things. The poison that was thought to ensure the instant death of the body mirrors the like effect of sin upon the soul. And just as the Christian who would be physically sound must avoid even a touch of such venom, so too must the one who would be spiritually worthy avoid even the gentlest brush with deadly sin.

The toad also represents the unpleasant journey the body must take after death, when it is left to decay and to provide food for vermin in accordance with biblical predictions. This theme was, of course, popular in every art form during the Middle Ages, and received especially poignant treatment in the visual arts in pieces designed to contrast the beauty of youth with the repugnance of death. The theme is nicely executed in figure 4 ("Death and the Young Man," a late fifteenth-century German engraving by the Master of the Housebook), in which the toad sits just at the feet of Death.

The aspect of the toad that is perhaps most remarkable in the twentieth century is its energetic feeding on the body, regardless of the state of decay. By doing so, the toad becomes a representative of the devil, and the activity becomes an extension of the demonic prerogative of eating sinners and then ejecting them in one way or another. Perhaps this theme gets its fullest literary treatment in *The Vision of Tundale*, a verse narrative from the twelfth century, but it appears frequently, for example, in the thirteenth-century homily "Sawles Warde." Tundale is a rich but evil man whose spirit is shown both the pains and pleasures of the afterlife. When he sees Lucifer, the evil one is bound with iron chains to a grid suspended over a pit of burning coals. Each time Lucifer sighs he inhales and then exhales sinners; some he actually swallows and "with the reek and stink of brimstone / The souls that passed out at his end / Fell into the fire and burned."[40] The author of "Sawles Warde" also warns against the pains of hell, where hideous dragons swallow sinners whole "and spew them out afterward before and behind, all the while tearing them to pieces and chewing every bit of them" (251).[41] Medieval torments are intimately connected with things of the flesh and have to do with physical pain. This physicality reflects a general concern with the flesh as the outer reflection of man's soul and as the material element that inclines the spirit to transgress. Yet an age so fond of paradox also understood the sustaining power of the Eucharist and the fact that Christ entered this world as the word of God made flesh. The body was at once the charnel house of sin and the temple of the Holy Spirit. The devil—in whatever form—that feeds on a human body mimics the good Christian who consumes the Eucharist, and the physical pain of the former is the antithesis of the spiritual enrichment of the latter. In such an era, religious instruction was meant to help the faithful understand that one form of eating may preclude the other.

The toad appears in an intensely resolute body of literature that reflects the unwavering religious zeal of the Middle Ages. Both literary and visual depictions of death and its consequences became more elaborate as the period progressed. The effects of the plague made death an intermittant companion and focused the attention of the population concretely on the frailty of the flesh. It became increasingly difficult for an artist to find imagery extreme enough to shock a population for whom the smell and appearance of a decomposing body had become familiar.

The heyday of the toad image ended with the Middle Ages and the type of didactic literature for which the animal was so well suited. As a literary reference and as a representative of death or the demonic, however, the image persists today. Shakespeare honored the animal in his plays, especially with purpose in *Richard III*. The title character is called a "poisonous bunch-backed toad" (I, iii, 245) by Queen Margaret and "that bottled spider, that foul bunch-backed toad" (IV, iv, 81) by Queen Elizabeth; in the same vein and also referring to Richard, Lady Anne states that "never hung poison on a fouler toad" (I, ii, 147). In *Paradise Lost*, when the angels Ithuriel and Zephon search Eden for the serpent, they find him "squat like a Toad, close at the ear of Eve" (IV, 800). Not to be outdone by artists in earlier centuries, Günter Grass published a novel entitled *The*

Call of the Toad (1992), which has as one of its themes modern attitudes toward death. The toad has thus become a literary image as inextricably linked with death as the lily with purity.

An early fourteenth-century statue at Nürnburg Cathedral depicts the devil as tempter or seducer. Here the devil has the pleasing aspect of a young man from the front. He stands in his crown and robes, holding out an apple. From the back his true nature is visible; he is filled with vermin in the forms of snakes and toads that crawl up and down his body.[42] He contemplates the apple in his hand and recalls man's first transgression. His appearance mirrors the state of a Christian who has a pleasing outer aspect but whose soul is filled with sin. To be sure, the image of the toad in the literary and visual arts of the Middle Ages, like the apple held by the demonic prince of Strasbourg cathedral, provided the Christian with food for thought. Both images offered man a homely reminder of his own frailty and a warning that what is bought in this world must be paid for in the next.

NOTES

*Grateful acknowledgment is made to Dover Publications and the Dover Pictorial Archive Series for allowing illustrations from *Devils, Demons, Death and Damnation* (Ernst and Johanna Lehner, 1971) to be reprinted here. The illustration from *The Ship of Fools* is by permission of the Houghton Library, Harvard University.

1. See Max Wellmann, *Paulys Realencyclopädie Der Classischen Altertumswissenschaft* (Stuttgart: Alfred Druckenmuller, 1910), band VII, I, col. 113.

2. Aristotle, *Parts of Animals*, trans. A.L. Peck (London: William Heinemann, 1968), vol. XII, bk. III, xii, 30.

3. Horace, *The Odes and Epodes*, trans. C.E. Bennett (London: William Heinemann, 1968), ll. 17–19. [iubet cupressus funebres / et uncta turpis ova ranae sanguine / plumamque nocturnae strigis.]

4. Virgil, *Georgics*, trans. H. Rushton Faircloth (London: William Heinemann, 1967), vol. I, bk. I, 176–86. [et vertenda manu et creta solidanda tenaci, / ne subeant herbae neu pulvere victa fatiscat, / tum variae inludant pestes . . . inventusque cavis bufo et quae plurima terrae / monstra ferunt.]

5. Virgil, *Georgics*, ed. R.A.B. Mynors (Oxford: Clarendon Press, 1990), 42.

6. Pliny, *Natural History*, trans. H. Rackham (London: William Heinemann, 1947), vol. III, bk. xi, ll. 280–1. [et aqua vinumque interimit salamandra ibi inmortua, vel si omnio unde biberit potetur; item rana quam rebetam vocant: tantum insidiarum est vitae!]

7. Pliny, *Natural History*, trans. W.H.S. Jones (London: William Heinemann, 1940), vol. VIII, bk. xxxii, ll. 50–2. [grandissimae cunctarum, geminis veluti cornibus, plenae veneficiorum.]

8. Juvenal, *Juvenal and Persius*, trans. G.G. Ramsay (London: William Heinemann, 1969), Satira I, ll. 69–72.

9. Juvenal, ll. 169–70. [tecum prius ergo voluta / haec animo ante tubas: galeatum sero duelli / paenitet.]

10. Juvenal, Satira II, ll. 149–52. [Esse aliquos manes et subterranea regna / et contum et Stygio ranas in gurgite nigras, / atque una transire vadum tot milia

cumba / nec pueri credunt.]

11. *Two of the Saxon Chronicles*, ed. Charles Plummer (Oxford: Clarendon Press, 1892; rpt. 1965), 264. [Hi dyden heom in quarterne þar nadres & snakes & pades waeron inne. & drapen heom swa.]

12. T.H. White, trans. *The Book of Beasts, Being a Translation from a Latin Bestiary of the Twelfth Century* (London: Jonathan Cape, 1954), 217.

13. Albert the Great, *Man and the Beasts: De Animalibus (Books 22–26)*, trans. James J. Scanlan (Binghamton, N.Y.: Medieval and Renaissance Texts and Studies, 1987), 213.

14. See Mary C. Dickerson, *The Frog Book* (New York: Dover Books, 1969), 63–116.

15. Novatian, *Novatian*, trans. Russell DeSimone (Washington, D.C.: Catholic University of America Press, 1974), 146–51.

16. *Saint Patrick's Purgatory*, trans. Jean-Michael Picard (Dublin: Four Courts Press, 1985), 58–9. [Latin text from *St. Patrick's Purgatory*, ed. Robert Easting (Oxford: Oxford University Press, 1991): Istos inter autem et alterius campi miseros hec erat diuersitas, quod illorum quidem uentres, istorum dorsa terre herebant. Dracones igniti super alios sededbant et quasi c(om)edentes illos modo miserabili dentibus ignitis lacerabant. Aliorum autem colla uel brachia uel totum corpus serpentes igniti circumcingebant et, capita sua pectoribus miserorum inprimentes, ignitum aculeum oris sui in cordibus eorum infigebant. Buffones etiam mire magnitudinis et quasi ignei uidebantur super quorundam pectora sedere et, rostra sua deformia infigentes, quasi eorum corda conarentur extrahere. Qui ita fixi et afflicti a fletu et eiulatu nunquam cessabant. / Demones etiam inter eos et super eos transcurrentes flagris eos uehementer cedendo cruciabant. Finis huius campi pre sui longitudine uideri non potuit nisi in latitudine, qua intrauit et exiuit; in transuersum enim campos pertransiuit. "Hec," inquiunt demones, "que uides tormenta patieris, nisi ut reuertaris assenseris." Cumque eos contempsisset, conati sunt, sicut et superius, clauis eum figere, sed non potuerunt, audito Ihesu nomine. (ll. 393–410)]

17. Giraldus Cambrensis, *The Historical Works of Giraldus Cambrensis*, ed. Thomas Wright, trans. Thomas Forester (London: H.G. Bohn, 1863), 48. [Latin text from *Rerum Britannicarum Medii Aevi Scriptores*, ed. J.S. Brewer (London: Longman, Green, Longman, and Roberts, 1861): "Inter omnia vermium genera, solis non noeivis Hibernia gaudet. Venenosis enim omnibus caret. Caret serpentibus et colubris; caret bufonibus et ranis; caret tortuis et scorpionibus; caret et draconibus." (*Topography* XXVIII, 62) "Corrigiae quoque terrae istius, non adulterinae sed verae, et de eoriis animalium quae hic nata sunt factae, contra serpentum bufonumque morsus, in aqua rasae et potae, efficax remedium fere solent." (XXXI, 64)]

18. Giraldus Cambrensis, *The Historical Works of Giraldus Cambrensis*, ed. Thomas Wright, trans. Richard Hoare, 422–3. [Latin text from Brewer ed. (see note 17): "Hoc itaque nostro tempore contigit (scilicet) juvenem quemdam, de finibus his oriundum, tantam a bufonibus in aegritudinis lecto persecutionem fuisse perpessum, ut omnes totius provinciae tanquam ex condicto in ipsum concurrerent. Et cum a custodibus et amicis ipsius interfecti fuissent intiniti, semper tamen undique confluentes tanquam Hydrae capita sine numero succreverunt. Tandem vero, lassatis universis tam necessariis quam extraneis, in arbore quadam excelsa, mutilata frondibus et levigata, in loculo quodam est sublimatus. Nec ibi venenosis tutus ab hostibus; immo certatim in arborem rependo petitus, et usque ad ossa consumptus interiit." (*Itinerary* II, 110–1)]

19. Caesarius of Heisterbach, *The Dialogue on Miracles*, trans. H. Vone, E. Scott, and C.C. Swinton Bland (London: George Routledge and Sons, 1929), bk. IV, chap. lxvii. [Hic tempore quodam iuuentutis suae dum in agro tribulos aridos levasset, bufonem sub eis magnum offendit. Qui cum se contra eum in pedes suos

posteriores quasi ad pugnam erexisset, ille iratus arrepto ligno vermem occidit. Mirabile dictu. Cum Theodericus nihil minus suspicaretur, vidit bufonem extinctum sua insequi vestigia. Quem cum denuo transfodisset, et multatiens concremando incinerasset, non tamen profecit. Non fuit locus adeo remotus, adeo mundus, qui ei ad·dormiendum esset tutus. Noctibus per clipeum timore illius ad trabem suspendebatur. Cum tempore quodam equitaret cum quodam venatore socio suo, eique tanta mirabilia conquerendo recitaret, ecce vermem eundem ille vidit caudae equi eius inhaerentem, celeriusque ad eum scandentem. Qui mox exclamavit: Cave cave, en diabolus equum tuum ascendit. Mox ille desiliens, occidit eum. Alio itidem tempore sedente eo cum sociis suis, conspicatur saependictum vermem in poste proximi parietis. Ecce, inquit, ubi diabolus ille. Nunquam ab eo liberabor, nisi se vindicaverit. Moxque nundata coxa, sinebat vermem accedere. Quem cum momordisset, mordentem manu iactavit, ipsumque morsum celerius rasorio ad hoc praeparato abscidens, longius proiecit. Mox mirum in modum ipsa praecisura ob infectionem veneni ad instar pugni intumuit, et crepuit. Sicque liberatus est a verme illo immundissimo. (*Dialogus Miraculorum* [Cologne: J.M. Heberle, 1851; rpt. Ridgewood, N.J.: Gregg Press, 1966.])]

20. "Sawles Warde," in *Old English Homilies and Homiletic Treatises of the Twelfth and Thirteenth Centuries*, ed. Richard Morris (London: Trubner and Company for the Early English Text Society [E.E.T.S.], 1868; rpt. New York: Greenwood Press, 1969), 249. [his leor deaðlich. ant blac ant elheowet.]

21. "Sawles Warde," 249. [fearlic ich hatte. ant am deaðes sonde. ant deaðes munegunge ant am icumen biuore hire to warnin ow of hire cume.]

22. "Sawles Warde," 249. [Ich cume . . . of helle.]

23. "Sawles Warde," 250. [þe laðe helle wurmes. tadden ant froggen. þe freoteð ham ut te ehnen. ant te nease. gristles. ant snikeð in. ant ut neddren. ant eauraskes. nawt ilich þeose her. ah hundret siðe grisluker et muð. ant et earen. ed ehnen. ant ed neauele. ant ed te breoste holke as meaðen iforrotet flesch eauergete þickest.]

24. Illustration can be found in Kathleen Cohen, *Metamorphosis of a Death Symbol* (Berkeley: University of California Press, 1973), 78.

25. *Old English Miscellany*, ed. Richard Morris (London: N. Trubner for E.E.T.S., 1872; rpt. New York: Greenwood Press, 1969), 224, l. 58. ["deueles bestes," (l. 50); "Todus., Neddres., Snakes. mony mo; / And þe synful soules. in hidȝ, / Eten. and gnowen" (ll. 60–2).]

26. Richard Rolle, *Prose and Verse*, ed. S.J. Ogilvie-Thomson (Oxford: Oxford University Press for E.E.T.S., 1913; rpt. 1988), 68. [Bethynke the, thou wreched kaytif, how hit shal be of þe when þou shalt be cast in a pitte vndre þe erthe, whan todis, w(or)mys, snakys and other venymous bestes shal ete þi eighen, (thy nose), þi mouth, thy lippes, thi tonge, thy hede, thy hondes, thy (fete), and al þi body. Who shal þan be thy helpe, thy comfort and thy refuyt? . . . Therfor, þou wreched kaytif, now, whan tyme is of mercy and of pite, ren to þat derward lord Ihesu, and say "Mercy, der Ihesu."]

27. *Caxton's Mirrour of the World*, ed. Oliver H. Prior (London: Oxford University Press for E.E.T.S., 1913; rpt. 1966), 100. [Yf the tode, Crapault or spyncop byte a man or woman, they be in daunger for to dye; it hath be ofte seen. The spttle of a man fastyng sleeth comynly the spyncoppe and the tode yf it touche them.]

28. *Middle English Sermons*, ed. Woodburn O. Ross (London: Oxford University Press for E.E.T.S., 1940; rpt. 1960), 299–300. [he that beres enuye aboute in his hert, sore hym forthynkes of mennes welfare, and he is glad and ioye-full of mennes euell fare. And thus he may be lykened to the fende of hell. . . . Grete payn were to such enuyus men if they were in heuen. . . . And therfor bot if they amende hem, þere com they neuer. And therfore are they lykened to a foule tode, þat mey not se the bryght sonne bot if it hym sore noye.]

29. Guillaume De Deguileville, *The Pilgrimage of the Life of Man*, trans. John Lydgate, ed. F.J. Furnivall (London: Kegan Paul, Trench, Trubner for E.E.T.S., 1904),

ll. 15650–2. (crepaud, from O.F. *crapault*.) [When Ire doth myn herte myne, / I am so venymous (in soth), / I bolle as any crepawd doth.]

30. *Old English Homilies*. ["Blake tadden and habbe atter uppon heore heorte" (51); "Þos blaca tadden þet habbeð þet atter uppon heore heorte. bitacneð þes riche men þe habbeð þes mucheles weorldes ehte and na ma en noht itimien þar of to eten ne to drinken ne na god don þer of for þe luue of god-almihtin þe haueð hit heom al geuen. ah liggeð þer uppon alse þe tadde deð in þere eorðe þet neuere ne mei itimien to eten hire fulle. swa heo is afered leste þeo eorðe hire trukie" (53).]

31. Janetta R. Benton, *The Medieval Menagerie: Animals in the Art of the Middle Ages* (New York: Abbeville Press, 1992), 169.

32. *Fasciculus Morum: A Fourteenth-Century Preacher's Handbook*, ed. and trans. Siegfried Wenzel (University Park, Penn.: Pennsylvania State University Press, 1989), 353. [Unde narratur de quodam ususrario qui hoc modo multas congregabat divicias, qui cum ad mortem infirmabatur et ab uxore ut testamentum conderet fuisset sepius admonitus, constanter negavit, set fecit uxorem suam iurare quod post mortem eius ligaret circa corpus eius de huiusmodi lucro triginta marcas, quas in thesauro reposuisset, dicens ei: "Ne timeas pro me. Quamcumque enim terram introiero, si hanc pecuniam mecum habuero, bene negociabor et caute." Sepulto ergo eo cum pecunia, cito post venit curie legatus et hec audiens precepit sacerdoti qui eum sepelierat a sepultura fidelium extrahi et in campum proici et comburi. Qui cum eius familiaribus accessisset, in loco ubi denarii fuerant ligati invenerunt bufones teterrimos corpus miserum et horridum corrodentes et vermes innumerabiles in braccale peccunie. Quo viso ignem apposuerunt, et multi illius fetore interierunt. (pars IV, vii, 107–19)]

33. Cohen, 41, 43.

34. *Fasciculus*, 353–5. [Ad idem eciam narracio de eodem legato, magister Robertus nomine, cum in sua visitacione apud Werdeley venisset et sibi idem intimatum fuisset de quodam usurario nuper defuncto, quem cum exhauriri iussisset, amoto lapide superiori viderunt corpus eius nigrum et fetidissimum, et quendam bufonem supra eum sedere, qui tenuit ad os eius quasi eius nutrix nummos ardentes et ipsum ad modum nutricis pavit cum illis. Quod cum vidissent, perterriti fugerunt, et venerunt demones et corpus cum tumba asportabant, nec usquam comparuit. (pars IV, vii, 120–7)]

35. Johannes Mirkus, *Mirk's Festial* (London: Kegan Paul, Trench, Trubner for E.E.T.S., 1905), 85. [Þen sygh he a passyng grete tode, as blake as peche, wyth een brennyng as fyre, þat had vmbeclypped wyth hyr foure fete hys fadyrs þrote, and gnof fast þeron. Þen, when þe sonne segy þys, he sayde: "O fadyr, moche swete mete and drynke haðe gon downe þat þrote; and now þou art strangult wyth a foule helle-best!"]

36. *Fasciculus*, 639. [Ad litteram enim dicitur quod de corpore humano post mortem nascuntur tria genera vermium: de capite enim et collo nascitur bufo, de spina dorsi scorpio, et (de) ventre et stomacho gurgullo. (pars VI, iii, 76–8)]

37. *A Revelation of Purgatory by an Unknown, Fifteenth-Century Woman Visionary*, ed. Marta P. Harley (Lewiston, N.Y.: Edwin Mellen Press, 1985), 74. [Than me þoȝt þe deuelles to(k) out har tonges and set addres þer-on and todes, and þan seid þe deuelles, "Take ȝe þis for ȝour fals lechery and foul wordes and foul contenaunce and bakbytynge and sclaundrynge."(74)] [wer putte on spittis and rostet, and as many addres and snakes and todes, and also mychel foul venym as myȝt swarm about ham, was set on ham to sowk ham and to gnaw ham. And þan wer þay taken of þese spittis, and þe deuelles drew ham þroȝ-out þe fyr with hard sharp hokes. . . . And þay al for-drow har hertis and har most pryue membres. Than seid þe deuelles to ham, "Take ȝe þese peynes for ȝe disused ȝour-self in þe foul lust of lechery." (75–6)]

38. "Lazarus," in *The Towneley Plays*, ed. George England and Alfred Pollard (London: Oxford University Press for E.E.T.S., 1897; rpt. 1966), ll. 138–40. [A

shete shall be youre pall / sich todys shall be youre nowche; / Todys shall you dere, / ffeyndys will you fere.]

39. "Lazarus," in *The Towneley Plays* ("paddok" from O.N. *padda*, toad). [Wormes shall in you brede / as bees dos in the byke, / And ees out of your hede / Thus-gate shall paddokys pyke.]

40. *The Vision of Tundale*, ed. Rodney Mearns (Heidelberg: Carl Winter Universitätsverlag, 1985), ll. 1408–10. [Wyth þe reke & stynke of brymstone / Tho sowles þat passed owte at hys ende / Fell into þe fyr & brende."]

41. "Sawles Warde," 251. [ant speoweð ham eft ut biuoren and bihinden. oðer hwile torendeð ham ant to cheoweð ham euch greot.]

42. Illustration can be found in Philippe Aries, *Images of Man and Death*, trans. Janet Lloyd (Cambridge, Mass.: Harvard University Press, 1985), 237.

Human Animals of Medieval Fables

Joyce E. Salisbury

The medieval world was populated with many animals. There were animals that were essential as labor, that provided hides and food, that served as hunting partners. Interaction with these animals dominated humans' experiences. However, these ubiquitous real animals were not the most influential ones in shaping medieval people's perception of themselves in relation to the animal world. After the twelfth century, animals of the imagination strongly affected people's views of themselves and the animal world.[1] Literature that portrayed animals as offering examples for human behavior became increasingly popular in monasteries and courts and spread, via preachers' sermons, to the unlettered masses. This literature included bestiaries, animal fables, and beast epics like the popular *Reynard the Fox*.

While these texts seem to be about animals, in fact, the works use animals to discuss human society, to mirror humanity. When we study these texts, we learn very little about animals and a great deal about what medieval thinkers thought of themselves. In this essay, I shall look at two such animal works, the fables of Marie of France and those of Odo of Cheriton. In these fables, we can see reflected the social concerns of the fabulists, their political stance, and their view of society. The animals in the tales become the humans that populated the medieval worlds of Marie's court and Odo's church.

In addition to portraying animals as reflections of humans, these two works also reveal how images of animals in the exemplar literature imposed a value on real animals. Animals that were portrayed as models for ideal human behavior (like lions) became more valued and respected. Animals that were portrayed with less desirable traits (like dogs) became despised in the literature despite the fact that real dogs were plainly more useful and indeed more "humanlike" than lions. However, animals of the imagination shaped people's view of animals so much that if you wanted to insult someone, you would call him a dog; whereas if you wanted to praise someone, you would call her a lion. This essay will offer some insights into the ways fable animals mirrored human society and, in doing so, transformed humans' views of real animals.

One of the most important figures in the spread of fables to courtly society was Marie of France. We do not know much about this twelfth-century literary figure. She identified herself in her works by giving the barest information: "Marie is my name and I am of France." Her writings reveal her to be well educated in the classics (including classical fables). She probably lived in Norman England, and her works were likely read in the English court of Henry II and his educated and cultured wife, Eleanor of Aquitaine. Marie's collection of fables (written between 1155 and 1189) contains 103 verse tales with morals written at the end of each. Many of the fables are derived from a medieval collection of Phaedrus's fables. The rest seem to be drawn from literary and folk traditions.[2]

This collection was influential in bringing fable literature out from behind monastery walls into the wider society. Marie wrote her fable verses in French, when all the other collections were in Latin. The large number of surviving manuscripts testifies to the popularity of this French collection: there are more medieval manuscripts of Marie's fables than those of any other author.[3] Marie's genius lay partly in her brisk verse style, which converted stories preserved largely for rhetorical exercises into vehicles for courtly entertainment. Additionally, however, she transformed the fables themselves into tales that belonged to twelfth-century society rather than to the classical world that had produced them originally.

The other fabulist I shall discuss lived a century after Marie and in a different setting. Odo of Cheriton was born about 1185 into a wealthy English landowning family (Cheriton was the name of one of their properties). Odo was called to the religious life, attended the University of Paris, and completed a doctorate in theology. He traveled extensively through France and Spain, and obviously spent a great deal of time at monasteries. Although he was particularly concerned with abuses in the Cistercian order, there is no evidence that he was a member of any order.[4] When Odo drew from the classical fables, he modified them to mirror the ecclesiastical society that surrounded him. Instead of becoming courtiers, the animals became monks and churchmen.

Both these fabulists inherited Greco-Roman animal fables, but they departed significantly from their classical predecessors. One of the principal differences between ancient and medieval fables was that in the ancient world, Aesopic fables were largely tales designed to criticize the social order. Phaedrus, the first-century Latin fabulist, explicitly defined fables as literature invented by slaves to allow them to speak critically without censure.[5] This definition of fables as vehicles of social criticism underlies much fable analysis. However, in the twelfth century, when classical fables were made newly popular, they were not rediscovered by the lower classes. Court and church brought fables back into circulation, and when fables were used by people in power, they were transformed from a literature of social criticism to a literature of social conservatism.

Medieval fables (and Marie's fables in particular) have been criticized for imperfectly fulfilling a goal of social criticism. H.J. Blackham wrote that medieval fables, while "lively," were not able to escape control of the church to fulfill adequately a fable's purpose.[6] A.C. Henderson wrote that Marie was "attempting to do at once two contradictory things"—stand outside her social class and write specifically of her society—and was successful at neither.[7] I disagree with such authors. We might not agree with medieval fabulists' socially conservative viewpoint, and we might not agree that this is an appropriate use of fables, but I believe we must acknowledge that these fabulists did a remarkable job of transforming fables into meaningful tales for the ruling classes.

Once fables had been co-opted by those in power, they were transformed into a powerful and popular force to preserve the status quo. Marie, Odo, and other medieval fabulists modified the animals, the morals, and the tales, and thus transformed the classical fables into a literary source that expressed a conservative view of society. This change from social criticism to social conservatism made fables both extremely influential in their own times and valuable historical tools. Their use by society's elite made the animals in the tales reveal a sharp image of how the authors viewed the medieval hierarchy. The fables' socially conservative message led ruling groups to promote the spread of the fables. Finally, the widespread distribution and popularity of the tales increased the degree to which their view of animals shaped medieval society's images of people and animals. Marie began these transformations, and by looking closely at the changes she made, one can see the ways fable animals came to mirror hierarchic medieval society.

One of the most obvious changes Marie introduced into the fable tradition she inherited was to transform the fables from commenting on the ethical conduct of individuals to having them comment on society as a whole. In a classical fable, a weak animal represented a weak person; for Marie a weak animal represented powerless groups: peasants or servants. Similarly, a strong animal no longer represented just a strong person; Marie converted such an animal into a strong social class: the nobility or the rich.[8] After her modification, these fables were no longer products associated with a semibestial slave, who was outside society and thus could be critical of it. Marie's fables were of and for the court, for people in power who were strongly committed to maintaining the social hierarchy that placed them in power.

Odo, too, used animals to represent types. His fables were populated by animals that represented greedy churchmen, ungrateful underlings (especially ecclesiastical ones), and those who desire worldly things.[9] As you can see, his types represent his ecclesiastical interests, but as we shall see, they express a socially conservative view of society as surely as the fables of Marie.

The world both these authors advocated in their fables was one populated by a static, well-ordered, hierarchic society. Those of noble birth ruled, but their rule should be benign, marked by integrity and compassion for the powerless in their charge. Subjects in this society should be loyal and enduring, content with their place and not desirous of change. Odo's ecclesiastical world was equally hierarchic; it would be virtuous and would especially avoid hypocrisy. Odo seemed particularly critical of those whose actions did not match their words, clearly a concern for preachers.[10] Obviously, both fabulists lived in a world in which Christian religion was central, for they felt all in society would trust in God,[11] thereby ensuring the security of the social order.

Beyond converting the tales from individual lessons to collective ones, Marie and Odo expressed their political conservatism by modifying classical fables in two main ways: their choice of animals, and their choice of the morals they appended to the tales.

One can see Marie's interest in the ruling classes by comparing the animals she used most frequently with those in the classical fables. For example, in Babrius's fables, the "lower class" animals (ox, dog, and ass) were represented with as much frequency as predators, which medieval authors viewed as noble. This reinforces the traditional notion that classical fables were a genre of social criticism. With Marie, the frequency with which courtly noble animals are mentioned increases dramatically, showing a shift toward her political interests.

In medieval society it was noble to be a predator. After all, war—the predatory occupation—was the privilege of the noble class; it was their reason for existence. That class favored their hunting animals over all others, and in their fables and symbols they placed the lion, which they considered the master predator, above all others. In Marie's fable world, society was ruled by those born to do so. Lions and eagles were appropriate rulers, since they were the strongest and most "noble" of the animals. In the classical fables, lions were most often shown as hunters or hunted, only occasionally as kings. Thus, for the ancients, as in reality, lions could be both predator and prey. This ambiguous role seemingly did not suit Marie's vision of society. For her (and subsequent fabulists including Odo) the lion was always the king. Not only was he king, but he was almost always portrayed as a just and noble king, sometimes aging but usually sympathetic. For example, when Marie retold a classical fable of an evil king, she changed the lion of the original fable to a wolf, thus preserving a social order that saw lions as just and proper kings.[12] Marie's portrayal had little to do with lions as animals and everything to do with her ideal of kingship. Kings were noble, just, above the fray, and—perhaps like lions—somewhat distant and unknowable. Birds in the fables also had a rightful king, and Marie's description of the eagle showed the qualities Marie saw as inherent to the role:

> The eagle's grand and glorious,
> And he's especially valorous,
> And very staid and dignified. (143)

In Marie's fables social ills were caused by predators (also noble animals) who did not adhere to the rules of correct behavior for the ruling classes. These vicious animals were wolves, and the medieval fabulists from Marie on vilified this creature. The wolf was shown as an evil, greedy, gluttonous, murderous thief. As you can see from these adjectives, the heart of the problem with the wolf was greed. He was dissatisfied with his lot in society and wanted more; he violated the noble behavioral principle of generosity. For Marie, this breach of noble behavior is what caused disruption in the social order. In fables, wolves become a metaphor for nobility gone astray.

The fable of the preacher and the wolf shows how appetite dominated the character of the fable wolf. In this tale, a preacher attempts to teach the wolf the alphabet (perhaps to try to improve his character). The wolf concentrats long enough to get to the letter c, but when he is asked what that might spell, he answers "lamb," revealing that his mind remains at the level of his stomach (217). Such greed threatened the hierarchy that placed nobility at the top, and the fabulists criticized such rapacity in their portrayal of men acting as wolves. They did not advocate violating a social order in which noble predators ruled, but they tried to insist on moderation, which after all would be the only way to preserve such a social order.

The next most popular animal in medieval animal exemplar literature as a whole was the fox.[13] (Its popularity reflects, in part, the immense popularity of the *Reynard the Fox* beast epics.) The fox, as a predator, represented someone of high social status, though not as powerful as lions or wolves. Foxes in fact and fable were known for their cunning. When they were hunted, foxes could outwit many dogs, and this reputation entered the fable lore from bestiaries to fables to beast epics, making foxes symbolize wit and trickery. Marie did not emphasize foxes or their cleverness as much as later authors did. Of her 103 fables, only 11 featured a fox, and of these only 5 used the fox as an example of craftiness. The rest of the fables showed the fox as greedy, poor, evil, and even stupid. Seemingly, in Marie's political construct a predator living by its wits instead of its legitimate power was not given much respect.

A society with rulers who were strong and counselors who were wise is not complete. The tales, like society itself, were populated with the meek, the poor, the victims. The proportion of the rich to the poor in the medieval fable literature, however, never matched that in real society. Medieval fabulists were much more interested in the activities of the powerful. The victims or domestic animals were there to provide opportunity for the powerful to exert their power. Chanticleer the cock existed for Reynard to exploit; lambs existed for Isegrim the wolf to eat. Within this category of animals, which includes everything from lambs to hares to asses to dogs, there are no fully sympathetic animals. Even in the fables of Marie, which show a great deal of sympathy for the powerless, none are particularly admirable creatures. Many are portrayed as stupid, especially when they aspire to a higher estate than that of their birth.

Marie included a number of fables with people instead of animals as protaganists. Most of these human fables deal with the lower classes, who are treated in much the same way as Marie treats powerless animals. For example, she tells of a peasant who was not content with one horse, prayed for two, and lost the one he had. Marie concludes unsympathetically: "Nobody ought to pray, therefore, to have more than his needs call for" (161). Marie tells another tale in which a peasant had an inflated sense of his own importance. He had abdominal pains because of a beetle that had crawled up his anus, and was convinced that he was going to give birth to an important child. Marie warns:

> This example serves to say
> The ignorant are oft this way;
> Believing that which cannot be,
> They're swayed and changed by vanity. (135)

In this case, the peasant was as deluded as the flea (in another of Marie's fables) that presumed to think it disturbed the camel on which it rode (127). So, even though Marie is best known among the fabulists for her compassion for the poor, it nevertheless was a compassion that assumed a static social order with an obedient lower class. Her stories mirrored her ideal society.

Perhaps because of his pastoral concern for the poor, Odo did not portray the poor with such disdain. He seems to have been more interested in condemning the greed of the rich[14] than in entertaining courtly society with tales of ignorant peasants. However, like Marie's, all his fables reveal an ideal static society. For example, Odo advised against subordinates attempting to take advantage of even incompetent rulers. He wrote a fable of a goat who was an ass's servant. The goat tried to take advantage of the simple ass and climbed on its back to take a ride. The ass was enraged and threw itself backward, crushing the goat. Odo concluded: "When an ass is your lord, don't think you can ride him" (152–3).

One particularly striking example of the degree to which all the medieval fabulists held the lower classes in disdain may be seen in their treatment of lambs. From earliest Christianity, lambs were heavily laden with symbolism. Christ was both the lamb of God and the good shepherd gathering the faithful into the flock. The lamb remained the symbol for the best in self-sacrifice in the Christian tradition. St. Francis (always sympathetic to all animals) was particularly fond of lambs because, as his biographer St. Bonaventure wrote, lambs "present a natural reflection of Christ's merciful gentleness and represent him in Scriptural symbolism."[15] For Francis, the symbolic quality of lambs led him to be kind to individual real lambs. This represents a logical application of Christian symbolism. However, medieval people seldom bothered following the logical consequences of their metaphors, and in a literature that made predators heroes, lambs were natural victims.

Lambs (and the poor) were "fleeced" by unscrupulous wolves:

The wolf then grabbed the lamb so small,
Chomped through his neck, extinguished all.
. . . .
They [rich people] strip them [the poor] clean of flesh and skin,
As the wolf did to the lambkin.[16]

Odo used the same fable to conclude: "Thus rich men, for no cause at all—and regardless of how the poor respond—devour them" (95).

Odo continued to be more interested in using his fables to teach rulers how to care for their charges than in the plight of the "poor sheep" in their care. For example, he tells a tale of a wolf that was put in charge of a flock of sheep. The wolf, of course, devoured them. For Odo, the moral of this story was that corrupt priests would be punished for not caring for their flock (94–5). The accent was on those in charge not on those consumed. The poor were passive in society. In the hands of the fabulists, if innocent lambs were occasionally an object for sympathy, they were not admired. Sheep (and lambs) were considered stupid and cowardly,[17] almost deserving of whatever they received.

So, if even the most sympathetic of the nonpredators was portrayed in a way that only the most pious or self-effacing would want to emulate, other domestic animals had no chance to be shown in any but a negative light. Dogs, the faithful servants (and the key word here is *servant*), were loyal. One of Marie's fables tells of a dog that refused to accept a bribe from a thief to relax his vigilance in guarding sheep.[18] This loyalty is shown in only one of Marie's fables. In the rest, dogs were shown as greedy, litigious, and garrulous. One of the most repeated medieval fables was that of the dog that lost the cheese he was carrying by reaching for his reflection in the water.[19] This fable was a comment on greed as an attribute of dogs. Canines were repeatedly vilified for greed, for it was said to drive them to return to eat their own vomit (a characteristic that preoccupied medieval commentators).[20] Early medieval thinkers consistently attributed disagreeable characteristics to man's best friend. Tertullian wrote that dogs were impure, and Boethius called them restless and always barking.[21] In patristic discussions of the seven deadly sins, the dog often represented envy.

Odo was even more disparaging of man's best friend than Marie. For the churchman, dogs were scavengers and filthy. Odo's fable illustrating the dangers of evil companions reveals his disdain for dogs (at least literary ones):

> Now there was a dog who wanted to take a crap right on top of a cluster of rushes. And one rush gave that dog's rear a good, stinging thrust. Then the dog retreated a fair distance and bayed at the rushes. The rush answered back: "I'd rather have you bay at me from a distance than defile me in close."[22]

For Odo, the dog represented the worst of evil companions, one who could defile one by its company.

Thus, in medieval metaphoric ranking, dogs had lost the high status accorded them for being carnivores, because they were servants. As the medieval social order became the model for evaluating the animal world, dogs were placed in a lower social class than the free predators, even though they were more useful.

By looking at Marie's choice and depiction of the animals in her fables, one can see her courtly appreciation of a hierarchic society. Although Odo stressed ecclesiastical ideas (which I shall discuss more fully below), he nevertheless shared the hierarchical value system articulated first by Marie. Predators were noble; servants were not. The animals that adhered to this principle were also favored, and in this way, her animals were re-created to reflect her values. In addition to changing the stories somewhat to re-create a model of a conservative society in their fables, Marie and Odo also changed the morals to articulate some of society's values.

In the morals to their fables, both Marie and Odo insisted that the ruled should be loyal to their proper lords. This emphasis was absent in the classical fables, which offered more possibility for social criticism. Medieval fables stressed values that would yield a preservation of the status quo, and loyalty to rulers is one of those values. For example, in the classical tale of the bat that, during the war between animals and birds, kept changing sides to try to be with the winner, the moral was aimed at individuals, who were warned that "anyone who wants to remain blameless in the eyes of two parties wins the favor of neither."[23] Marie changed the moral to make it specific to a feudal society in which loyalty to one's lord was central:

He should give honour to his lord
And should be loyal, keep his word.
And when his master is in need,
He should join others and bring aid. (91)

Odo, too, advocated loyalty by repeatedly reprimanding ungrateful underlings. For him this was especially true of clergy who did not show proper respect to their superiors. He has fables that warn "against prelates who give too much power to subordinates" (91), and writes about "supposedly obedient monks and laymen who . . . are always scheming how to devour their chaplains and superiors" (96). Both Marie and Odo repeatedly urged loyalty and obedience as a way to preserve an ordered society.

In their vision of a stable conservative society, Marie and Odo advocated more than loyalty. They believed people should also keep their place, both socially and geographically. Marie repeatedly urged people to be content with their social class. For example, in the fable of the ass that wanted to frolic with its master like a lapdog, the classical moral said, "The fable shows that all do not have the same natural aptitudes."[24] Marie turned this fable of individual talents to social commentary, concluding:

Those who to raise themselves aspire
And who a higher place desire—
One that's not fitting to their girth
And most of all, not to their birth.
The same result will come to pass
For many, like the beaten ass. (71)

Perhaps even more strongly, Marie used the fable of the hare that wanted to have horns like a deer to comment:

Folks covetous and miserly:
They always start such projects as
They think will raise their social class.
What they attempt through foolishness
Turns back on them, injurious. (247)

Odo, too, has several examples of fables that urge people not to aspire to be what they were not born to be. One fable described a boy who died trying to imitate his strong father. Odo concluded: "Brother, if you were made to be such as a great ox, then give praise to the Lord. If you were made a frog (that is, a poor or modest man), be content; don't ask to be made into an ox."[25]

For Marie and Odo, then, people should not aspire above the station into which they were born. But further, they should not even desire to move about. This monastic ideal of staying in one's space and being content with it permeates both fabulists' writings. For example, in the classical fable of the rabbits and the frogs, the author says the rabbits, despairing of their own cowardice, were going to commit suicide until they saw that the frogs feared them. The classical moral again was an individual one: "The misfortunes of others serve as consolations for our own troubles."[26] Marie changed the fable to have the rabbits search for a land in which they would feel safe and, seeing the frogs' fear, decide to stay home. Marie concluded:

Those folk who wish to move away,
Abandoning their ancient home—
They'd best take heed of what could come.
No kingdom will they ever find
Anywhere known to humankind
Where everyone lives free of fear,
Where toil and sorrow disappear. (87)

Similarly, Odo told the tale of the tortoise that wished to leave its "dwelling in places which were damp and deep" and to soar like an eagle. The eagle took it aloft only to dash it against the rocks. Odo entitled this fable "Against the Curious," warning people of the dangers of leaving their place (76–7). In another fable, Odo tells of a stork that tried to leave, to escape the consequence of an injury it had inflicted. Odo's moral is an explicit advocacy of *stabilitas*: "This exemplum demonstrates that change of place does not produce holiness" (81–2).

While lessons of loyalty and stability seem to be primarily directed to lower classes, the medieval vision of a conservative, stable society required that ruling classes also behave in particular ways and adhere to certain moral standards. Marie's and Odo's lessons were not only for the lower classes. Marie was particularly firm with rulers. She believed that some people were destined to rule, but she consistently reminded them that they were to rule justly:

> A prince should be well-rested too;
> In his delights not overdo;
> Nor shame himself or his domain,
> Nor cause the poor folk undue pain. (143–5)

Beneath the rulers, the rich and noble should govern society, but they, too, should govern with compassion for the poor. The fable of the lion that freed a mouse he had caught and, in return, is freed from ropes by the same mouse, caused Marie to conclude:

> And so this model serves to show
> A lesson wealthy men should know
> Who over poor folks have much power.
> If these should wrong them, unaware,
> The rich should show them charity. (75)

Marie wrote that the spirit of *noblesse oblige* should govern those who govern, and she reinforced this lesson by indicating that the ruled would eventually take vengeance on an unjust ruler (57). This moral, however, seems not a cry for social revolution but a reminder to rulers not to abuse their power.

Odo, too, warned those in power not to abuse their power, and in some of his fables he reveals the kind of detail that shows that he witnessed and disapproved of medieval injustice. For example, Odo told a fable of a raven who held a dove's chick captive until the dove would sing a beautiful song. Since it was not in the dove's capacity to sing beautifully, the raven ate the chick. Odo offered the following explanation of this tale:

> It is just the same when wealthy lords and their bailiffs seize the cow or sheep of a simple peasant, then levy a charge of crime or fraud against him. Seeking the hostage or the terms of its freedom, the simple man comes before the powerful. He pledges five coins—more or less up to the very limit of his ability. "My brother," the bailiff says, "you don't know how to sing better than that? Unless you can sing more sweetly, you won't have the hostage back." "Indeed," the simple man replies, "I haven't learned how to sing better—nor can I, for I am needy and poor. I just can't give you more." Then the rich man either keeps the animal hostage or, otherwise, butchers it. And it is thus that he devours the poor peasant. (114–5)

By offering such specific detail in his moral, Odo not only brings to life medieval injustice, but he also warns masters against exploiting the poor in their charge. Like Marie, he does not advocate social revolution, but he does warn lords of the hatred they will incur when he concludes another fable by saying "And that's when the poor man can exclaim: "May God bring destruction upon all lords.""[27]

In Odo's political system, it would not be social revolution that would redress social ills, but God's power. As he warned cruel lords that the poor would call down God's wrath upon them, he wrote another fable that warned of God's vengeance. He told of a rich man who had many cows but coveted the single fat cow of a neighboring widow. He had that cow taken from the woman and brought to him. His servant roasted it, and the moment the rich man took a bite of his ill-gotten meat, he choked and died. Odo concluded "This rich fellow got the cow by plundering, and the Devil plundered his soul" (116–7).

Thus, rich and poor alike were to live by the rules and moral principles that both Marie and Odo felt were suitable to a Christian and conservative society. Odo shared many of Marie's attitudes, and both used animal fables to advocate preserving the social order. However, Odo's collection of fables differed from that of Marie. The differences derive primarily from the fact that Odo was a churchman, and the social order he was interested in commenting on and preserving was an ecclesiastical order. As I look at the specific ways Odo's collection differed from that of Marie, I can highlight the ways animals were used to mirror either the courtly or the ecclesiastical worlds of the Middle Ages.

One of the first contrasts between Marie's collection of fables and that of Odo is that Odo's ecclesiastical bias caused him to make subtle changes in the portrayal of the animals. For Odo, none of the animals was particularly noble. Even the ruling lions and the predatory hawks were held up as models to avoid. Churchmen followed church fathers and scholastic theologians in claiming that people and animals were qualitatively different,[28] and thus all animals were for Odo representatives of the bestial and nonhuman. Odo kept Marie's hierarchy and re-created human society in his animal population. However, he wanted to urge people to rise above the bestial by not portraying animals quite as sympathetically as Marie had done.

Another indication of Odo's ecclesiastical interest was his inclusion of a number of tales that his translator, Professor J.C. Jacobs called "moralized animal lore."[29] Unlike regular fables in which one may draw a moral from the imagined, anthropomorphic actions of animals, Odo draws an allegorical lesson based solely on the character or characteristic behavior of an animal. For example, Odo's tale of the wild colt is succinct: "A wild colt throws himself into the water or into a pit, unless he is held back by a bridle." Here we do not have a fable with a story but, instead, a statement of the characteristic actions of a colt. Odo follows that with a great deal of analysis about the necessity of "the bridle of Christ's restraining nails" to keep humans from falling into the pit of hell (112–3). Here we can see Odo's debt not only to the *Physiologus* and bestiaries but also to ecclesiastical education, which established a pattern of thinking in this form of allegory. This way of thinking shaped his view of the appropriate use of animals and separated him from Marie, who remained more wedded to the narrative form for her courtly audience. Certainly, Odo's brief allegorical statements were well suited to preaching and instructing the unlettered, who made up the greater portion of churchmen's charges.

Another indicator that Odo was interested in revealing a world different from that of Marie is in the animals Odo featured in his fables. Odo did not use the noble courtly animals as often as Marie had. Odo explored a world that was much wider than that of a court dominated by metaphoric lions and wolves preying on sheep. Perhaps for this reason, his fables feature a greater array of animals, from birds to toads.

Not only did Odo change the frequency of the appearance of these animals, but he changed their portrayal as well. For example, Odo had even less praise than Marie for the wily fox. In his hands, the fox remained crafty but he was also dirty and evil. The fox repays a favor by urinating on his own tail and flicking it into the eyes of his benefactor. Elsewhere, Odo equates the fox with the Devil and with "anyone who is both poor and a deceiver."[30] The fox is portrayed less sympathetically in Odo's fables than he is in beast epics like that of Reynard. Seemingly, unlike some of his ecclesiastical counterparts, Odo did not admire people living by their wits. He preferred more simple Christian virtues. Again, Odo's perspective and social values shapes the animals.

Domestic animals are much more popular with Odo than with Marie. Cats appear eight times and their adversaries, mice and rats, seven times. Dogs and asses appear five times each. His interest in humble domestic animals is perhaps indicative of the fact that he was a preacher and involved with common people. The increase in domestic animals recalls the classical world's fables, in which domestic animals appear more frequently than they do in Marie's collection.

Instead of featuring noble animals and their prey, Odo used birds much more often in his examples. Of 117 fables, birds are featured in approximately 35. Odo's emphasis on birds further points to his ecclesiastical interests. Birds have traditionally been associated with spiritual things,[31] and it is likely that Odo encountered Hugh of Fouilloy's *Aviarium*, a treatise that used birds to illustrate moral lessons. Hugh composed his *Aviarium* in the twelfth century, and it spread quickly through the monastic community. It was particularly popular in Cistercian houses in the regions through which Odo travelled.[32] While the *Aviarium* drew moral lessons and animal lore from many of the standard medieval sources (Pliny, Isidore of Seville, Aelian), Hugh's predominant sources were nevertheless biblical or patristic.[33] This text shows the strong tradition in monastic circles of drawing moral lessons from birds. Odo followed directly in this tradition. Unlike Marie, Odo wanted his audience drawn upward to spiritual ideas, and he most often used birds to carry that message. This spiritual application is perhaps most apparent in Odo's treatment of the eagle. As we have seen, Marie used the eagle as a noble predator, a king of the birds. Odo makes no mention of that role. Instead, his fable on the eagle is really pure allegory such as one might find in the bestiary: "When the eagle has chicks, she turns their heads up toward the sun. She saves and nurtures that chick who gazes at the sun's direct rays. But anyone unable to contemplate the sun is cast out of her nest." Odo concludes by equating the mother eagle with God, who casts out "those too ignorant to look on any except earthly things" (80–1). Neither Marie's nor Odo's eagle bears any resemblance to a real eagle, nor were they intended to. Both eagles reflect the author's social interest, whether court or church. Odo's eagle was used as moral allegory, showing his desire to use animals in the service of religion.

Odo also transformed the morals of many of the fables, to bring them into service of religion. Both Marie and Odo told the familiar tale of the frog and the mouse. In the classical story, the frog lured the mouse into a pond, promising to keep it safe by tying the mouse's leg to its own. As the frog was dragging the mouse underwater to drown it, a bird swooped down and consumed both. Marie transformed this story for her own purposes. She had the bird eat only the evil frog saving the trusting mouse. The moral Marie gave to this fable warned that evildoers who "think that others they'll ensnare, will find that they place themselves in peril" (35–41). In the same fable, Odo returned to the original tale in which the mouse and frog were both killed by the bird. He concluded with the moral: "This is what happens when a parish has been given to someone who is foolish and weak. The Devil comes along and carries off both, the chaplain and the parish" (92). The same story was used to reflect the concerns of both worlds. Marie warned evildoers at court who lured the trusting to peril, and Odo warned of the spiritual dangers of incompetent churchmen.

Odo similarly reinterprets the familiar fable of the country mouse who would rather eat simple fare in safety than rich food in the presence of a cat. Odo somewhat stretches this story to make it a lesson against "simoniacs and usurers" who eat their "unjustly acquired morsel" in the presence of the Devil, "the cat who devours souls" (87–8). In both of these well-known fables, one can see how flexible the stories are in allowing Odo to bring a religious message and to address the issues that preoccupied him in his ecclesiastical setting.

Just as Marie used prey animals to provide a foil for the noble predators that dominated her tales, Odo has particular animals that he used as a contrast to the spiritual birds. To offer examples of animals that are "stuck in the mire of sin," he uses insects, toads, and frogs. For example, he tells of a beetle that flew over and ignored beautiful flowering plants and fruits to land "on a dunghill made from the droppings of horses and cattle," and the beetle declares to his wife that it is the most delightful place on earth. Not surprisingly, Odo equates the beetle with those who "savor the dung of sin, the places of the Devil" (102–3). He features these animals frequently in his collection. As the birds represent spirituality, these animals represent the evils of sin.

Preachers and fabulists after Odo continued to use insects and toads to represent sin and decay. It may well be that the ecclesiastical fabulists' association of these animals with sin has influenced our image of them. If so, this is an example of the degree to which our ideas about actual animals have been molded by their portrayal in fables. It is hard to imagine having anything but negative associations about insects and amphibians, but we are likely to have them because we are imbued with attitudes formulated during the Middle Ages. There are cultures that value such animals, so our revulsion cannot be taken for granted. More research is needed to determine the origins of our attitudes toward these animals, but it is certain that their treatment by medieval fabulists did nothing to improve their reputation.

Marie populated her literary world with predators and prey, just as her courtly world was dominated by these characters. As we have seen, Odo's world certainly had its share of oppressive lords and exploited poor, but Odo's world was dominated by sinners and those aspiring to virtue. Although Odo's vision was as politically conservative as Marie's, he was primarily interested in giving spiritual not social warnings.

In the works of both fabulists, the animals were not animals at all. They were metaphors for classes and types that made up human society. Since both these authors were part of the ruling establishment, they made their fables and animal protagonists carry a socially conservative message. The politically conservative quality of medieval fables made them more readily distributable throughout society, and makes them fine reflections of how certain medieval thinkers viewed their society and its values. Furthermore, the medieval popularity of fables and related animal exemplar literature helped contribute to forming a valuative hierarchy of animals in which "the right" people aspired to be as strong as a lion, as crafty as a fox, or as fierce as a wolf, or to soar spiritually like an eagle. Animals of the imagination were powerful metaphors, especially in the hands of skilled fabulists like Marie de France and Odo of Cheriton.

NOTES

1. For a fuller discussion of people's relationship with animals and their perceptions of themselves as animals, see Joyce E. Salisbury, *The Beast Within: Animals and Bestiality in the Middle Ages* (New York: Routledge, 1994).

2. H. Spiegel, ed. and trans., *Marie de France: Fables* (Toronto: University of Toronto Press, 1987), 3–5, 7. All citations to Marie's fables are from this edition.

3. G.C. Keidel, "The History of the French Fable Manuscripts," *Publications of the Modern Language Association* 24 (1909), 218.

4. Odo of Cheriton, *The Fables of Odo of Cheriton*, trans. J.C. Jacobs (Syracuse: University of Syracuse Press, 1985), 10–15 (all citations from Odo's fables are from this edition); and Albert C. Friend, "Master Odo of Cheriton," *Speculum* 23 (1948), 641–58.

5. Phaedrus, in B.E. Perry, *Babrius and Phaedrus* (Cambridge, Mass.: Harvard University Press, 1965), 255.

6. H.J. Blackham, *The Fable as Literature* (London: Athlone Press, 1985), xx.

7. A.C. Henderson, "Animal Fables as Vehicles of Social Protest and Satire: Twelfth Century to Henryson," *Proceedings, Third International Beast Epic, Fable and Fabliau Colloquium*, ed. J. Goossens and T. Sodmann (Cologne: Böhlau Verlag, 1981), 164.

8. Henderson, 163.

9. Against greedy churchmen, see Odo of Cheriton, 86–7, 92, 94. Against ungrateful underlings, see 76, 91, 95, 152. Against people desiring worldly things, see 101–2, 104, 118–9.

10. Odo of Cheriton, 73–4, 78, 96, 150.

11. Spiegel, *Marie de France*, 253.

12. Spiegel, *Marie de France*, 103–7, 10.

13. While it would be inappropriate to discuss the Reynard stories in detail here, the literature on these tales is abundant. A good starting point is D.B. Sands, ed., *The History of Reynard the Fox* (Cambridge, Mass.: Harvard University Press, 1960).

14. Odo of Cheriton, 116–7.

15. Bonaventure, "Life of Francis," in A. Linzey and T. Regan, *Animals and Christianity: A Book of Readings* (New York: Crossroad, 1988), 28.

16. Spiegel, *Marie de France*, 35.

17. See Beryl Rowland, *Animals with Human Faces* (Knoxville, Tenn.: University of Tennessee Press, 1973), 138.

18. T.H. White, ed. and trans., *The Bestiary* (New York: G.P. Putnam's Sons, 1960), 61–5; Spiegel, *Marie de France*, 81.

19. Spiegel, *Marie de France*, 43; Odo, 138–9.

20. White, 66–7.

21. Tertullian, "On the Soul," in *Tertullian: Apologetical Works and Minucius Felix Octavius*, trans. E.A. Quain (New York: Fathers of the Church, Inc., 1950), 255; Boethius, *The Consolation of Philosophy* (New York: Penguin, 1980), 125.

22. Odo of Cheriton, 120; see Odo of Cheriton, 92, for dogs as scavangers.

23. L.W. Daly, *Aesop without Morals* (New York: Thomas Yoseloff, 1961), 257, 305.

24. Daly, 133, 277.

25. Odo of Cheriton, 140–1. See also Odo of Cheriton, 147–9, 152–3 for other fables that offer the same moral.

26. Daly, 151, 283.

27. Odo of Cheriton, 129. For other fables that warn against unjust exploitation of the poor, see Odo of Cheriton, 77, 93, 95, 114, 116, 124.

28. See Salisbury, *The Beast Within*, for a full explanation of this Christian attitude toward animals.

29. Odo of Cheriton, 55–7.

30. Odo of Cheriton, 121, 71, 72.

31. Hugh of Fouilloy, *The Medieval Book of Birds: Hugh of Fouilloy's Aviarum*, trans. W.B. Clark (Binghamton, N.Y.: Medieval and Renaissance Texts and Studies, 1992), 3.

32. Hugh of Fouilloy, 25, describes the popularity of the text and its influence in monastic houses. See Odo of Cheriton, 15, for Odo's travels and his close association with Cistercians.

33. Hugh of Fouilloy, 12, 35.

Parodic Animal Physicians from the Margins of Medieval Manuscripts

David A. Sprunger

In the margins of many medieval manuscripts, amazing *drôleries* contrast sharply with the serious verbal texts around which they appear. The rabbit skins the hunter; a band of rabbits captures and imprisons a knight; the warrior flees from a snail; the cow milks the dairy maid; and the ox dismembers the butcher.[1] Such illustrations suggest what Ernst Curtius labels the *adynata* topos, the portrayal of impossibilities, an *inversus mundi* with the order of the world turned upside down.[2] Some of these illustrations extend into the realm of parody, and of these, one pattern stands out: the animal physician. Pictures of the animal practitioner and his patient fit into the broad categories of parody and *inversus mundi*, but a closer examination suggests that these scenes are shaped additionally by society's concern about human physicians.

Attacks on doctors, their medicines, and their fees in historical record and literature extend back to the first recorded practitioner. By the fourteenth century, satire on doctors, like that in the verbal portrait of Chaucer's physician, had visual offshoots in the margins of medieval manuscripts. By transferring the iconographic traits of human physicians to animals and showing them in often predatory situations, the medieval artist could nonverbally express society's suspicion of doctors.

Public antagonism toward physicians as a group in the Middle Ages stems from age-old concerns still present in contemporary society: doctors live well at the expense of the sick, people question the ability of a practitioner to diagnose accurately and effectively to cure a disorder, and people resent the cost of receiving such treatment. Jill Mann notes in her *Chaucer and Medieval Estates Satire* that doctors frequently come under attack for "chicanery and malpractice" resulting from the "inefficiency and indeed dangerousness of medical practice."[3] The public's greatest concern is no doubt whether the learned physician would really be able to identify and vanquish a malady. Such concerns appear in proverbs, for example, and although they date from later than the images this essay explores, these proverbs provide an anthology of popular wisdom from the Middle Ages. Such proverbs range from scepticism ("God heals and the physician takes the fee") to outright distrust ("The physician is more dangerous than the disease"). Other proverbs focus on the physician's interest in his fee ("redie monie, redie medicine") or the more explicit concern that "he is a fool that makes his physician his heir."[4] In Sebastian Brant's *Ship of Fools* (1494), a catalog of foolish behavior, we find another instance of the tension between academic medicine and some unspecified, but apparently more practical, treatment:

> A fool is he, of little skill,
> Who tests the urine of the ill
> And says: "Wait, sir, and be so kind,
> The answer in my books I'll find."
> And while he thumbs the folios
> The patient to the bone yard goes.[5]

Such distrust of the medieval physician is not confined to western Europe. A view from Islamic culture provides a graphic, wry perspective on the perils of medieval European medical therapy. The Syrian emir Ousâma Ibn Moundkidh (1095–1188) tells of the physician Thâbit, who was called to treat some serious cases among the crusaders at Al-Mounatiria. He returned after only ten days and reported that his therapies had been interrupted by a European physician:

> They brought before me a knight with an abscess which had formed in his leg and a woman who was wasting away with a consumptive fever. I applied a little plaster to the knight; his abscess opened and took a turn for the better; the woman I forbade certain food and improved her condition. It was at this point that a Frankish doctor came up and said: "This man is incapable of curing them." Then, turning to the knight, he asked, "Which do you prefer, to live with one leg or die with two?" "I would rather live with one leg," the knight answered. "Bring a stalwart knight," said the Frankish doctor, "and a sharp hatchet." Knight and hatchet soon appeared. I was present at the scene. The doctor stretched the patient's leg on a block of wood and then said to the knight, "Strike off his leg with the hatchet; take it off with one blow." Under my eyes the knight aimed a violent blow at it without cutting through the leg. He aimed another blow at the unfortunate man, as a result of which his marrow came from his leg and the knight died instantly. As for the woman, the doctor examined her and said, "She is a woman in whose head there is a devil who has taken possession of

her. Shave off her hair!" His prescription was carried out, and like her fellows, she began once again to eat garlic and mustard. Her consumption became worse. The doctor then said, "It is because the devil has entered her head." Taking a razor, the doctor cut open her head in the shape of a cross and scraped away the skin in the centre so deeply that her very bones were showing. He then rubbed the head with salt. In her turn the woman died instantly. After having asked them whether my services were still required and obtained an answer in the negative, I came back, having learnt to know what I had formerly been ignorant of about their medicine.[6]

This account reminds us of the most crucial thought underlying most criticism of the medical profession: more accurate, more effective diagnosis and therapy must exist, but for reasons of pride, profit, or incompetance, the physician will not use them.

Acknowledging this widespread mistrust of the physician helps us to view the animal physicians more accurately, but to better understand the motif, we must first consider another important aspect: the iconographic tradition associated with human physicians.

In illustrations of human physicians, three iconographic strategies abound. The first is to show them in the act of diagnosis, usually taking a patient's pulse or inspecting the patient's urine in a distinctive flask. Second, this flask or jordan became so firmly associated in the public mind with the physician that its presence alone is enough to denote a medical doctor. And finally, sometimes a physician may be identified by a distinctive costume that sets him apart from others in the scene.

We see these strategies of diagnosis, flask, and dress in the famous portrait of the Physician from the Ellesmere manuscript of the *Canterbury Tales* (figure 1). Chaucer's verbal portrait of the Doctor of Physic emphasizes his wide knowledge of medical authorities and his business arrangements.[7] Yet, to illustrate the scene, the unknown artist has reached to traditions outside the text. We see the Physician ambling along on his palfrey, his occupation clearly identified by the large urine flask he carries in his hand.

In the *General Prologue*, Chaucer details the Physician's rich clothes: "In sangwyn and in pers he clad was al, / Lyned with taffata and with sendal"[8] [In red and Persian blue cloth was he entirely clad / Lined with taffeta and with silk]. Chaucer is not alone in associating physicians with such outward signs of wealth. We find other references to well-clothed doctors in the writings of his contemporaries. For instance, in his *Testament of Cresseid*, Robert Henryson presents Mercury as an ideal physician, a "Doctour in Phisick cled in ane Skarlot goun, / And furrit weill, as sic ane aucht to be"[9] [Doctor of Physic clad in a scarlet gown / One well furred, as such a one ought to be]. In *Piers Plowman*, Hunger speaks of forcing the Physician to sell his "furred hood" and "cloke of Calabre with alle the knappes of golde"[10] [A cloak of Calabrian fur with all the buttons of gold], and a sixteenth-century Spanish proverb remarks that "physicians of Valencia have long robes and little skill."[11] By the later Middle Ages, people still associated physicians with their fancy clothing, an element so closely connected with their rise in social status that physicians and their wives were exempted from the sumptuary laws that restricted opulence of dress.[12]

As mentioned earlier, the association of the urine flask with the physician is so strong that the jordan alone becomes the primary iconographic marker of a physician. To some degree, this association reflects the visual uniqueness

Figure 1. Portrait of the physician from the Ellesmere Chaucer (ca. 1410). San Marino, California: Huntington Library, EL 26 C 9, fol. 137. Reproduced by permission of the Huntington Library.

Figure 2. Marginal detail (enlarged) from a lower border in the Metz Pontifical (French, ca. 1316). Cambridge: Fitzwilliam Museum, MS. 298, fol. 81. Reproduced by permission of the Syndics of the Fitzwilliam Museum, Cambridge.

of the flask. While members of other professions might have worn equally rich clothes, no other group is ever displayed with the flask. This identification also indicates the importance of urinoscopy to medieval medicine. The medieval physician was able to discern much from examination of a patient's urine: its appearance, smell, and sometimes taste provided important clues to the patient's condition. In certain cases, physicians would even diagnose a patient's illness and prognosis from urine samples alone without even seeing the patient.[13]

This skill is reflected in an anecdote of Notker, the ninth-century medical monk of St. Gall. Wanting to test Notker's medical prowess, the Duke of Bavaria substituted a glass of urine from a pregnant woman for his own sample. Notker announced that God was to perform a miracle, for the duke would give birth to a boy within thirty days, and the duke, adequately impressed, named Notker the ducal physician.[14]

To reinforce the physician's occupation, the artist of the Ellesmere manuscript also shows the physician in the act of diagnosis: he holds the flask at its base in his left hand and has the back of his right hand against the neck. The right hand does not appear to help him secure the flask, although such security would seem advisable when riding a horse and carrying a bottle of urine. Perhaps the physician is shading the sample so as to see its color more accurately. In any case, the patient has ignored the proverbial advice to "piss clear and defy the physician,"[15] and the prognosis appears grim, since the sample is a muddy red color.

In figure 2, we see how a medieval artist might apply these human attributes to animal actors. In this border detail from the Metz Pontifical (ca.

1316), an ape wearing a hat and sitting on a chair consults a jordan and simultaneously takes the pulse of a stork. The illustrator of this manuscript was particularly fond of using animals for human parody, for on almost every page of the volume we find them engaging in human activity, evidence that "the artist has felt himself at liberty to indulge his exuberant fancy by pictures and caricatures of the life around him, and by the creation of legions of delightful animals which gravely mimic the doings of mankind."[16] Yet, one may ask, why has the artist specifically chosen an ape to portray the physician?

With their physical resemblance to humans and their capacity to mimic but not understand human behavior, apes have long been used for human parody. From the twelfth century onward, manuscript illumination and the plastic arts depict apes engaged in human activity, clearly showing the folly of their human counterparts, particularly those in the aristocracy, the clergy, and the teaching professions.[17] Apes fight battles, copy manuscripts, preach to congregations, lecture to classes, and especially from the mid-fourteenth century, practice medicine. In a carving from the early fifteenth century, an ape in an academic hood gestures to a urine flask and lectures on medicine to some fox pupils, one of whom follows along in a book.[18]

A number of cues in the illustration suggest the ape-physician's high social prestige. The hat gives the ape both a more human appearance and suggests the fashion of the upper classes of the Middle Ages. Although there is no evidence of a particular hat associated with physicians, the ape's pointed hat is very similar to one worn by a doctor in a German fifteenth-century manuscript, which Peter Jones suggests might also signal the practitioner's Jewish identity.[19] That the ape sits on a thronelike chair atop a dais further suggests his social superiority to the patient. An illustrated *Trésor* of Bruno Latini (early fourteenth century) contains a miniature with personifications of various professional positions (canon law, medicine, civil law, and so forth), and in each frame, the practitioner sits in a chair to conduct business.[20]

The hat and the seated position mark a professional man, but the role of the physician, however, is made most evident by the dual acts of diagnosis: scrutiny of the urine flask mentioned earlier and the taking of a patient's pulse. Examination of the pulse stands second only to urinoscopy among the diagnostic tools of the medieval physician, and treatises on the pulse passed from classical medicine to the medical students' curriculum. Jones notes that "it is a measure of the powers of their discrimination that some of the symptomatic pulses [that medieval physicians] identified were still used in diagnosis up to the introduction of the electrocardiograph."[21] The ape even uses the proper technique, placing his hand upon the patient's left wrist.[22]

Figures 3a and 3b. Marginal details from the Smithfield Decretals (fourteenth century). London: British Library, Royal MS. 10 E. IV, fols. 54 and 54v. Reproduced by permission of the British Library.

Unlike his human counterpart, the animal physician never appears in illustrations without a patient, and the choice of patient is an important element in the parody. In this illustration, the crane or stork is no doubt deliberately paired with the simian physician. Apes and cranes are found together in other medieval illustrations, but their connection in this scene is of special significance. In his discussion "Apes and Birds," Horst Janson identifies three typical patterns of illustration, the ape's response varying according to the kind of bird.[23] Apes try to capture small songbirds, they are companions of owls, and they battle large wading birds. This latter relationship may linger from classical descriptions of cranes battling pygmies.[24] In any case, if we consider the figures in this tradition, we find a hint that the ape's motives for treating the patient may not be to the patient's advantage and that the crane patient may, in fact, be in some peril.

We find similar ideas brought together more sharply in figure 3, a pair of marginal illustrations from the Smithfield Decretals.[25] In the first, a fox wearing a belt, from which hang several small pouches, leans on a staff while taking the pulse of a wolf who lies back with a bandaged head. Turning the leaf, a reader finds the doctor leaving the patient, who now lies flat on his back with his paws in the air, apparently dead. Rather than showing sorrow for the patient's demise, the fox's open mouth grins, as if jeering at the wolf.

An exact interpretation of these scenes is impossible. Kenneth Varty argues convincingly that an entire series of fox illustrations scattered throughout the Smithfield Decretals are meant to illustrate the story of Reynard the Fox from the *Roman Reynard*.[26] As such, this particular pair of pictures would correspond most closely to an episode in which Reynard gets the better of his nemesis the wolf by impersonating a physician and prescribing that the ailing King Noble, the lion, wrap himself in a fresh wolfskin.[27] However, if the artist meant to illustrate that incident accurately, in the first picture Reynard should be taking Noble's pulse rather than the wolf's, and in the second we would expect to find clearer evidence that the wolf had been skinned, either by its bare appearance or by a depiction of Reynard taking the skin with him.

In portraying a medical encounter between traditional enemies, the artist has let other attitudes toward physicians and patients overshadow a literal adherence to the text. His interest in medical diagnosis appears elsewhere in the manuscript, for example, in an illustration in which a fox ex-

Figure 4. Marginal detail from a Book of Hours (second half of the fourteenth century). Reprinted by permission of the Edinburgh University Library, MS. 305, fol. 25v.

amines a urine flask before a seated wolf.[28] The result of these sequential pictures, regardless of context, is a clear reminder that a visit from the physician is not a good thing for the patient.

A more explicit suggestion that nature pits doctor against patient occurs in a detail from a Book of Hours from the second half of the fifteenth century (figure 4). Amidst the marginal illustrations, a dog in a blue hood studiously consults a urine flask at the side of a bedridden cat wearing a nightcap.[29] In their natural role, dogs were thought to have medicinal power. The bestiary credited a dog's lick with healing wounds, an idea that Janetta Rebold Benton notes has some medical validity because of the relative acidity of dog saliva.[30] In this illustration, however, we see no indication of such a tradition. Instead, this dog provides human parody, and a close examination of the medical hound demonstrates how the artist has drawn upon the iconographic traditions associated with the human physicians.

Although not specifically linked to medicine, the dog's hood—like the ape's hat in the Metz Pontifical—provides an iconographic connection to academia in general. Once a staple item of clothing for members of all classes and genders, by the mid-fourteenth century the hood was becoming entrenched in public thought as an emblem of the academic community. The hound's hood is highly stylized; protocol of the early academic hood distinguished degree and rank by shape and cut of the hood, not color, and from this hood we cannot infer connection to a particular degree or institution. In his study of academic dress, W.N. Hargreaves-Mawdsley notes that the hood also signifies the conservative nature of academic institutions: "It is typical of the growth of specialized costume that a fashion abandoned in everyday life is appropriated by institutions, themselves strongholds of conservatism."[31]

That the physician's patient is in this case a cat is also important, for it again shows the physician as a natural enemy of the patient, a theme we have seen echoed in other cases of the animal physician.

A marginal detail from another fifteenth-century Flemish Book of Hours reverses the positions of power but retains the same message about patients and doctors (figure 5).[32] Here, the physician with his urine flask is a bespectacled rabbit and his patients are dogs, although in this case they are perhaps less threatening to him because they walk with canes and crutches.

The rabbit's spectacles (lenses linked by a leather strap) function in a way similar to the dog's hood in the Edinburgh Book of Hours. At a practical level, the artist places a piece of distinctly human equipment on an animal. But more significantly, although glasses are not linked specifically with the practice of medicine, they associate the wearer with academic life and the elite social class. The origins of eyeglasses in medieval Europe are uncertain,

Figure 5. Marginal detail from lower border in a Book of Hours (fifteenth century). Reprinted by permission of The Pierpont Morgan Library, New York: M. 358, fol. 20v.

but most scholars agree that they probably originated in Italy at the end of the thirteenth century.[33] A seventeenth-century reference to a sermon from 1285 describes them and speaks of their invention having occurred within the previous twenty years, and from the fourteenth century onward the spectacle was regarded as a symbol of "scholarship and educational superiority."[34]

We may also consider the pairing of rabbit physician with canine patients. When medieval readers encountered this illustration of upright dogs in human poses, John Block Friedman speculates that they would think first of Dominican friars because of a well-known pun on the name of the order.[35] Saint Dominic's mother dreamt during her pregnancy of a dog carrying a lighted torch in its mouth, and thus the Dominican order, or Dominicani, was interpreted as the *domini cani*—the dogs of the Lord.

Although they may have thought of the Dominicans, readers encountering the dog and rabbit would have found an additional message about the physician-patient relationship. The traditional role of the hounds as pursuers of rabbits in the natural world has been reversed, and the dogs are now dependent upon the hare for their physical health. This inverted relationship is consistent with the *inversus mundi* theme, but such a reversal also reiterates the perilous relationship between doctor and patient in the human world: even a person who might normally rule over the physician must submit to him in a time of sickness or injury.

Perhaps because public perception of the physician had improved, or perhaps because printed books had supplanted manuscripts with their marginal illustrations, the parodic animal physician largely disappeared by the close of the sixteenth century. A late example survives, however, in an early seventeenth-century painting by Pieter Quast entitled "Der Wundartz" or "The Surgeon" (figure 6).[36]

Here a surgeon performs an operation on a seated patient. In several respects this operation suggests a "stone operation" as seen in the late fifteenth-century Hieronymus Bosch painting "Cure for Folly." This procedure was a staple of quack medicine, in which a physician, or more likely a charlatan, would make an incision in a patient's head and then display some pebbles that he would claim to have extracted from the wound. These "stones of folly" were seen as manifestations of the patient's illness.[37]

In this particular painting, onlookers gawk from the doorway as a man in a chair is held down by the physician's assistant while the surgeon cuts into his head. In the shadows, a picture on the wall shows an ape performing the same operation on an owl. While the animal parody is not in a margin *per se*, the frame that encloses the figures and its relegation to the background and shadows put it in a similar position.

We have already seen how medieval thought dealt with the ape, but definitive interpretation of the ape's pairing with the owl remains elusive, for the owl has many different iconographic roles. In its depiction with Athena, goddess of wisdom, the owl signifies sagacity; the medieval bestiary, on the other hand, looked less favorably upon the owl as "symbolic of the Jews, who repulse our Saviour when he comes to redeem them, saying 'We

Figure 6. Pieter Quast, "Der Wundartz." Early seventeenth century. Bamberg: Außengalerie, Inv. Nr. 2148. Reproduced by permission of the Bayerische Staatsgemäldesammlungen.

have no king but Caesar.'"[38] As late as the early sixteenth century, owls had connotations of folly, drunkenness, and lechery.[39]

When the owl and ape appear together, the pairing usually suggests a single response. For instance, Janson notes that much late medieval decoration linked the owl with the ape as symbols of vice or evil, partly because each is a species rejected by other animals in its own domain.[40] A character in Chaucer's *Nun's Priest's Tale* equates foolish and unbelievable things with men dreaming "alday of owles or of apes."[41]

Whether we choose to see the owl as wise or wicked, in either case the illustration on the wall provides a commentary on the action in the foreground, suggesting at one extreme that the patient is wiser than the physician or that the patient and physician are both rogues.

In the other illustrations we have seen, the parodic physician and his patient appear in the margins of manuscripts whose content is neither medical nor zoological. Instead, the illustrations stand by themselves and provide general, gentle reminders of the ways doctors interact with their patients. In "Der Wundartz," Quast uses the marginal illustration in a much more focused way. Gone is the subtle parody we saw in the manuscripts. Here the presence of the animal physician encourages our outright ridicule of the human practitioner and his duped patient in the foreground. This shift from indefinite, widespread parody to focused ridicule is indicative of the shift from general "carnival" laughter to bitter derision noted by Mikhail Bakhtin in literature of the sixteenth century:

> [Carnival laughter] is, first of all, a festive laughter. Therefore it is not an individual reaction to some isolated "comic" event. Carnival laughter is the laughter of all the people. Second, it is universal in scope; it is directed at all and everyone, including the carnival's participants. The entire world is seen in its droll aspect, in its gay relativity. Third, this laughter is ambivalent: it is gay, triumphant, and at the same time mocking, deriding. It asserts and denies, it buries and revives. . . . The satirist whose laughter is negative places himself above the object of his mockery, he is opposed to it. The wholeness of the world's comic aspect is destroyed, and that which appears comic becomes a private reaction.[42]

Quast's iconographic strategy clearly works in this way, using a once gentle image to signal his disapproval of both he who performs the operation and he who submits to it.

Throughout its history, the parodic animal physician has always invoked laughter. The very audacity of the image suggests the *inversus mundi* in several ways: first, in the absurdity of depicting an animal engaging in one of the most complex human arts; and second, in showing an animal caring for the physical health of a traditional nemesis. It is this second aspect that goes beyond mere humor and reflects widespread suspicion of the physician-patient relationship, and thus the image of the parodic animal physician reminds us that truth can lie not at the center of things but at the edges.

NOTES

1. Lilian Randall includes a multitude of examples in *Images in the Margins of Gothic Manuscripts* (Berkeley: University of California Press, 1966). For a discussion of how such marginal illustrations relate to the page as a whole, see Michael Camille, *Image on the Edge: The Margins of Medieval Art* (Cambridge, Mass.: Harvard University Press, 1992). The idea of the *inversus mundi* is discussed by Malcolm Jones in "Folklore Motifs in Late Medieval Art, I: Proverbial Follies and Impossibilities," *Folklore* 2 (1989), 201–17. David Kunzle discusses and reproduces later permutations of the theme in "World Upside Down: The Iconography of a European Broadsheet Type," in *The Reversible World: Symbolic Inversion in Art and Society*, ed. Barbara Babcock (Ithaca, N.Y.: Cornell University Press, 1978), 39–94. Also of interest is Jean Klene, "Chaucer's Contribution to a Popular Topos: The World Upside-Down," *Viator* 11 (1980), 321–34.

2. Ernst Curtius, *European Literature and the Latin Middle Ages*, trans. Willard Trask, Bollingen Series 36 (1952; Princeton: Princeton University Press, 1973), 94–8.

3. Jill Mann, *Chaucer and Medieval Estates Satire* (Cambridge: Cambridge University Press, 1973), 91–2. For a list of medieval complaints against physicians, see 250, n. 24.

4. Morris Tilley, *A Dictionary of the Proverbs in England in the Sixteenth and Seventeenth Centuries* (Ann Arbor, Mich.: University of Michigan Press, 1950), M1091, P267a, F483.

5. Sebastian Brant, *The Ship of Fools*, trans. Edwin Zeydel (1944; New York: Dover Books, 1962), 188.

6. Ousâma Ibn Moundkidh [Usamah Ibn Murshid], *The Autobiography of Ousâma*, trans. George Potter (London: George Routledge and Sons, 1929), 173–5.

7. Those interested in this physician should consult Walter Clyde Curry, "Chaucer's Doctor of Physyk," *Philological Quarterly* 4 (1925), 1–24 (revised as a chapter in *Chaucer and the Medieval Sciences*, rev. ed. [New York: Barnes and Noble, 1960]); or Huling Ussering, *Chaucer's Physician: Medicine and Literature in Fourteenth-Century England*, Tulane Studies in Literature 19 (New Orleans: Tulane University, 1971).

8. *Riverside Chaucer*, 3rd ed., ed. Larry D. Benson (Boston: Houghton Mifflin, 1987), l. 439–40.

9. Robert Henryson, *The Testament of Cresseid and Other Poems*, ed. Hugh MacDiarmid (Harmondsworth: Penguin Books, 1973), l. 250–1.

10. William Langland, *Piers Plowman: The B Version*, ed. George Kane and E. Talbot Donaldson (London: The Athlone Press, 1975), Passus vi. 269–70. Another reference to a physician's furred hood occurs in xx.176.

11. Tilley, P275.

12. Barbara Tuchman, *A Distant Mirror: The Calamitous 14th Century* (New York: Ballantine Books, 1978), 19–20, 106. For more on medical dress, see also Augustin Cabanès, *Le costume du médecin en France des origines au XVIIe siècle* (Paris: Longuet, 1921).

13. For a complete history of urinoscopy, see René Küss and Willy Gregoir, *Histoire Illustrée de l'urologie de l'Antiquité à nos jours* (Paris: Les Editions Roger DaCosta, 1988). Additional information appears in Peter Murray Jones, *Medieval Medical Miniatures* (Austin: University of Texas Press, 1984), 58–60; and John Murdoch, *Album of Science: Antiquity and the Middle Ages* (New York: Charles Scribner's Sons, 1984), 260–1.

14. Marjorie Rowling, *Everyday Life in Medieval Times* (1968; New York: Dorset Press, 1987), 178.

15. Tilley, P289.

16. Francis Wormald and Phyllis M. Giles, *A Descriptive Catalogue of the Additional Illuminated Manuscripts in the Fitzwilliam Museum*, vol. I (Cambridge: Cambridge University Press, 1982), xvi. This manuscript was probably produced by the same workshop that did the Verdun Breviary, vol. I of which is now in the British Library (Yates Thompson MS. 8); vol. II is in the city library of Verdun (MS. 107).

17. The best study remains that of H.W. Janson, *Apes and Ape Lore in the Middle Ages and the Renaissance* (London: The Warburg Institute, 1952). Although Janson traces the ape motif to some twelfth-century works, he argues that the theme didn't flourish until the "Gothic era" (165).

18. Parish church in Knowles, Warwickshire. Reproduced in Kenneth Varty, *Reynard the Fox: A Study of the Fox in Medieval English Art* (New York: Humanities Press, 1967), figure 112.

19. Figure 22 in Jones, *Medieval Medical Miniatures*. For more discussion of the distinctive headgear, see Ruth Mellinkoff, *Outcasts: Signs of Otherness in Northern European Art of the Late Middle Ages*, 2 vols. (Berkeley: University of California Press, 1993), particularly I, 91–4 and II, pls. 120–31; and John Block Friedman, "Bald Jonah and the Exegesis of 4 Kings 2.23," *Traditio* 44 (1988), 125–44, especially 128–9.

20. London, British Library, Additional MS. 30024, fol. 1v. See the reproduction in Jones, 57.

21. Jones, 60. For much information on the role of the pulse in determining etiology of disease, see especially 24–6 and 57–60. For even more pulse lore, consult John Murdoch, *Album of Science: Antiquity and the Middle Ages* (New York: Scribner's, 1984), who discusses this illustration in conjunction with the importance of the pulse to diagnosis in medieval medicine (307).

22. Jones, 60. See also his comments on plate V.

23. Janson, 174.

24. Janson, 184.

25. The canon-law edicts of Pope Gregory IX, written in Italy and illustrated in England, second quarter of the fourteenth century. London, British Library, Royal MS. 10 E. IV, fols. 54 and 54v.

26. Kenneth Varty, "Reynard the Fox and the Smithfield Decretals," *Journal of the Warburg and Courtauld Institutes* 26 (1963), 347–54. Varty amplifies this argument in the chapter "The Fox Physician," in *Reynard the Fox: A Study in Medieval English Art*, 68–75.

27. For more on the Reynard stories, see especially N.F. Blake's introduction to *The History of Reynard the Fox; translated from the Dutch original by William Caxton*, EETS, o.s. 263 (London: Oxford University Press, 1970); and Thomas Best, *Reynard the Fox* (Boston: Twayne Publishers, 1983).

28. Figure 98 in Varty, *Reynard*.

29. Edinburgh University Library, MS. 305, fol. 25v. Written in the southern Netherlands in the second half of the fifteenth century. For a description, see N.R. Ker, *Medieval Manuscripts in British Libraries*, vol. II (Oxford: Clarendon Press, 1977), 597–8. This manuscript was formerly cataloged as MS. Db.3.30, and I thank John Howard, Special Collections Librarian at Edinburgh University Library, for providing me with the updated shelfmark.

30. *The Medieval Menagerie: Animals in the Art of the Middle Ages* (New York: Abbeville Press, 1992), 93.

31. W.N. Hargreaves-Mawdsley, *A History of Academical Dress in Europe until the End of the Eighteenth Century* (Oxford: Clarendon Press, 1963), 6–7.

32. New York, Pierpont Morgan Library, MS. 358, fol. 20v. John Plummer dates this manuscript ca. 1440–50, and although he reports that scholars have argued variously for origins in Flanders, Luxembourg, Picardy, Anjou, and Provence, he finds more stylistic evidence for the latter. A full bibliographic description of the book appears in Plummer, *The Last Flowering: French Painting in Manuscripts, 1420–1530, from American Collections* (New York: Pierpont Morgan Library, 1982), 28–9.

33. Charles Panatti, *Extraordinary Origins of Everyday Things* (New York: Harper and Row, 1987), 264.

34. Benjamin Gordon, "The Invention of Spectacles," *Medieval and Renaissance Medicine* (New York: Philosophical Library, 1959), 288–98. In his overview on the invention of spectacles, Panatti suggests that early eyeglasses became status symbols because of their scarcity and corresponding cost (267).

35. Private correspondence, 25 February 1993. Friedman expands on the parodic significance of this *bas de page* in his article "The Friar Portrait in Bodleian Library MS. Douce 104: Contemporary Satire?" in *The Yearbook of Langland Studies* 8 (1994), 177–84.

36. This painting is on wood, 37.5 cm. × 54 cm.

37. For much lore on the stone operation and on reference to "stones of folly" in folklore, see D. Bax, *Hieronymus Bosch: His Picture-Writing Deciphered*, trans. M.A. Bax-Botha (1948; Rotterdam: A.A. Balkema, 1979), especially 270–5. Bosch's piece is on wood, 48 cm. × 37 cm.

38. T.H. White, trans., *The Book of Beasts, Being a Translation from a Latin Bestiary of the Twelfth Century* (1954; New York: Dover, 1984), 134. Further elaboration on the evils of owls appears in the debate poem "The Owl and the Nightingale."

39. Bax, 208–13.

40. Janson, 181–4.

41. *Nun's Priest's Tale*, l. 4282.

42. Mikhail Bakhtin, *Rabelais and his World*, trans. Helene Iswolsky (1965; Cambridge, Mass: M.I.T. Press, 1968), 11–2.

Making Animals Mean

Speciest Hermeneutics in the
Physiologus of Theobaldus

Lesley Kordecki

> It seemed to me only proper that words
> Should be withheld from vegetables and birds.
> . . . .
> Let them leave language to their lonely betters
> Who count some days and long for certain letters;
> We, too, make noises when we laugh or weep,
> Words are for those with promises to keep. (ll. 3–4, 13–16)
>
> W.H. Auden, "Their Lonely Betters" *

When the owl argues with the nightingale about who is more valu-able, the late twelfth-century English poem deals with the specifics of each animal, down to the keen eyesight of the owl and the aesthetic abundance of the nightingale's song. Most readers assume that the text only marginally concerns these birds, whose debate elaborately encodes matters actually about humans.[1] I believe this to be true, but wish to examine more closely a medieval text that helps to authorize centuries of animal appropriation, one of the many documents that ulti-mately make animals "mean." In the medieval bestiary, we observe the subversion of the world of nature (constituted in the distinct form of ani-mals) to the world of discourse, and the semiotic implications of this sub-version.

Many medieval texts exert great energy re-creating creatures into hu-man form, rewording the beast for a human agenda, so much so that ani-mals in these centuries, it seems, occupy a privileged hermeneutic position. We should not be surprised to find that they had the power of speech. Parliament was not confined merely to fowls but was often extended in poetry to all those creatures somewhat like humans but blissfully free of accessible discourse. Auden in our century ironically calls people "Their Lonely Betters," suggesting that subservient animals occupy a world less solipsistic and less contaminated by language. He perceives that their wordless world does not with "promises" and "letters" attempt to assume "responsibility for time":

> Not one of them was capable of lying,
> There was not one which knew that it was dying
> Or could have with a rhythm or a rhyme
> Assumed responsibility for time. (ll. 9–12)

This poem's appropriation and biased perception of nature, like that found in medieval texts, ultimately "talks" about humans not animals. After all, animals are here to serve Adam, who named (or worded) them. They frequently serve as textual instructors at one level or another. Even Chaucer, a writer not unaccustomed to consideration of worldly glory, uses an eagle to teach him the correct meaning of fame, which is merely the promise of future words. Today's questions about history and text take on a new dimension when these irresponsible wordless beings "figure" strongly in story.

Animals in a sense are the ideal textual agents of speech. Unlike women, whose problematic tongues complicate the elaborate falsehoods of patriarchal visions, animals mutely allow continued speciest fantasies by human authors. But one might speculate—might *want* to speculate—that beasts and birds will endure the travesty in a good-"natured" way, for their "natures" are touched upon not by the errors and arrogance of human discourse but by the ravages of human materialism, as we have been belatedly discovering. Indeed, like nearly everything in the world, animals on paper, on parchment, are most often reflections, distortions, models, subversions, scape"goats" if you will, for the human animal.

This relationship, I think, was more honest in the Middle Ages; the speech and action of animals were openly appropriated by writers. In fables beasts articulated their way into the human realm with persistent literary endurance. Even when "words [are] withheld from vegetables and birds," as in the bestiary, we find their actions speaking louder. In addition, bestiaries predicate themselves upon a comfortable suspension of accuracy, as do many interesting discourses. The "world" of the descriptive sections of the bestiary becomes subverted under the "word" of its allegorical passages. And taken as a whole, the dual, glossed text awaits a magnified, multiplied signified in the mind of the reader to accompany the tricky signifier sequence provided.

Critics are becoming more aware of how speech, or the lack thereof, empowers characters in narrative. Sometimes the success of the story hinges on the verbal prowess or perversion of an animal character. The crow in Chaucer's *Manciple's Tale*, for example, becomes the locus wherein the entire collection of tales begins to deconstruct. The crow talks too much and talks about cuckolding (the stuff of many of the tales). Its punishment is eternal, etiological silence, the strongest weapon of poetry. The tale's message exhorting silence ("Kepe wel thy tonge and thenk upon the crow") is highlighted by its nearly terminal position in the sequence of tales. Even more interestingly, the Parson's antiliterary prologue directly follows: "For Paul . . . Repreveth hem that weyven soothfastnesse / And tellen fables and swich wrecchednesse"[2] [For Paul . . . reproaches them who turn aside from truth and tell stories and such wretchedness.] The crow becomes essential in a series of assertions that seem to undercut the whole of the *Canterbury Tales*.

I am interested in how animal books, with their overt hermeneutic directives, present the process of interpretation imbedded within the text. This process, I believe, occurs in many other written accounts from the Middle Ages. We have known for some time that medieval writers did not define "literary" texts in our post-Romantic way but grouped all discourse together in much the same manner as poststructuralist precepts now advise us to do.[3] We can productively reexamine hermeneutic discourses present in some medieval texts by applying the lesson provided by biblical commentary, whose basic characteristics are found in the combination of any text and its interpretation. This model of a gloss supplementing a base text helps us examine the dynamics involved in the category of discourse that we call bestiaries. I would argue that a major attraction of these documents (in addition to the sometimes elaborate illustrations) is the inclusion of interpretation with text. The flagrant intertextualism of these books calls attention to the effort to construct a bridge between text and life, between word and world. The difficult and dogged relationship of written discourse with the world outside articulation can be fruitfully sought in the context of an age when the world itself was universally acknowledged as an articulation—an articulation of the godhead. The "symbolist mentality" of the Middle Ages, in which the empirical world represents the spiritual world, might simply be another way of describing the "prison house" that language is said to construct.[4] Language, whether we like it or not, is the offspring of ideologically constructed humans. As a child of our own desires and wills, it bites the hand that feeds it, but can never quite separate itself from human agency enough to represent fully what is outside us. If the world is God's Word, created solely to lead us to him, then such ontological gymnastics enabled medieval thinkers to accept the deconstruction of not only their texts but also their world as a matter of course. The frequency of glossed texts—those texts that most overtly further the process of interpreting the world, i.e., the articulated and ultimately deconstructed Word of God—begins to make more sense.

Medieval writings glossed more than stories and descriptions of animals, as we well know. A habit of supplying one text with another which expanded, clarified, and ultimately changed the former can be seen in various discourses. Medieval subtexts were provided for classical materials; heroic configurations are often found in hagiography. Homiletic writings appended and transformed their rhetoric with exempla, reversing the text and gloss sequence of the bestiary. More subtle are the interpretive moves of allegorical texts, which intertwine text and gloss. Eugene Vinaver, moreover, compares some monologues in medieval romances to biblical commentary, and prophecies in these texts often serve this function.[5] Ovid, too valuable to lose, required, it seems, substantial moralizing. Significantly, classical fables, already supplied with glosses or morals to mediate the animal stories, were little changed by medieval writers. Perhaps most self-consciously, classical encyclopedias (like those of Pliny, Solinus, and Aelianus) and early medieval compilations (like Isidore's *Etymologiae)* in their glossed versions were adapted into bestiaries and lapidaries. Here descriptions or stories of creatures or minerals were accompanied by assertive statements that purported to give the text relevance.

I would like to examine in this essay the rhetorical function of the *moralitas* sections of the bestiary and how this glossing supplements and attempts to determine the sense of the work's descriptive passages or *proprietas* portions, material often borrowed from Pliny or Isidore. I hope to demonstrate that although the Latin verse *Physiologus* attributed to Theobaldus (late eleventh or early twelfth century) makes statements about natural science and theology, it more significantly makes statements about interpretation shaping narrative, word shaping world, and maybe even about the delight of allowing the gloss or margin to usurp the text.

The influence of the Bible and its glosses on other literature has been well established for decades by critics following the lead of D.W. Robertson, Jr.[6] These comparative studies, however, have mostly been about content not form. For example, because of the simple equation of dragon and devil in the Apocalypse, the creature in medieval literature often performs the function of the devil—something we can easily see in saints' lives.[7] The dragon's demonic characteristics appear frequently in exegetical writings even as early as the ninth-century *De rerum naturis* of Hrabanus Maurus. This work is an interesting combination of Isidore's seventh-century *Etymologiae* material with the standard theological interpretations found in later exegesis and bestiaries. Following Isidore's description of the dragon, Hrabanus forms what might be one of the earliest concise medieval symbolic statements on the creature, which he glosses as the devil or persecutor of the church.[8] But we see a different exegetical tradition operating in one of the amateur hermeneutical flourishes of Chaucer's Wife of Bath, as she recalls the cunning attributes associated with the dragon in the antifeminist passage of Ecclesiasticus 25:23:

"Bet is . . . thyn habitacioun
Be with a leon or a foul dragoun,
Than with a womman usynge for to chyde."
(*Canterbury Tales*, *Wife of Bath's Prologue*, III, 775–7)

[Better your habitation be with a lion or a foul dragon than with a woman accustomed to chiding.]

The biblical passage to which the Wife refers reads:

Et non est ira super iram mulieris.
Commorari leoni et draconi placebit,
Quam habitare cum muliere nequam. (Ecclus. 25:23)

[There is no wrath greater than the wrath of a woman. I would rather dwell with a lion or dragon than with a woman.]

The Wife may simply be repeating Scripture, but the passage becomes richer if Chaucer also had in mind biblical commentary that most definitively positions "woman" as a category more heinous than that of lion or dragon. Hugh of St. Cher, for instance, in his thirteenth-century commentary on this Ecclesiasticus passage echoes Augustine's exegetical distinction between the lion and serpent as representing overt and covert anger (his gloss of Ps. 90:13), and if known to Chaucer, Hugh's distinctions make the lusty Wife's allusion particularly apt: Hugh tells us that a lion or dragon can only hurt the body. A woman is like a lion because of her heat, wrath, and passion; and like a dragon because, as a dragon pursues an elephant (the symbol of purity), so a woman pursues the chastity of men. A lion harms openly while a dragon harms secretly, but a woman harms in both ways.[9] Chaucer seems to be influenced by both text and gloss. Malory similarly exploits the same exegetical connotations in Percival's dream, in which he sees two ladies—one riding a lion and the other, a dragon.[10] The lion represents open anger and the serpent/dragon represents covert anger in exegesis and, subsequently, in the Arthurian romance.

To provide further illustrations would only belabor a point well made years ago. I want to emphasize that not only the content of exegesis but also the form of its presentation can provide "telling" things about other writings. Glossed Bibles reveal a structural strategy of discourse which informs other genres, most notably the bestiary.

Beryl Smalley's painstaking study of the remarkable hermeneutic fervor of the later Middle Ages led to the assertion that exegesis often contributes to the literal exposition of the Bible, not just the spiritual exposition, and that we should not reject gloss as simply pious meditation or religious teaching.[11] In this impressively long and complicated tradition, we see that text comes to be prized eventually not only for its ultimate authority—its divine authorship—but also for its assertive commentary, which unites the stories and sermons of the Bible to other discourses. The Bible became standardized in Jerome's translation, and its explication became standardized in the phenomenon of the *Glossa ordinaria*. This text and gloss, at times supplying revered patristic commentary, became for Christians the most impressive example of text (or texts) relating to primary text in Western culture.

The bestiary presents us with a more popularized version of a dual text in which one part becomes a hermeneutic directive for the other. Although many versions of the bestiary would demonstrate my point, Theobaldus's Latin *Physiologus*, like its Greek source, is short enough (slightly over 300 lines) to discuss in a more limited space. Both its use as a school primer and its earlier date than many noted bestiaries[12] recommend this version as a model for the discourse as a whole, although it remains distinctive in a few important elements.

Theobaldus's poem offers descriptions of the natural characteristics (which he calls *naturas)* of thirteen creatures: the lion, the eagle, the serpent, the ant, the fox, the stag, the spider, the whale, sirens, onocentaurs, the elephant, the turtledove, and the panther. Each entry (except for that of the sirens) links characteristics with appropriate allegorical interpretations, or *figuras,* of varying length. The first lines of the beginning chapter, the lion, explain with economy the scheme of the entire text:

> Tres leo naturas et tres habet inde figuras,
> Quas ego, Christe, tibi ter seno carmine scripsi.
> Altera divini memorant animalia libri,
> De quibus apposui, que rursus mystica novi,
> Temptans, diversis si possem scribere metris;
> Et numero nostrum complent simul addita soldum.

[The lion has three natural characteristics and hence three allegorical interpretations, which I have described for you, Christ, in a poem of eighteen verses. Holy books record the other animals, about which I have added the mystic allegories I have got to know, trying to see if I could write in different metres; and, at the same time, additions fill up our sum-total.][13]

Here we learn that the poem will purposely have several meters and will include material taken from other texts as well as new material. Eighteen lines will be devoted to the lion entry. Most important, the first line tells us that since the lion has three natural characteristics, then it follows that (*inde*) it must have three *figuras*. This simple assertion of causal relation suffices for Theobaldus. The *natura* of the lion then follows:

> Nam leo stans fortis super alta cacumina montis,
> Qualicunque via descendit vallis ad ima:
> Si venatorem per notum sentit odorem,
> Cauda cuncta linit, que pes vestigia figit,
> Quatinus inde suum non possit querere lustrum.
> Natus non vigilat, dum sol se tertio gyrat,
> Sed dans rugitum pater eius suscitat illum.
> Tunc quasi vivescit, tunc sensus quinque capescit,
> Et quotiens dormit, sua nunquam lumina claudit. (I, 1–9)

[The lion, then, standing in his might above the towering mountain peaks, descends by any path he chooses to the depths of the valley: if, through the familiar scent, he senses a hunter, he smoothes with his tail over all the tracks his feet imprint, so that the hunter cannot then track out his lair. After birth he does not wake up until the sun circles for the third time, but his father rouses him by giving a roar; then, so to speak, he comes alive, then he takes hold of his five senses, and he never shuts his eyes however often he sleeps.]

The lion is allegorized in a traditional manner as Christ who, like the lion descending from a mountain, descends into Mary's womb. The second *natura*, the lion's father awakening the lion with a roar, is glossed as Christ's father making him rise ("surgere fecit") after his death on the cross. And finally, like the lion in sleep, Christ never shuts his eyes but guards us as his flock.

With this one entry, we are clearly able to appreciate the exegetical impulse of the age. Recent attention to the action of glossing and discourse analysis procedures has made us more sensitive to interpretive maneuvers in writing and the internal dynamics of intertextualism in all nonmonologic texts. In one sense, the gloss here, the *figuras* of the lion, limits meaning by asserting that the lion ultimately exists in this world as a sign for Christ. Much can and has been written on how the Church controlled discourse and, thereby, perception with such glosses. The political ramifications of these theological power plays are not to be denied, but I am more concerned in this essay with the effect of the dichotomous text that mediates the reader's prerogative for interpretation by supplying, in an intrusive level of discourse, ready-made signifieds (mental images) for the signifier (the word itself), here "lion" or more precisely "leo." The linguists' useful division of the sign into its two parts, signifier and signified, is forcefully anticipated by decoding texts like bestiaries and all other hermeneutical discourse. Of course, the *figuras*, functioning as prescribed signifieds for the animal, constitute their own sequence of signifiers, but their powerful manipulation of the animal as signifier is what the book is all about.

The signifieds, or mental images, suggested by the *figuras* in this case are nothing like the biological lion, of course. The program of the bestiary is such that the writer and, presumably, the reader no longer care about signifiers in the same way as less overtly hermeneutic books would have. The lion becomes something other (or more) than a lion, so much so that it transforms itself into Christ, and the interpretive distance between signifier and signified (i.e., the lion who descends from the mountain is like Christ who descends into the womb) widens, shifting emphasis from the world to how it can be construed. Prose versions of bestiaries display the often doctrinal quality of the *moralitates* in an even stronger medium for the modern reader accustomed to factual information being relayed in prose. Verse, however, somewhat mitigates the correspondences between word and world, and softens the semiotics as the post-Romantic reader adjusts to the allegorical mode and abandons scientific discursive requirements. For this reason, the verse *Physiologus* of Theobaldus frees the text or, perhaps more accurately, the reader from prescribed responses to the intent of the discourse. The reader can suspend empirical knowledge of the animal and embrace the didactic more easily. Thus, as a "poem" the text is allowed to proceed in its interpretive special pleading in a way that fails for the numerous prose versions (but perhaps only for modern readers).

The three distinct behaviors of the lion (descending from mountain peaks, rising after three days, and sleeping with open eyes) prepare the reader for the allegory that follows and, like many of the *proprietas* sections, maneuver the reader into a hermeneutic position even before encountering the *moralitas*:

Sic tibi, qui celsi resides in culmine celi,
Cum libuit tandem terrenam visere partem,
Ut genus humanum relevares crimine lapsum,
Non penitus notum fuit ulli demoniorum
Viscera Marie tibi, Christe, fuisse cubile.
Et qui te genuit, triduum post surgere fecit,
Cum mortis vindex mortem crucis ipse subires.
Tu nos custodis, tu nullo tempore dormis,
Pervigil ut pastor, ne demat de grege raptor. (I, 10–18)

[In the same way, when it was your pleasure, you who dwell at the
summit of the lofty sky, finally to visit the region of earth to lift up
mankind fallen through sin, it was not fully known to any of the devils
that your cradle, Christ, was Mary's womb. And he who begot you
made you rise three days after the time when you, death's conqueror,
yourself underwent the death of the cross. You are our guardian, you
never sleep at any time, like the shepherd watching to stop the raider
stealing from the flock.]

Interestingly, the lion's gloss does not mention some of the details of
the description. Presumably both the animal's clever deception of covering
his tracks from the hunter with his tail and his father's roaring after three
days do not lend themselves easily to the Christian allegory. On the other
hand, certain particulars—like the death on the cross and, notably, the shepherd watching his sheep (an odd image which casts the predator lion in the
role of *pastor*)—are added in the exegesis, showing a sort of verbal free play.

The many bestiaries in the Middle Ages present, on the whole, a curious picture of medieval credulity and, more to the point here, medieval
hermeneutic posturing. They are useful in providing bits of received material about animals to explicate other, perhaps more interesting texts for some,
but the plenitude of bestiaries suggests that they were indeed more than store-
houses of interpretations or lexical footnotes. Something more innate about
the action of perceiving the "out there" or the external, extrahuman is en-
acted in the texts of bestiaries. The world of animals is subsumed egocen-
trically by the human in human interpretive terms. These texts show a reor-
dering of the "other" in astounding, often bizarre formulations that demonstrate a pure love of assigning a plethora of interpretations unencumbered
by rules of selection or confirmation, certainly with little sense of plausibil-
ity. We surely cannot think that the poet believed the short descriptive sections adequately delimited the creatures named. Bestiaries are interpretive

playgrounds, seemingly pat moves in the curiously open-ended game of constructing pattern and meaning.

What kind of writer labors at these equations? The heavily proselytizing Christian message apparent in the bestiary becomes, of course, most offensive in such anti-Semitic comments as "the ant furnishes us with a model of toil when she carries her usual food in her mouth, and in her doings she indicates spiritual qualities which the Jew does not love—and so he stands accused" (IV.1–4). Similarly, the *moralitas* for the eagle weighed down by old age reads, "Because of sins which take their origin from the mother, man is like the eagle here." (II.15–6). These sentiments help define the attributes of the poet (as well as the period), the interpreter whose voice produces the *figuras* text and thus molds the *naturas* text to its specifications. The voice is in one sense a composite of bestiary and classical encyclopedia traditions: Isidore of Seville is often heard in bestiaries, and in another sort of essay, his exact contribution would be an important historicist note. But this poetic moralist also defines himself as masculinist, defining the sins of "man" as those "which take their origin from the mother." We begin to unfold the double layering of the interpretive process of the explicator through whose eyes and morality we perceive animals and, hence, the world.

All bestiaries are two texts in one, the *naturas* and the *figuras*, the physical characteristics and their symbolic approximation. The specifics of the *naturas* are in many ways as artificial as the ethical interpretations assigned them. Following the cognitive alleys created in such an entry as "the lion equals Christ," we see that the signifier "lion" is provided with a signified "Christ" in the *figuras* text that glosses this entry. The second text inserts an additional level of semiotic development, one that posits Christ as signifier, leaving the reader with the decision of the ultimate (and decidedly mediated) signified. After all, we are told how to appropriate the lion in a speciest, masculinist, Christian, moralist way. The second text complicates and undermines the signifier/signified thread by multiplying the initial process. This leads to a less disguised unlayering of connections, making the more simplistic hermeneutic demands of the bestiary descriptive of the interpretive requirements of other texts.

In the interpretation of the lion, we perceive a slippage of the signifier, not only the kind brought about by positing that the lion might be a person strong in faith as well as Christ himself, but also a different kind of indeterminancy, one that arises out of the knowledge of the verbal game afoot at the very core of the bestiary. The lion becomes no longer a thing of the world. The information used to construct the *naturas* section of the lion entry is collected from an earlier work or previous *Physiologus* passage, the elements of which ("mountain," "valley," "hunter," "three days") produce in the *figuras* matching attributes of Christ's birth and death, not a curious choice for a book dedicated to Christ, but a questionable one considering this work's clear applicability to the ethical pathways of humans. In other words, more parts of the bestiary adhere to the moral rather than the anagogical level of signification. The entries exhort proper behavior for humans based on highly selective habits of animals. For that matter, the animals slip into a shadowy realm of fictive endeavor where the narratives look constituted by the morals that are applied. The skewing of the natural world leads to the distortion produced by the entire enterprise. One rereads the two texts side by side and begins to see that the dominance of the second exerts a peculiar power over the banality or artificiality of the first. We see fiction masquerading as fact, but not quite that. The intrusive reader, the glossator, the selector of *naturas* and explicator of narrative, forms the fact to fit the fiction, but in this case the fiction is the meaning or *figuras*. The narrative, in a sense, is lost in a semiotic sequence that no longer needs it. In this patent way, the gloss's meanings shape or figure the discourse in the first part, which is presented as a description of the exterior world. This world becomes circumscribed through the narrow eyeglass of the poet in a text that self-consciously attempts to unite world and word.

Moreover, I wonder *how* one reads a bestiary with both its levels of discourse representing differing human attempts to understand the world—its *naturas* sections closer to the world itself and its *figuras* sections closer to the spiritual subtext of the world, that subtext that theologically deconstructs the world for the believer. Clearly, the bestiary strives to explain the world around the reader by having its allegorizations dogmatically determine meaning. One could argue, however, as Foucault does, that text and gloss relate paradoxically. He stresses both the finality and repetition of the original in all its glosses, but also the infinity of discourse generated by the base text.[14] Fredric Jameson reminds us that "a text can have no ultimate meaning, and that the process of interpretation, of unfolding the successive layers of the signified, each of which is then in its own turn transformed into a new signifier or signifying system in its own right, is properly an infinite one."[15] The *figuras* sections, presumably designed to enclose meaning, can actually enhance indeterminancy by attempting to relate word to world. By constituting the middle ground held by exegesis or interpretation, the bestiary shows an active attempt to schematize meaning's generation. The reader of the bestiary is of course always at the least the second reader, one who reads the glossator's reading as well as, at times, that of a previous explicator or observer.

A logical help might be Augustine's *De doctrina Christiana*, the patristic handbook on signs. The work purports to guide glossators toward constructing correct exegesis; it is Augustine's textbook exhorting proper hermeneutic procedure so people could learn through words, signs "whose whole use is in signifying."[16] While biblical exegesis is the human commentary on or decoding of God's word, the bestiary's exegetical passages occupy a different dialectical space. The *moralitas* functions as the human commentary on or decoding of nature, which—although ultimately God's Word—has been filtered through the human observer, the person who first gave a description of the animal behavior or characteristics that eventually found their way to the unknown source called *Physiologus* (whether person or text). In a sense, the bestiary's two discourses actually reverse the descending movement found in the glossed Bible, in which the base text (erroneously so named in this example) is the Word of God interpreted in a lower form of discourse (exegesis). The bestiary—whose "base" text is more properly just that, a text written by faulty humans describing the world—provides in its accompanying glosses a higher form of discourse (exegesis) to combine world with Word of God.

The terms themselves that the *Physiologus* uses to distinguish between the two levels of discourse are revealing. The first line reads "Tres leo naturas et tres habet inde figuras." Because the lion has three "natures," it will have three "figures." The first word, *naturas*, is etymologically related to "birth," to the biological condition of life in this world, whereas *figura* connotes shaping something already in existence in this world. More directly, *figura* has a specialized identity in rhetoric, meaning the shaping of words. Again we see the world/word dichotomy born(e) out as the bestiary contributes to the yoking of experience with the authority of written texts.

Augustine not only advises on hermeneutic strategy; he also warns of variant meanings of texts:

> Thus one thing signifies another thing and still another either in such a way that the second thing signified is contrary to the first or in such a way that the second thing is entirely different from the first. . . . Thus the serpent appears in a good sense in "wise as serpents," but in a bad sense in "the serpent seduced Eve by his subtlety."[17]

The serpent entry in Theobaldus clearly demonstrates Augustine's point. The creature is described as old ("senex serpens" [III.1]), and eager to shed his old skin. Yet the *figura* equates this old snake not with the devil but with humans eager to change their ways (III.21–44), although in the stag entry, the serpent is glossed as the devil "with the deceit of the old serpent" ("prisci serpentis fraude" [VII.9]), demonstrating Augustine's contrary signifieds, the serpent operating in "a good sense" as well as "a bad sense." The panther's serpent also clearly represents Satan.[18] In this, the final chapter of the poem, the panther (Christ) rises from death after three days, and roars, and all believers follow him to heaven. Only the old serpent ("serpens antiquus") flees and hides, for he is not allowed to deceive people openly (XIII.13–22). Theobaldus, balancing the discourse, begins and concludes with a creature (the lion and the panther) equated with Christ, who sleeps for three days and arises after a roar.

I have argued elsewhere that because of their contradictions, biblical glosses taken as a whole perhaps ironically do more to expand meaning than to enclose it.[19] The static bestiary presents a much more simplified verbal project. No reader should be confused about the meaning of the serpent in the panther section. The serpent does mean the devil in this entry, but the emphasis on the connection between the two parts of the text makes the bestiary more a model of interpretation rather than a determined doctrine, since the serpent chapter tells us to "always imitate the snake when you grow old" (III.23–24). It seems that serpents are not always fixed signifiers.

Augustine's attention to *how* animals become signs for people does draw us closer to an appreciation of the bestiary enterprise. He reminds us:

> Just as a knowledge of the nature of serpents illuminates the many similitudes which Scripture frequently makes with that animal, an ignorance of many other animals which are also used for comparisons is a great impediment to understanding.[20]

Animals, it seems, constitute an especially fruitful category of signs for the exegete. Here we approach the question that perhaps presupposes all others in the study of bestiaries: why are selected behaviors and characteristics of animals so pregnant with meaning? A complex literary tradition accounts for the handing down of familiar narratives, but why do these illustrated texts specifically on animals become the handbook on divine signs for the common reader?

Bestiaries tell us that animals iconically represent the entire nonhuman world in medieval discourse. When God threatened to destroy his evil creation in the Old Testament, Noah was charged with saving animals not plant clippings. The range of attributes found in the animal kingdom provides endless narrative for beginning the hermeneutic chain.

The *Physiologus* equates both the lion and the panther with Christ, but the other entries help trace the exegetical trends of the poem more fully. Of the other eleven entries, animals represent Christ in only one, that of the elephant, a creature that also signifies the first man, Adam. The whale is likened to the devil, and the sirens interestingly have no *figura* section. The remaining animals represent a person or a person's soul or some attribute of a person that should be encouraged or eschewed. It seems that animals, closest to humans on the chain of being, have diverse *naturas* that are similar enough to our own (or the narratives are adjusted enough to make animals appear like us) that they provide clever models for bestiary writers to exploit in their glossing. The abstracted, reduced account of nature found in the descriptive passages of the bestiary becomes rich fodder for the hermeneutic imperative voiced in the *moralitas* sections. In these early verbal acts of exploitation, writers used natural traits to substantiate ethical ones. The same diminishment and distortion of nature (as well as tautological argumentation) is found today when we assert that particular traits are "naturally" masculine or feminine. Our easy deconstruction of the ideological power moves inherent in the discourse of the medieval Church can be paralleled by the not-so-easy deconstruction of our own agendas in evaluating (or any kind of inscribing of) the natural world.

The entry on sirens gives us one further clue. Like the section on onocentaurs (whose bodies are half like a human being and half like an ass), these monsters are referred to in the plural, as a marvelous race of humans might be. The other animals are handled in the singular, as a type. Sirens, being composite creatures (this time half-maiden, half-bird) like the onocentaurs, already participate partly in human nature in the descriptive passage that merely defines their composition, offering no other narrative. The *moralitas* section explains that they represent two-faced humans who have two natures. These entries might include whole races of creatures and not the individual representing the type because their natures are too close to human for the overriding hermeneutic strategy to be effective. In other words, because sirens and onocentaurs are already partially human, they present a less tidy, less observable part of the world from which to draw human moralization.

Moreover, the omission of a *figura* for the sirens entry suggests that these unconfirmed creatures, replete with a narrative of great ancestry like most animals in the bestiary, perhaps function differently as signs. The bestiary attempts to explain and gloss animal inhabitants of this world, providing a discourse that can enable people to read the world in a spiritual and morally directive way. Sirens and onocentaurs, little seen members of this world, have perhaps slipped into a verbal realm to such an extent that they become less direct examples of the interpretive aims of the bestiary. This is not to say that fabulous creatures do not have a place in later, more expanded bestiaries. Their half-human composition merely makes their glossing less clearly delineated. Because the reader does not encounter them directly as a part of this world, they become too much a part of discourse, or word, to enhance the bestiary's *natura* passages.

Bestiaries display the static clarity of typing, the peculiar rhetoric of the emblem, the individual who represents the universal, and do not display groups with their messy diversity nor the particular, naturalistic individual possessing idiosyncratic interest but not iconic power. We hear of *the* stag, *the* ant, *the* whale, *the* spider, and *the* thing or person known as Physiologus. This representative universality attempts to counteract time, to make the discourse float in an emblematic and a somehow truer (because perennial), "now." Theobaldus himself shares this ambiguous quality. We know little about him,[21] and he does little to correct this other than to provide the subscript at the end:

> Carmine finito sit laus et gloria Christo,
> Cui, si non alii, placeant hec metra Tebaldi. (*Subscriptio,* 1–2)

> [Now that the poem is finished, praise and glory be to Christ: may these metres of Tebaldus please him if no one else.]

The author becomes the composite anthologist/exegete whom all good bestiaries require, down to the last lines, in which he challenges the reader to dislike his production. Bestiaries are group projects, like biblical commentaries, with their dialogic texts striving for universal types. Theobaldus openly acknowledges his debt to previous explicators ("Altera divini memorant animalia libri" [I.3]) but retains the universal not particular quality of authorship.[22]

Lately, we "lonely betters" are even more self-consciously assuming "responsibility for time." As we look back on the strange equations perpetuated for centuries about the meaning(s) of the world, and look forward to the ones we are configuring now, we at times remember that we are indeed "capable of lying." I see nothing new or alarming about this, as long as one of the promises we keep is that of acknowledging that language, our (if we can claim ownership?) tricksy spirit, has more to do with us than with the ephemeral construct we "name" the world.

* From W.H. Auden: *Collected Poems*. Edited by Edward Mendelson. Copyright © 1951 by W.H. Auden. Reprinted by permission of Random House, Inc., and Faber and Faber, Ltd.

1. "The birds abuse each other about their nature as birds, and all the time the standard is man," *The Owl and the Nightingale*, ed. Eric Gerald Stanley (Manchester, England: Manchester University Press, 1972), 31.

2. IX(H) 362, X(I) 32–34. All Chaucer passages are taken from *The Riverside Chaucer*, ed. Larry D. Benson, 3rd ed. (Boston: Houghton Mifflin, 1987).

3. Actually, this loosening of traditional definitions of literature proves modest indeed in light of Michel Foucault's revamping of all notions of discipline in *The Archaeology of Knowledge* and *The Discourse on Language*, trans. A.M. Sheridan Smith (New York: Pantheon Books, 1972); (*Archaeology* orig. publ. in French, 1969; *Discourse* orig. publ. 1971). More specifically, see Terry Eagleton, *Literary Theory: An Introduction* (Oxford: Basil Blackwell, 1983), 1–16; and Lee Patterson, *Negotiating the Past: The Historical Understanding of Medieval Literature* (Madison, Wisc.: University of Wisconsin Press, 1987): "There is no inherent, ahistorical essence that marks one written document as literary and another as non-literary" (41).

4. See M.-D. Chenu, "The Symbolist Mentality," in *Nature, Man and Society in the Twelfth Century*, ed. and trans. J. Taylor and L. Little (France, 1957; rpt. Chicago: University of Chicago Press, 1968), 99–145; and Fredric Jameson, *The Prison-House of Language: A Critical Account of Structuralism and Russian Formalism* (Princeton: Princeton University Press, 1972). See also Gerald Graff, "Literature as Assertions," *American Critics at Work: Examinations of Contemporary Literary Theories*, ed. Victor A. Kramer (New York: Whitson, 1984), 81–110.

5. Eugene Vinaver, *The Rise of Romance* (Oxford: Clarendon Press, 1971), 26–7.

6. See D.W. Robertson, Jr., *A Preface to Chaucer: Studies in Medieval Perspectives* (Princeton: Princeton University Press, 1962).

7. See the *Acta Sanctorum*, 1615–1915, ed. Hippolyte Delehaye from the original French (Paris: V. Palme, 1863–1940): Romanus 59:74–103; George 12:101–65; and Matthew 46:194–227.

8. Hrabanus Maurus, *De universo*, PL 111, 229–30. Hrabanus Maurus glosses the dragon as the Antichrist in Apoc. 12:3, the spirit of evil in Isa. 34:13, the Jews in Jer. 14:6, and the Gentiles in Isa. 43:20 in *Allegoriae in sacram scripturam*, PL 112, 906.

Isidore's description of the dragon can be found in Isidori Hispalensis Episcopi, *Etymologiarum sive originum, liber xx*, ed. W.M. Lindsay (Oxford: Oxford University Press, 1911), XII, iv, 4–5.

9.   Super aspidem et basiliscum amulabis
     Et conculcabis leonem et draconem (Ps. 90:13)

[You will walk on the asp and basilisk and crush the lion and dragon.]

All biblical passages are from *Biblia sacra iuxta Vulgatam Clementinam*, eds. Alberto Colunga and Laurentio Turrado (Madrid: Biblioteca de Autores Christianos, 1959; rpt. 4th ed., 1965), translation mine.

Augustine's comment on this passage is found in *De civitate dei*, in PL 37, 1168: "The lion attacks openly; the dragon lies in ambush secretly." Hugh [Hugues] de Saint Cher, *Opera omnia in universum vetus et novum testamentum* (Venice: Nicolaus Pezzana, 1732), III, 223 recto.

10. *The Works of Sir Thomas Malory*, ed. Eugene Vinaver, 2nd ed. (Oxford: Clarendon Press, 1947, 1967: rpt. 1971, 1977), XIV, 6.

11. Beryl Smalley, *The Study of the Bible in the Middle Ages* (Oxford, 1952; rpt. Notre Dame, Ind.: University of Notre Dame Press, 1964), 2. See also Susan

Noakes, *Timely Reading: Between Exegesis and Interpretation* (Ithaca, N.Y.: Cornell University Press, 1988).

12. The third and fourth "families" of bestiaries are written later in the twelfth and in the thirteenth centuries. See Frances McCulloch, *Medieval Latin and French Bestiaries* (Chapel Hill, N.C.: University of North Carolina Press, 1962). For recent work on bestiaries and animals, see *Beasts and Birds of the Middle Ages: The Bestiary and Its Legacy*, ed. Willene B. Clark and Meradith T. McMunn (Philadelphia: University of Pennsylvania Press, 1989); and *The Medieval World of Nature: A Book of Essays*, ed. Joyce E. Salisbury (New York: Garland Publishing, 1993).

13. I, Prologus, 1–6. All passages of text and translation of this bestiary are from P.T. Eden, *Theobaldi Physiologus* (Leyden: E.J. Brill, 1972).

14. Foucault, 221.

15. Jameson, 176.

16. Augustine, *On Christian Doctrine*, trans. D.W. Robertson, Jr. (New York: MacMillan, 1958), 1.2.2.

17. Augustine, *On Christian Doctrine*, 3.25.36. See also Rita Copeland and Stephen Melville, "Allegory and Allegoresis, Rhetoric and Hermeneutics," *Exemplaria: A Journal of Theory in Medieval and Renaissance Studies* 3 (1991), 157–87, in which the authors cite the commentary on *Aeneid* 6 attributed to Bernardus Silvestris, which stresses "verbal equivocation and polysemousness" ("equivocationes et multivocationes"). Copeland and Melville maintain that "[r]esponsibility for producing meaning has shifted to the reader: the multiple meanings of a word, name, or motif (e.g., 'the descent into the underworld'), or, conversely, the manifold ways of expressing a single meaning, give the reader the responsibility of fitting the discourse to the particular circumstances of interpretation and receptivity" (173–4).

18. Theobaldus also tells us earlier that the fox is like the devil (see V.18).

19. See Lesley Kordecki, "Let Me 'telle yow what I mente': The *Glossa ordinaria* and *The Nun's Priest's Tale*," *Exemplaria: A Journal of Theory in Medieval and Renaissance Studies* 4 (1992), 365–85.

20. Augustine, *On Christian Doctrine*, 2.16.24.

21. See Eden, 5–7.

22. Karlheinz Stierle calls this "institutionalized reading": "From the Alexandrian commentaries up to the end of the Renaissance or, to be more precise, up to the shift in reading that was caused by the development of the printed book, commentary was the basic form of institutionalized reading. Commentary is a place of institution-bound understanding." See Karlheinz Stierle, "*Studium*: Perspectives on Institutionalized Modes of Reading," *New Literary History* 22 (1991), 116.

ON THE QUESTION OF A
PHYSIOLOGUS TRADITION IN
EMBLEMATIC ART AND WRITING

*Dietmar Peil**

In the preface to one of the most important aids to emblematic research, the manual *Emblemata*, the editors point out "the connection of the emblematic tradition with the symbolic thought of the Middle Ages embodied in the herbals and bestiaries which transmitted a wealth of motifs to the books of emblems. This is particularly true of the Greek *Physiologus*, which was compiled in the second century A.D., probably in Alexandria. It was copied, adapted and translated into Latin and into various national languages throughout the whole Middle Ages."[1] They further maintain: "Many *res pictae* of the emblem books can already be found in the *Physiologus*."[2] It is in complete accordance with this thesis that in the manual's appendix an "Index rerum notabilium" to the *Physiologus graecus* is printed even before the index to the *Hieroglyphica* of Horapollo.[3] This suggests that both sources are of equal importance to the emblematic tradition. Repeatedly in the list of sources for each entry, the respective parallel in the *Physiologus* is indicated, as is to be expected.

However, the theory of the widespread influence of the *Physiologus* (*Physiologus* is understood in this sense as the title of a written work, not as the term for a genre characterized by descriptions of animals and accompanied by allegorical exegesis) does not remain unqualified: "But it [i.e., the *Physiologus*] did not in all cases really serve as the source. Sometimes the description of an animal in this work and the corresponding picture of an emblem can be traced independently back to the Bible or writers in classical antiquity."[4] This reservation has clearly been ignored in subsequent research. William S. Heckscher and Karl-August Wirth already list the following sources for the pictures of the emblems: "illustrated works of a more or less scientific character, such as bestiaries, herbals and the *Physiologus* as well as their more specialized successors (manuals on birds, herbs and the like)."[5] Other articles in encyclopedias and compendia are worded similarly.[6]

Without question there is evidence for the exegetical method of medieval allegorical interpretation both in the *Physiologus* and in the emblematic tradition, but the theory that the *Physiologus* directly influenced the emblem books must nevertheless be examined more closely. In the following pages I will first compare the account of the sources given in the manual *Emblemata* with its index of the *Physiologus*, and examine in what form the *Physiologus* was accessible in the sixteenth century. Then I will examine quotations said to be from the *Physiologus* in a sampling of emblem books and sift them for *Physiologus* motifs that are not marked as quotations. Finally, I will try to reconstruct ways in which *Physiologus* motifs may have been transmitted, using the example of the rejuvenation of the eagle.

The manual *Emblemata* is a compendium containing more than 3,000 emblems drawn from 47 emblem books, most of them from the sixteenth century. The index to the *Physiologus* printed in the manual *Emblemata* includes 66 entries, not counting the cross-references. The sources given in the manual correspond only to 15 of the animals, stones, and plants named in the *Physiologus*, some occurring more than once.[7] Compared with the number of total entries (the manual lists 3,713 emblems in all), this represents such a small fraction that the *Physiologus* can by no means be viewed as an important source of the emblem books. One should also note that the *Physiologus* is always named together with other sources.

There is another problem here. The *Physiologus graecus* as edited by F. Sbordone[8] was not known in the sixteenth century. During the Middle Ages the Latin *Physiologus* had been used as a school book,[9] but the work lost its influence to a great extent, when the manuscript tradition of the Latin versions petered out. Printed encyclopaedias, such as the *Speculum naturale* of Vincent of Beauvais or the *De genuinis rerum coelestium, terrestrium et inferarum proprietatibus libri XVIII* of Bartholomaeus Anglicus, do offer *Physiologus* quotations now and then alongside information taken from many other sources, but as a rule they leave out the exegetical interpretation.[10] Only the *Physiologus Theobaldi* and the version by Epiphanius of Constantia (died 402) were printed. The *Physiologus Theobaldi* only treats twelve (or thirteen) animals. Latin incunabula containing it were published in the period between 1487 and 1500.[11] They are not likely to have been much read as late as the sixteenth century. That applies even more so to the German prose translation printed in the period between 1482 and 1484.[12] The version by Epiphanius was first published in an edition in Greek and Latin in 1587 and ran through several editions.[13] This work is furnished with woodcuts (figure 1) and includes not only descriptions but also the respective exegetical interpretations;[14] however, its twenty-five chapters treat only twenty different animals.[15] This is the only version of the *Physiologus* that seems to have been used by the authors of emblem books, but they did so with great restraint. In the manual *Emblemata* Epiphanius is only given among the sources for five animals, seven times altogether.[16]

Figure 1. Epiphanius, Ad Physiologum, *Rome 1587. (From Santiago Sebastián,* El Fisiólogo *attribuido a San Epifanio [Madrid, 1986], 39.)*

A look at the emblem books themselves confirms the theory that the *Physiologus* was little known. Hadrianus Junius, whose *Emblemata* appeared in 1565 (i.e., more than twenty years before Epiphanius's *Physiologus*), does not mention the *Physiologus* in his notes to those emblems that might be traced back to the *Physiologus* tradition (such as the pelican or the viper). Instead, he cites Isidore and Jerome, or Pliny and Horapollo, as his sources.[17] More than thirty years after the edition of Epiphanius, Schoonhovius proceeds in a similar manner.[18] Joachim Camerarius gives a reference to Epiphanius's version three times, listing it among his sources for the first time in the third Centuria.[19] Filippo Picinelli also quotes Epiphanius three times,[20] while Julius Wilhelm Zincgref does not refer to it more than once.[21] In each case Epiphanius is made use of only sporadically. The *Physiologus* itself, as an independent work, is never mentioned.

How do the authors of the emblem books treat their source? Joachim Camerarius brings in Epiphanius for the first time in his notes to the emblem of the eagle (III, 16), which shows the bird trying to renew itself (figure 2). First Camerarius quotes Aristotle and, as additional authorities, Pliny and Horapollo, who only say that as the eagle grows older, the upper half of its beak starts to curve inward so strongly that it finally dies of starvation. Epiphanius, however, has more to tell. The aging eagle has trouble not only with its beak but also with its eyes, which darken. The eagle, finding itself thus beset, flies up high into the air, whets its beak on a rock, dives into cold water, and finally experiences rejuvenation in the rays of the sun.[22] As further proof of this account of the rejuvenation of the eagle, Camerarius draws from the commentaries on the Psalms by Augustine, as well as Jerome on Psalm 103:5, and cites Isaiah 40:31 as a parallel in the Bible.[23] Finally he returns to the comprehensive interpretation by Epiphanius, giving it as an indirect quotation:

Figure 2. Joachim Camerarius, Symbola et emblemata (Nuremberg, 1596) Centuria III, No. 16 (BSB Munich).

Figure 3. Epiphanius, Ad Physiologum *(Antwerp, 1588), 22 (UB Munich).*

Ait enim, si quis multitudine criminum fuerit oppressus, in altum debet ascendere, id est, in propriam conscientiam, et ad petram, hoc est, fidem orthodoxam se projicere, et deflere peccatorum multitudinem perpetuis aquis, id est, lachrymis ea abstergere, denique solis radiis incalescere, id est, in coetu fidelium et in Spiritu sancto ad calorem poenitentiae properare, squammas peccata nimirum abjicere. Statim enim renovabitur ut aquilae juventus tua, et justus vocaberis apud DEUM.[24]

[He says that if anyone is oppressed by the multitude of his offences, he must rise up towards the height (that is, towards his own conscience) and thrust himself at the rock (that is, orthodox faith) and weep over the multitude of his sins with ever-flowing water (that is, wash them off with tears) and finally grow warm in the rays of the sun (that is, rush towards the heat of penitence in the community of the faithful and in the Holy Spirit), throwing off his scales—his sins, of course. For at once your youth will be renewed as that of the eagle and you shall be called just before God.]

Not only does the commentary show that Epiphanius's version of the *Physiologus* was known to Camerarius, but its influence is clear in the design of the *pictura*. Camerarius's engraving looks like a copy (with the left and right sides reversed) of the woodcut in the Epiphanius edition issued in Antwerp in 1588, for which the illustrations were redone (figure 3).[25] Moreover, comparison with the manuscript containing the drafts of the emblems by Camerarius shows that Epiphanius obviously influenced Camerarius to change his original concept. In the manuscript, below the motto RENOVATA IVVENT[us] there is an eagle losing its feathers during its flight towards the sun (figure 4). In his commentary Camerarius quotes Jerome and explains:

> D. Hieronymus ubi psalmum 102 interpretatur. Reuocabitur ut aquila juventus tua etc. scribit, hanc alitem ubi consenuerit pennis supra modum grauari, ideoque fontem quaerere cujus aspergine pennas abjiciat quibus liberata et ad solem elevata calorem intra se reccolligere, sanarique tum primum oculos, mox quasi rejuuenescere. Ita quoque ad Christi sacratissimam disciplinam accessurus, ejusque diuina preacepta obseruaturus, omnem inprobitatem et affectus impios qui animam grauant, exuere et abluere, at nouum vestitum puritatem nempe et renouationem vitae induere debet.[26]

> [St. Jerome writes in the place where he interprets "Thy youth shall be renewed like the eagle," etc., in Psalm 102 that that bird is weighed down too much by its feathers when it grows old and, for that reason, looks for a fountain in which it can moisten itself and so throw off its feathers. Having freed itself of these and lifted itself up to the sun, it collects heat in itself. And then first its eyes are healed, soon it becomes young again, as it were, he writes. So also someone who wishes to attain to the most holy teaching of Christ and to observe his divine precepts must strip off and wash away all iniquity and wicked emotions which weigh down the soul, but must put on new clothes, namely, purity and the renewal of life.]

In the printed book Camerarius uses the motto for a similar pictorial subject, a moulting hawk (III, 34). This bird, however, is not shown flying straight up to the sun but sitting on a tree (figure 5). Only the epigram ("Exuviis vitii abjectis, decus indue recti, / ad Solem ut plumas renovat accipiter" [Throw off the garments of vice and dress yourself in the beauty of right, as the hawk renews its feathers in the sun]) and the commentary mention the sun and then give a moral or religious interpretation:

Figure 4. Stadtbibliothek Mainz, Hs. II/366, fol. 146.

GESNERUS ex pluribus autoribus, qui de Aucupio aliquid litteris mandarunt, tradit quo pacto Accipitres ad radios solares vitia pennarum, veteribus abjectis, et quasi rejuvenescere solent: docetque simul quae applicari debeant, ut hoc defluvium acceleretur, et eo celerius novae renescantur[!]. Quo indicatur, alicuius in flagitiis viventis propositum laudabile in mutando eo genere vitae in meliorem statum. Idque inprimis piis Christiana "metanoia" sese ad DEUM convertentibus convenit, qui nihil aliud cogitant, nec in votis magis habent, quam depositis omnis improbitatis et humanae depravationis sordibus, in vera innocentia et puritate secundum divinam voluntatem et mandata ipsius vivere.[27]

[Gesner, as one of several authors who wrote something about fowling, recounts the manner in which it is the habit of hawks to repair[?] the defects of their feathers in the rays of the sun, after they have thrown off the old ones, and to become young again, as it were, and he also teaches what means must be applied so that the falling out is accelerated and the new ones are reformed the sooner. By this, the praiseworthy decision of someone living in iniquity to change that way of life to a better state is indicated. This applies particularly to the pious who turn to God in Christian "metanoia" [change of thought, repentance], who do not think of anything else and have no greater wish than to put off the dirt of all wickedness and human depravation and live in true innocence and purity according to the divine will and its commands.]

While Camerarius in his notes to the eagle emblem takes over the description of the facts of natural history as well as the exegesis from Epiphanius, in his explanation of the emblem of the pelican he quotes the pertinent passage from Isidore, since none of his other sources knows of the pelican's sacrifice of its own blood.[28] Isidore himself also reveals that he is a little doubtful of this tradition:

Figure 5. Joachim Camerarius, Symbola et emblemata *(Nuremburg, 1596), Centuria III, No. 34 (BSB Munich).*

Quamquam vero de sauciante proprio rostro pectus, et pullis ex eo sanguinem excipientibus apud veteres scriptores (quantum ego scio) nulla fiat mentio, et Isidorus quoque lib. XII. orig. dubitanter de hoc loquatur, ubi ait: Fertur enim, si verum est, eam occidere suos natos, eosque per triduum lugere et deinde seipsum vulnerare, et aspersione sui sanguinis vivificare filios.[29]

[However, there is no mention among the old authors, as far as I know, of its wounding its breast with its own beak and its children's receiving blood from it, and Isidore also speaks doubtfully of this in the twelfth book of his Origins, where he says: For it is supposed, if that is true, to kill its own children and mourn them for three days and then wound itself and bring its sons to life by sprinkling its blood over them.]

As a secular interpretation of the pelican, Camerarius offers the motto of the *impresa* of King Alfonso of Aragon; for the religious interpretation he cites the Fathers and Epiphanius:

Quare sancti patres hoc mystico sensu ad CHRISTI nostri Salvatoris unici sacrosanctam passionem pie admodum retulerunt, ut videre est apud D. Hieronymum, et D. Augustinum, ac inprimis in physiologo S. Epiphanio ascriptus.[30]

[This is why in mystical interpretation the holy fathers related this, piously enough, to the most sacred passion of Christ, our only saviour, as can be seen in St. Jerome and St. Augustine and especially in the *Physiologus* ascribed to St. Epiphanius.]

That the phoenix should immolate itself is as difficult for a modern reader to believe as that the pelican should sacrifice its own blood, but this had been transmitted, with varying reservations, by numerous authors since classical antiquity. Camerarius ends his third Centuria with the phoenix emblem and gives more room to annotation this time, since tradition reveals that there were many different views on this and because the bird has been utilized for many famous emblems. Epiphanius appears among the long list of authors who have written on the phoenix. The roll call starts off with Herodotus and ends with Conrad Gesner and lists the following names:

Herodotus, Philostratus, Horapollo, Plinius, Solinus, Seneca, Tacitus, Aelianus, Lucianus, Sextus Aurelius Victor, Suidas, Xiphilinus, Glycas,

Artemidorus, Æneas Platonicus, Aristides, Marc Aurel, Oppian, Ovid, Claudian, Lactanz, Tzetze, Statius, Gregor v. Nazianz, Basilius, Tertullian, Cyrill, Cyprian, Epiphanius, Eusebius Pamphilius, Rufinus, Ambrosius, Isidor, Albertus Magnus, Volaterrenus, Scaliger, Pierius Valerianus, Erasmus, Hadrianus Junius, Conrad Gesner.[31]

Epiphanius is only one name among many here. In the discussion of the several differing accounts, he is not taken into consideration. He does not appear again until the series of emblems, where he is mentioned as one of the authors who see the hope of resurrection symbolized in the phoenix.[32] Thus there is no evidence that Camerarius was markedly conscious of a tradition going back to the *Physiologus*.

Filippo Picinelli seems to be as unaware of any special debts to the *Physiologus* as Camerarius. It is true that Picinelli includes Epiphanius in his index of authors, but he quotes Epiphanius's version of the *Physiologus* only in the chapters on the phoenix, the lion, and the viper and then only once in each chapter.[33] On the other hand, even in the chapters dealing with animals that appear in the *Physiologus*, he refers twice as often to the bestiary *De bestiis et aliis rebus* mistakenly attributed to Hugh of St. Victor.[34] However, Picinelli is apparently unmoved by the fact that Pseudo-Hugh sometimes quotes the *Physiologus* by name.[35] Clearly, the authors of the emblem books did not connect the name "Physiologus" with the idea of the title of a work of its own.

Even though in emblematic art and writing there is no evidence for the awareness of a tradition going back to the *Physiologus*, the question remains whether information typical of the *Physiologus* might not have found its way into the emblem books in other ways, as a *Physiologus* tradition below the threshold of consciousness, as it were. However, only a few motifs can be isolated that were exclusively transmitted only in the *Physiologus* and not by classical natural history at the same time. According to Perry's discussion of this subject (see note 1 below), apart from the rejuvenation of the eagle already mentioned, the following motifs belong in this category:

1.　The whelps of the lion are born dead and are brought to life three days after their birth by the breath of the male lion.

2.　The snake fears a naked human being, while it attacks one who has clothing on.

3.　The panther is friendly to other animals and is hostile only to the dragon, according to the *Physiologus*. (Authors of classical antiquity, on the other hand, say that the panther attracts the other animals by its pleasant smell in order to kill them.)

4.   Elephants eat of the root of the mandragora before coition; their offspring are born in the water.

5.   The heron has only one nest and does not eat carrion.

If we leave the rejuvenation of the eagle out of consideration, we cannot help but observe that none of the emblem books accounted for in the manual *Emblemata* utilizes the *Physiologus* motifs just listed for its interpretation. Although Camerarius shows his elephant in the water,[36] the scene has nothing to do with its birth, deriving instead from a passage in Solinus. The pleasant smell of the panther is interpreted unfavourably by Camerarius (in line with classical natural history) as a warning of defilement by debauchery.[37] The many-coloured spots of the panther, which relate to the many good traits of Christ in the *Physiologus*,[38] Camerarius interprets in a bad sense, as a sign of the immutability of evil.[39]

The analysis of the encyclopedia of emblems by Picinelli yields a similar result. He also, as we have seen, only rarely quotes the *Physiologus* according to Epiphanius's version, but he appears to have become aware of some special motifs in other ways, too. He introduces the chapter on the lion with several emblems based on a variant motif, according to which the lion brings his dead whelps to life not with his breath but with his roar. However, he quotes Antonius of Padua, not Epiphanius, as authority for this idea.[40] He interprets the pleasant smell of the panther not only *in malam* but also *in bonam partem* and, in doing so, cites Pseudo-Hugh of St. Victor.[41] The other motifs from the *Physiologus*, however, are not known to Picinelli either, or at any rate, he does not refer to them in connection with designs for emblems.

While Camerarius took over the motif of the rejuvenation of the eagle from Epiphanius and therefore poses no problems as far as reconstructing the textual transmission is concerned, other authors clearly used deviating sources for their variations on the account. Juan de Boria has the eagle on its flight to the sun as a symbol of renewal through God, the "sun of justice," in his *Empresas morales* of 1581 (figure 6). Man ought to try to renew himself by discarding the old, as Boria explains in his prose subscription, "just as it is said of the eagle that it flies so high and near the sun that [the sun] burns it with its rays and singes its feathers. With its feathers the eagle then immerses itself in water and thus receives new feathers and strength."[42] While Boria sees the flight to the sun as the beginning of the procedure of rejuvenation and concludes with the bathing and the consequent renewal, Nikolaus Reusner in his eagle emblem of 1581 (figure 7) changes the order of these elements: "When it [the eagle] is wearied because of its extreme old age, it bathes three or four times in clear water, flies upwards from there, and gains new life from the light of the sun and renews its feathers and its exhausted limbs."[43]

Compared with the description of the process of rejuvenation in Epiphanius, the accounts of both Boria and Reusner are deficient and contain gaps. Neither of them mentions the crippling growth of the eagle's beak and of its growing blindness. Moreover, Reusner does not present a clear concept of how the feathers are renewed. Boria arranges the eagle's course of treatment as a procedure in three stages: the soaring flight is followed by the burning of the feathers, and these are then renewed by immersion. Reusner contents himself with two stages. He seems to consider the function of the bathing rather in the light of purification. This is followed by the flight towards the sun, during which the eagle gains new feathers and strength in a way that is not described more precisely.

Figure 6. Juan de Boria, Empresas morales *(Brussels, 1680), 13 (BSB Munich).*

Renouata iuuentus.

EMBLEMA XXXIIX.

Ad Philippum, Ioach. F. Camerarium
Iurisconsultum.

A Lituûm regina potens, & fulminis expers:
　Sola aquila est summi fida ministra Iouis.
Quæ si longæua nimium sit tarda senecta:
　Flumine se liquido terg, quaterg, lauat:
Subuolat hinc, Solisq, capit de lumine lumen:
　Et renouat pennas, membraq, fessa sibi.
Qui pius est sacro lustratus fonte salutis:
　Fulmineo nunquam læditur igne Iouis.

Namg,

Figure 7. Nikolaus Reusner, Emblemata Partim Ethica, Et Physica: Partim vero Historica & Hieroglyphica *(Frankfurt am Main, 1581), rpt. M. Schilling (Hildesheim: Verlag Georg Olms, 1990), 101.*

The fact that the process is described only in a rudimentary way makes it difficult to identify the respective sources. Any evidence that might demonstrate potential ways of transmission with regard to this motif is complicated even more by the existence of variant traditions going back to different adaptations of the *Physiologus*. On one hand, the version by Epiphanius offers a relatively complex plot, which is, however, coherent in itself. There are five stages: deformation of the beak and loss of sight, the soaring flight, whetting the beak, immersion, and renewal in the sun. The motif of burning the feathers is missing. On the other hand, the older version as transmitted by the Latin *Physiologus* has only four phases. The eagle's blindness is followed by its soaring flight. This, in its turn, leads to the burning of the eagle's feathers and the cure of the weakness of its eyes. Finally the eagle immerses itself three times and achieves rejuvenation. This sequence of motifs is supplemented in the Latin version by a quotation from Augustine, which describes the healing of the crippled beak. The chapter concludes by returning to a variant that is ascribed to Jerome. The aging eagle burns its wings in the fire of the region of the aether and then precipitates itself into its nest, where it is supported by its young until it renews itself. Each variation of the motif receives its own interpretation.[44] The *Physiologus Theobaldi* omits the variant by Pseudo-Jerome and only mentions impairment of vision in connection with the process of healing; only from the passage containing the interpretation can it be deduced that the eagle submerges itself three times.[45] The *Novus Phisiologus*, which interprets the eagle against the background of the Evangelist symbols, knows nothing of its going blind but otherwise accounts for all phases like the *Physiologus Theobaldi*.[46]

The medieval bestiaries present further contamination and reduction of motifs. In his book on birds, which has been transmitted under the name of Hugh of St. Victor, Hugh of Fouilloy (died 1272/3), who cites Gregory (?), records only the whetting of the beak without mentioning any other symptoms of age or their cure.[47] Thomas of Cantimpré (died after 1263) is more thorough but omits the exegetical interpretations. In his account, which relies on a certain Adelinus,[48] the aging eagle first seeks out a very cold spring and then soars above the clouds, where the weakness of its eyes is dispelled in the heat of the sun. The eagle, which is very hot, throws itself into the spring, dives three times, and finally seeks safety in its nest among its offspring. The drop in temperature leads to a fever, during which the eagle loses its feathers. Its offspring then support it until its feathers are renewed. The treatment of the beak is appended by Thomas to this account as a quotation from Augustine that is unconnected with the preceding material.[49]

Bartholomaeus Anglicus (died 1275)[50] refers to Augustine and Pliny for his version, which follows the shorter variant of the *Physiologus*, but deviates sharply at one point. The feathers do not burn but fall out, because the pores open up due to the heat of the sun and the effort of the eagle's soaring flight. During the eagle's immersion the feathers are renewed, the dimness of the eyes disappears, and the eagle gains new strength. The whetting of the beak is again seen by Bartholomaeus as connected with the aging of the eagle, but he quotes this motif according to Augustine without grouping it with the other means of rejuvenation.[51]

Vincent of Beauvais (died 1264) repeats nearly all the variants, but he, too, leaves out the exegetical interpretations. The quotation from Augustine is followed, after some other evidence, by the shorter of the two *Physiologus* versions. The chapter concludes with the version of Thomas of Cantimpré.[52] Albertus Magnus, too, is clearly close to Thomas of Cantimpré, but he is extremely sceptical about his source: he quotes Iorach[53] in addition to Adelinus:

> Quod autem dicit Jorach et Adelinus de hac aquila, non sum expertus. Dicunt enim hanc aquilam quando senescit tempore quo pulli iam grandes facti venari sciunt et possunt, considerare fontis limpidi et latae scaturitionis ebullitionem et super illam directe in altum extolli usque ad tertium aëris interstitium quod aestum vocavimus in libro Metheororum: et cum ibi incaluerit et quasi exuri videtur, subito demissis et retractis alis ruere in fontis frigiditatem ut ex frigido exterius restringente calor intrinsecus in medullis multiplicetur: et tunc exsurgere de fonte et ad nidum quem ibi vicinum habet, convolare et inter alas puellorum tectam resolvi in sudorem et sic exuere antiquitatis habitum depositis pennis veteribus, et rursus indui novis et interim donec recreverint, sustentari praeda pullorum. Sed ad hoc aliud nescio dicere nisi quia mirabilia naturae multa sunt: sed quod vidi in duobus herodiis in terra nostra hiis non concordat: quia illae domesticae erant et ad modum aliarum avium rapacium mutabantur.[54]

[Concerning what Jorach and Adelinus say about the eagle, however, I have not experienced it myself. For they say that when the eagle grows old, at the time when its young are grown and know how to hunt and are able to do it, it regards the upwelling of a clear fountain and ample, gushing spring and lifts itself up directly above it up to the third layer of air, which we named "aestus" (surging heat) in our *Liber Metheororum* (*Book on Astronomical Phenomena*). And when it is heated up there and almost appears to burn, it suddenly drops its wings and draws them close and precipitates itself into the coldness of the spring, so that, because of the coldness that constrains it from outside, the heat is intensified within in the marrow. And then it rises out of the spring and flies to its nest, which it has nearby, and is covered by the wings of its young, breaks out in sweat, and so puts off its trappings of old age, shedding its old feathers, and is clothed in new ones again and is meanwhile supported by the captured prey of its young until they are grown back, they say. But about that I cannot say anything except that the wonders of nature are many, but what I saw of two gerfalcons in our country does not agree with that, because they were domesticated and moulted like other birds of prey.]

The lore of the rejuvenation of the eagle is transmitted also in early modern books on natural history. Conrad Gesner in his book on birds, quoted several times by Camerarius, begins with the quotations from Jerome and Augustine and also a variant version, which he ascribes to a certain Rabi Sahadias.[55] At the end of the following quotation from Thomas of Cantimpré, its source is indicated as "Obscurus." He finishes the section with the relevant quotation from Albertus. The German translation, which is much abbreviated, has the quotation from Thomas without naming a source:

So der [Adler] aber mit Alter beschwehret wird / so fleugt er in die Höhe vber alle Wolcken / da wirt denn von der Sonnen die Tunckelheit seiner Augen verzehrt / vnd alsbald fällt er schnell mit derselbigen hitz herab / vnd tauffet sich dreymal in aller kältesten Wasser / denn stehet er widerumb auff / vnd fleugt alsbald zu seinem Nest vnder seine junge die jetzt starck worden sind / in der Qualitet vnd Eigenschafft der Natur kalt und warm / als ob er das Feber het / mit einem grossen schweiß läßt er seine Federn fallen / und wirt also von seinen jungen wider erquicket und ernehret / biß daß er seine Federn wider vberkommt / und also erjüngert wird.[56]

[When the eagle, however, is weighed down by age, it flies up high above all clouds. There the darkness of its eyes is then consumed by the sun, and at once it quickly falls down with that same heat in it and immerses itself three times in extremely cold water. Then it rises again and at once flies to its nest among its young, which have by then grown strong. In the quality and property of nature cold and warm, as if it had a fever, among much sweating it lets its feathers drop out and is thus restored and maintained by its young, until it gets its feathers back about it and so becomes young again.]

In the German adaptation of Pliny by Johann Heyden, several versions of the procedure of rejuvenation are found. Quoting Münster, Heyden briefly reports what is called the theory of Rabi Sahadius by Gesner: "Darüber schreibt Munsterus und setzt: Von der erneuwerung des Adlers / sagen die Hebreer / das er alle zehen Jar sich von dem hohen Himmel herab stürtzt in das Meer / vnd wachsen im neue Federn."[57] [Munsterus writes about this and says: Of the renewal of the eagle the Hebrews say that it precipitates itself from high up in the sky into the sea every ten years and grows new feathers.] Heyden follows up the relevant quotation from Augustine with extensive commentary by Iohannes Fabri and closes the chapter with three quotations which he ascribes to Papias and Iorath, probably relying completely on Fabri as his source. In fact, they are from the *Physiologus*, Iorath-Arnoldus, and Thomas of Cantimpré, and appear in the same sequence in Vincent of Beauvais. The quotation from Pseudo-Papias is especially revealing, because it has the motif of the feathers burning in the sun, and because it demonstrates how Vincent of Beauvais's naming of his source ("Physiologus dicit," i.e., "Physiologus says") was no longer recognized as such. Instead, it was understood and translated by Heyden (or Fabri) as an appeal to general authority ("Die naturforscher sagen" [The natural historians say]). There was no longer an awareness of the *Physiologus* as the title of a written work:

Ex Papia. Die naturforscher sagen / der Adler habe die art / wenn er alt werd / so werden jhm die flügel schwer / vnnd Augen dunckel / da suoch er denn ein Born lebendigs Wassers / und gegen demselbigen flieg er auff biß an die Sonnen hinan / und zünd allda seine flügel an / vnd brenn an jrem glantzen die tunckelheit seiner augen auß / danner laß sich entlich herab in den Born / vnd wird so bald gentzlich erneuwert / also / daß seine Flügel behafft vnd seine augen hell werden.

Jorath: Der Adler / wenn seine Federn alt / vnnd sein Gesicht stumpff wirt / so begibt er sich dreymal uber sich / und scherpfft sein Gesicht vnd Federn gegen der Sonnen / vnd lest sich so offt herab / vnd daucht in den Born Semoth / vnd scherpfft sein Schnabel an eim Felsen / vnd kompt jm also auf dreymal sein Gesicht / Federn vnnd Schnabel wider / wo ers aber zum vierten Mal vntersteht / so stirbt er.

Idem Iorath lib. de natura rerum: Der Adler ist ein groß und aller edelst Vogel / als der König der Vögel / welcher / so er mit alter beschweret wirt / fleucht er in die höhe vber alle Wolcken auß / und verzeret die hitz der Sonnen / die tunckelheit seiner Augen / vnnd bald lest er sich mit eim sturm also hitzig vnd brinnig herab / vnd felt zum drittenmal in gantz kalt Wasser / vnd von dannen stehet er wider auff / vnd macht sich so bald in das Nest / vnd thuot zwischen den Jungen / so jetzund starck zum Raub / da thuot er ein kelt vnd hitz / als mit einem Feder [= Feber] behafft / die Federn vonn sich / da erwermen vnnd ernehren jhn die Jungen / biß die Pflaumen vnnd Federn wider wachsen / vnd er erneuwert wirt.[58]

[From Papias. The natural historians say that the eagle has that property that when it grows old, its wings grow heavy and its eyes are darkened. So then it looks for a spring of living water and opposite to it flies up to the sun and kindles its wings there and burns out the darkness of its eyes with its glow. Then it finally descends into the spring and so is soon completely renewed so that its wings are restored and its eyes grow clear.

Iorath: The eagle. When its feathers grow old and its sight less keen, it rises up three times and sharpens its sight and feathers in the sun and descends as often and immerses itself in the spring Semoth and whets its beak on a rock and thus three times restores its sight, feathers, and beak, but if it tries that for the fourth time, it dies.

The same Iorath in his *Liber de natura rerum*. The eagle is a big bird and the noblest one, as king of birds. When it is weighed down with age, it flies up high above all the clouds and the heat of the sun burns away the darkness of its eyes, and soon it descends with a rush, thus heated and burning, and the third time it falls into very cold water and rises up again out of it and at once goes to its nest and puts itself between its young, which are by then strong enough to hunt their prey. There it grows as cold and hot as if a fever had befallen it and loses its feathers. Then the young warm and feed it, until the down and the feathers grow back and it renews itself.]

Apart from the bestiaries of the medieval and the early modern period, information on the rejuvenation of the eagle may have been imparted by exegetical works. Pierius Valerianus in his *Hieroglyphica* offers three relevant quotations from the Fathers, but neither Jerome nor Eucherius nor Augustine refer to the rejuvenating power of fire.[59] Petrus Damianus, on the other hand, seems to know the *Physiologus* account; he quotes it in his work *De bono religiosi status*.[60] It is, however, doubtful whether this piece was so widely known that it could have served to spread the idea that the eagle is rejuvenated by the burning of its feathers in the rays of the sun. The perusal of exegetical works leads one to suspect that the motif of the whetting of the beak was repeated largely due to its support by Augustine, while apparently no consensus was established on the changing of the feathers.[61]

If there are no essential elements missing in this short sketch of the tradition, and if the motif of burning during the eagle's rejuvenation is not to be explained as a loan from a different branch (the rebirth of the phoenix in the fire might be considered),[62] the eagle emblem in Boria ultimately goes back to the *Physiologus*. Possibly Reusner's eagle emblem does also. However, both authors owe to the *Physiologus* only the basic idea of the rejuvenating force of sunlight and bathing in water. The only conceivable intermediary by which the *Physiologus* tradition can have reached them is the *Speculum naturale* of Vincent of Beauvais, for that is the only way the relevant motifs of the *Physiologus* got into print before 1587.[63]

In spite of all the difficulties created by the history of the text and the transmission of the *Physiologus,* I would like to summarize my analysis as follows. The theory that the *Physiologus* widely influenced the emblematic tradition cannot be maintained. A printed text, the version by Epiphanius, was not available before 1587; and it did not transmit even half of the original motifs. It is true that some motifs may have passed into emblematic tradition by way of secondary transmission, such as encyclopaedic works, but on the whole the *Physiologus* offers comparatively little material to writers of emblem books. Motifs that are known only from the *Physiologus* tradition are very rare and are hardly ever taken up in the emblematic tradition. Wherever the *Physiologus* agrees with the natural history of antiquity and other classical literature, the authors of emblem books in the main cite the classical sources, not the *Physiologus*, which would appear to have been hardly known as an independent work. In this connection the Fathers and contemporaries are included among the "respectable" or authoritative sources, while witnesses of the High and Late Middle Ages are not cited. Whether these reservations may be interpreted as a symptom of humanism's dislike of the "dark" Middle Ages is a question requiring further examination. The fact that Picinelli now and then breaks away from this united front of rejection may indicate that he is conscious of a different tradition. As an Augustinian canon Picinelli felt himself more indebted to the Augustinians of St. Victor (after all, *De bestiis et aliis rebus* is transmitted under the name of Hugh of St. Victor) but also more indebted to other members of the orders in the Middle Ages than were the humanist authors of emblem books.

My observations are based on an analysis of the manual *Emblemata*, the encyclopaedia of emblems by Filippo Picinelli, a few selected emblem books (Camerarius, Junius, Schoonhovius), and a number of writings on natural history. More research, which would have to include above all the Italian literature of the *impresa*, will be necessary to confirm, correct, or even refute my results. But I would like to conclude for now by alluding to the motto that Julius Wilhelm Zincgref attached to his emblem of the key: "Non omnia possumus omnes."[64]

NOTES

*A shorter English version of this essay was offered for discussion at the 27th International Congress on Medieval Studies (May 7–10, 1992) in Kalamazoo, Michigan. A German version of this essay appears as "Zum Problem der Physiologus—Traditionen in der Emblematik" in *Mittellateinisches Jahrbuch* 29 (1994), 97–112. This English version is printed here with the permission of its editors. I am indebted to Inge Milfull (University of Eichstätt) for the translation of my original German version. The figures are reproduced here with the kind permission of Ediciones Turero, Madrid (figure 1), BSB Munich (figures 2, 5, 6), UB Munich (figure 3), Stadtbibliothek Mainz (figure 4), and the Verlag Georg Olms, Hildesheim (figure 7).

1. "(. . .) Zusammenhang der Emblematik mit dem Symboldenken des Mittelalters, dessen Herbarien und Bestiarien den Emblembüchern eine Fülle von Motiven geliefert haben. Vor allem gilt dies für den griechischen 'Physiologus', der im 2. nachchristlichen Jahrhundert vermutlich in Alexandrien zusammengestellt worden ist und dessen Abschriften, Bearbeitungen, Übersetzungen ins Lateinische und in die Nationalsprachen durch das ganze Mittelalter gehen." *Emblemata. Handbuch zur Sinnbildkunst des XVI. und XVII. Jahrhunderts*, ed. Arthur Henkel and Albrecht Schöne, 2nd ed. (Stuttgart: Metzler, 1976), xv. For the contents of the *Physiologus* and the complex history of its text and transmission see the article by B.E. Perry, "Physiologus," in *Realenzyclopädie der classischen Altertumswissenschaft* (Stuttgart: Druckenmüller, 1941), vol. XX, 1, cols. 1074–129; also Nikolaus Henkel, *Studien zum Physiologus im Mittelalter*, Hermaea 38 (Tübingen: Niemeyer, 1976); Christian Schröder, "Physiologus," in *Die deutsche Literatur des Mittelalters. Verfasserlexikon*, 2nd ed., vol. 7 (Berlin: de Gruyter, 1989), cols. 620–34.

2. "Viele Res pictae der Emblembücher finden sich bereits im 'Physiologus.'" *Emblemata*, xv.

3. *Emblemata*, cols. 2085–94.

4. "Aber nicht in allen Fällen hat er wirklich als Quelle gedient. Mitunter gehen eine Tierbeschreibung dieses Werkes und das ihr entsprechende Emblembild auch unabhängig voneinander auf die Bibel oder auf antikes Schrifttum zurück." *Emblemata*, xv. The views held by Albrecht Schöne in his *Emblematik und Drama im Zeitalter des Barock*, a pioneering publication in German emblematic research (first published in 1964), are much more cautious. He puts them as follows: "Häufig gehen die Tierbeschreibung des *Physiologus* und das ihr entsprechende Emblembild unabhängig voneinander auf die Bibel oder auf antikes Schrifttum zurück." [Often the description of the animal in the *Physiologus* and the corresponding picture of an emblem derive independently from the Bible or classical writing.] *Emblematik und Drama im Zeitalter des Barock*, 2nd ed. (Munich: Beck, 1968), 46.

5. William S. Heckscher and Karl-August Wirth, "Emblem, Emblembuch," *Reallexikon zur deutschen Kunstgeschichte*, vol. 5 (Stuttgart: Druckenmüller, 1967), col. 125.

6. Dieter Sulzer, "Emblem," *Enzyklopädie des Märchens*, vol. 3 (Berlin: de Gruyter, 1987), col. 1386: "Als weitere Bildquellen kommen neben der antiken Mythologie die spätantike Physiologus, hellenistische Allegorien, ma. Herbarien, Bestiarien, Steinbücher und die Heraldik hinzu." [As further sources of the pictures, in addition to classical mythology, the Physiologus of late antiquity, hellenistic allegories, medieval herbals, bestiaries, lapidaries, and heraldry must be added.] Wolfgang Harms, "Emblem, Emblematik," *Theologische Realenzyklopädie*, vol. 9 (Berlin: de Gruyter, 1982), 554, does not name the *Physiologus* itself but lists "Bestiarien, Herbarien, Lapidarien und allegorische Wörterbücher" as "exegetische Spezialliteratur" from which emblematic tradition may draw apart from the "exegetischen Verfahrensweise der

Allegorese . . . auch punktuelle Deutungsergebnisse" (i.e., bestiaries, herbals, lapidaries, and allegorical dictionaries are specialist texts of an exegetical nature from which, at some points, emblematic tradition may borrow the conclusions of a particular interpretation as well as the exegetical method of allegorical interpretation as such). This view may be presumed to be more in keeping with the facts.

7. *Emblemata*, cols. 400 (lion), 411 (elephant, twice), 413 (elephant), 417 (elephant), 422 (unicorn), 424 (unicorn), 460 (beaver), 463 (weasel), 470 (stag), 635 (snake, shedding its skin), 641 (snake, protecting its head), 661 (viper, coition), 662 (viper, birth), 671 (ichneumon), 733 (pearl), 739 (salamander), 776 (eagle), 777 (eagle), 796 (phoenix), 811 (pelican), 812 (pelican), 844 (partridge).

8. *Physiologi graeci singulas recensiones*, ed. Francesco Sbordone (Milan, 1936; rpt. Hildesheim, Olms, 1976).

9. N. Henkel (see note 1 above), 53–6; see also Nikolaus Henkel, *Deutsche Übersetzungen Lateinischer Schultexte. Ihre Verbreitung und Funktion im Mittelalter und in der frühen Neuzeit. Mit einem Verzeichnis der Texte*, Münchener Texte und Untersuchungen zur deutschen Literatur des Mittelalters (Munich: Artemis, 1988), esp. 283–5.

10. Compare Vincentius Bellovacensis, *Speculum naturale* (Douai, 1624; rpt. Graz: Akademische Druck- und Verlagsanstalt, 1964), Lib. 16, caps. 36, 44, 76, 96, 127, 131, 138–139, 144, 148, 149; Lib. 17, cap. 129; Lib. 19, caps. 30, 38, 48, 72–74, 99–100, 104, 122, 133; Lib. 20, caps. 48, 54. Bartholomaeus Angelicus (Anglicus), *De rerum proprietatibus* (Frankfurt, 1601; rpt. Frankfurt am Main: Minerva, 1964), 1003, 1043, 1050, 1096, 1100, 1113.

In the manuscript tradition of the encyclopaedia, exegetical interpretation is by no means left out altogether; see Heinz Meyer, "Zum Verhältnis von Enzyklopädik und Allegorese im Mittelalter," in *Frühmittelalterliche Studien* 24 (1990), 290–313.

11. The editions are listed by Arnold C. Klebs, "Incunabula scientifica et medica," *Osiris* 4 (1938), 1–359 (rpt. Hildesheim: Olms, 1963), under no. 956.

12. Dietrich Schmidtke, "Physiologus Theobaldi deutsch," in *Beiträge zur Geschichte der deutschen Sprache und Literatur* 89 (1967), 270–301; the text is printed on 290–301. The German version in rhyming couplets in clm. 5594 is printed in N. Henkel, *Physiologus* (see note 1 above), 118–28.

13. Epiphanius, *Ad Physiologum*, ed. Gonzalez Ponce de Leon (Antwerp, 1588). The preface is dated 1586. The first edition appeared in Rome in 1587, and a further edition appeared in Paris in 1621, before Petau edited the collected works of Epiphanius in 1622. The *Physiologus* of Epiphanius is printed without the commentary by Ponce de Leon in *PG* 43, cols. 517–34.

14. It is very doubtful indeed whether the fact that the chapter headings are followed by the woodcuts and they in their turn by the explanation in prose allows the conclusion that this print is a "ganz emblematisch aufgemachte Physiologus-Fassung" [a version of the Physiologus entirely adapted to emblematic conventions]; Schöne, *Emblematik*, 46. After all, texts of the *Physiologus* have been transmitted together with illustrations since very early times.

15. The various properties of some animals are each treated in a chapter of their own: lion (chs. 1–2), aurochs (3), elephant (4), stag (5), eagle (6), vulture (7), pelican (8), partridge (9), dove (10), phoenix (11), peacock (12), snake (13–16), ant (17–18), fox (19), owl (20), bee (21), frog (22), charadrius (23), woodpecker (24), stork (25).

16. Compare cols. 400 (lion), 635 and 641 (snake), 776 and 777 (eagle), 796 (phoenix), 811 (pelican).

17. Compare Hadrianus Junius, *Emblemata, ad D. Arnoldum Cobelium. Aenigmata ad D. Arnoldum Rosenbergum*, a reprint of the edition of Antwerp, 1565; Emblematisches Cabinet 14 (Hildesheim: Olms, 1987), 78f., 128.

18. Florentius Schoonhovius, *Emblemata Partim Moralia Partim Civilia*, reprinted from the edition of Gouda, 1618; Emblematisches Cabinet 7 (Hildesheim: Olms, 1975), 142, 150.

19. Joachim Camerarius, *Symbola et emblemata*, a reprint of the edition of Nuremberg, 1590–1604. With introduction and indices ed. Wolfgang Harms and Ulla-Britta Kuechen. Parts 1 (Centuria I through Centuria III) and 2 (Centuria IV, introduction, indices), *Naturalis Historia Bibliae* 2, Parts 1–2 (Graz: Academische Druck-und Verlagsanstalt, 1986–8); Centuria III, nos. 16, 37, 100.

20. Filippo Picinelli, *Mundus symbolicus* (reprinted from the edition of Cologne, 1687), ed. D. Donat (Hildesheim: Olms, 1979), 323, 403, 494.

21. Julius Wilhelm Zincgref, *Hundert ethisch-politische Embleme. Mit den Kupferstichen des Matthaeus Merian*, ed. Arthur Henkel and Wolfgang Wiemann (Heidelberg: Winter, 1986), Part I, no. 50.

22. Camerarius, Centuria III, fol. 16v: "Aristoteles lib. IX cap. III refert, Aquilis senescentibus rostrum superius accrescere et semper incurvari, ut tandem fame pereant. Quod Plinius quoque lib. X. cap. I confirmat, Vnde (ut in Horapolline lib. II. cap. XCVI. habetur) veteres senem fame pereuntem exprimere volentes, pinxerunt aquilam cum adunco rostro. Sed D. Epiphanius in physiologo addit, oculis jam caligantib. et rostro nimis incurvato, aquilam in sublime sese attollentem ad altam rupem conferre, et ibidem rostrum allidere, ac denique frigidis aquis immergere, quo facto se postea solaribus radiis exponere et sic quasi rejuvenescere." [Aristotle in the Ninth Book, Chapter Three, relates that when eagles grow old, the upper half of their beak grows and keeps getting more curved so that they finally die of starvation. This is also confirmed by Pliny in Book Ten, Chapter One. Therefore the ancients, when they wanted to portray the old bird dying of hunger, painted an eagle with a hooked bill, such as there is in Horapollo, Book Two, Chapter Ninety-Six. But St. Epiphanius adds in his *Physiologus* that when the eagle's eyes are already darkening and its beak is too crooked, it rises up high and goes to a steep cliff and hits its beak on it and then immerses itself in cold water; having done that, it then exposes itself to the sun's rays and thus, as it were, regains its youth.]

23. Loc. cit.: "Quod idem D. Augustinus quoque exponit in explicatione dicti ad Psalmum CIII. Renovabitur ut Aquilae juventus tua. D. Hieronymus tamen et alii in Psalmi huius expositione, renovationem hanc tantum de oculis et pennis ipsius intelligendam perhibent. Cum quo etiam dictum Isaiae, cap. XL. convenire videtur, ubi ait, Sustinentes DOMINUM mutabunt vires et renascentur eius pennae in modum Aquilarum." [The same thing is explained by St. Augustine in his commentary on the saying in Psalm 103: Thy youth shall be renewed like the eagle's. But St. Jerome and others in their explanation of this psalm show that the renewal is to be understood only as of its eyes and the feathers. The saying of Isaiah, Chapter Forty, also appears to agree with this where he says: They that wait upon the Lord shall change their strength and his feathers shall grow anew after the manner of eagles.]

24. Loc. cit.

25. The illustrations of the first edition are reproduced by Santiago Sebastián, *El Fisiólogo atribuido a San Epifanio. Traducción directa del latín: Francisco Tejada Vizuete*, Collección Investigación y Crítica 2 (Madrid: Ediciones Tuero, 1986) (kindly pointed out to me by José Julio García Arranz, Badajoz).

26. Stadtbibliothek Mainz, MS. II/366, 146. The quotation from Jerome is impossible to locate, at least in that exact wording. The natural historical description resembles Pseudo-Jerome, *PL* 30, col. 187A, where, however, the sun is not mentioned: "Aquila quando senuerit, gravantur ipsius pennae et oculi, quaeritque fontem, et erigit[?] pennas, et colligit in se calorem, et sic oculi ejus sanantur: et in fontem se ter mergit, et ita ad juventutem redit." [When the eagle grows old, its feathers and eyes are affected and it looks for a fountain and spreads [moistens?] its feathers and gathers heat into itself. And so its eyes are healed. And it immerses itself three times in the spring and so becomes young again.]

27. Camerarius, Centuria III, fol. 34v.

28. In this connection Eucherius of Lyon and Jerome should also be mentioned; compare Pierius Valerianus, *Hieroglyphica* (Lyon, 1626; first published in Basel, 1556),

Lib. XX, cap. viii, 201. For variant interpretations of the pelican, compare Christoph Gerhardt, *Die Metamorphosen des Pelikans. Exempel und Auslegung in mittelalterlicher Literatur. Mit Beispielen aus der bildenden Kunst und einem Bildanhang,* Europäische Hochschulschriften I/265 (Frankfurt am Main: Lang, 1979).

29. Camerarius, Centuria III, fol. 37v.

30. Loc. cit.

31. Camerarius, Centuria III, fol. 100v–101r.

32. Camerarius, Centuria III, fol. 101v: "Sic B. Tertullianus in libro de resurrectione carnis inquit, plenissimum ac firmissimum specimen esse huius spei (resurrectionis) ex hoc alite sumendum, quod B. Ambrosius quoque et Epiphanius in Physiologo asserunt." [Thus the Blessed Tertullian says in his book on the resurrection of the flesh that very complete and reliable evidence for this hope (of resurrection) is to be got from that bird, which is also assured by the Blessed Ambrose and Epiphanius in his *Physiologus*.]

33. Picinelli, Lib. IV, § 478; V, 500; VII, 113. Other writings of Epiphanius are also adduced (cf. V, 502; VII, 500).

34. Picinelli, IV, 239 (charadrius); IV, 247 (stork); IV, 500 (owl); IV, 535 (pelican); IV, 555 (partridge); V, 451 (lion); VIII, 23 (bee). Picinelli cites Pseudo-Hugh also with regard to other animals included in the *Physiologus* but omitted by Epiphanius; cf. III, 125 (siren); IV, 218 (heron); IV, 454 (swallow); V, 594 (panther).

De bestiis et aliis rebus is a compilation of four books; the first of these, a book on birds, is a work of Hugh of Fouilloy, who may have also composed the second part. The authors of the last two parts, however, are unknown (cf. N. Henkel, *Physiologus*, 156f.); for the book on birds see also Friedrich Ohly, "Probleme der mittelalterlichen Bedeutungsforschung und das Taubenbild des Hugo de Folieto," *Frühmittelalterliche Studien* 2 (1968), 162–201, reprinted in Friedrich Ohly, *Schriften zur mittelalterlichen Bedeutungsforschung,* (Darmstadt: Wissenschaftliche Buchgesellschaft, 1977), 32–92; and Charles de Clercq, "La nature et le sens du 'De avibus' d'Hugues de Fouilloy," *Methoden in Wissenschaft und Kunst,* ed. Albert Zimmermann, Miscellanea Mediaevalia 7 (Berlin: de Gruyter, 1970), 279–302.

35. The relation between this compilation and the *Physiologus* is treated by Francis J. Carmody, "*De Bestiis et Aliis Rebus* and the Latin *Physiologus,*" *Speculum* 13 (1938), 153–9.

36. Cf. Camerarius, Centuria II, 1. Thus the reference to the *Physiologus* (cap. 43) in the manual *Emblemata,* col. 411, is not justified.

37. Camerarius, Centuria II, 37.

38. Cf. Index, col. 2090. Perry, col. 1084f., does not mention this motif.

39. Camerarius, Centuria II, 38.

40. Picinelli, V, 414. Epiphanius has the breath motif; the reviving of the whelps by a roar had been transmitted as a variant since Isidore (*Etymologiae,* XII, 2.5). Cf. N. Henkel, *Physiologus,* 100, n. 139.

41. Picinelli, V, 594–5.

42. "[W]ie von dem Adler gesagt wird / daß er so hoch und nahe an die Sonne fliege / daß sie ihn mit ihren Strahlen verbrenne und die Federn versengte / mit welchen er hernach sich ins Wasser tauchte und also neue Federn und Kräffte bekäme." Quoted according to *Emblemata,* col. 776.

43. "[W]enn er von allzu hohem Alter ermattet ist, badet er drei- und viermal im klaren Wasser, fliegt auf von dort und gewinnt neues Leben aus dem Licht der Sonne und erneuert sein Gefieder und seine erschöpften Glieder." Quoted according to *Emblemata,* col. 777.

44. *Der altdeutsche Physiologus,* ed. Friedrich Maurer, Altdeutsche Textbibliothek, vol. 67 (Tübingen: Niemeyer, 1967), 86: "Dicit David in psalmo CII: Renovabitur ut aquile iuventus tua. Phisiologus dicit aquilam talem naturam habere, ut quando senuerit, graventur ale eius et oculi eius obducuntur caligine. Tunc vero querit fontem aque vive et contra fontem evolat in altum usque ad ignem solis, ibique incendit

alas suas simul et caliginem oculorum suorum emendat. Surgens autem de radio solis demum descendit in fontem ac tertia vice se mergit statimque renovata est. Ergo et tu homo dei Iudeus sive gentilis qui vestimentum habes vetus et caligantur oculi tui cordis secundum sensum spiritalem domini qui dixit: Nisi quis renatus fuerit ex aqua et spiritu sancto, non potest introire in regnum dei. Si ergo baptizatus fueris ex aqua et spiritu sancto, tunc renovabitur ut aquile iuventus tua. Item sanctus Augustinus de aquila ita disseruit dicens: Cum autem senuerit aquila, crescit illi rostrum superius, id est beccus ex quo tunc impeditur manducare. Pergens autem ad petram frangit illum sicque manducat et vivit quam diu deus vult. Sic et nos percutimur ad petram, idest Christum. Per rostrum intelligitur vetus tunica, quam de Adam taximus. Renovamur autem in baptismo et postea possumus comedere corpus domini. Item Hieronimus refert, quod quando aquila senuerit, petit altiora celi, hoc est usque ad ignem ethereum sumensque de illo comburit alas suas. Sicque cadens in nidum suum arescit per pennas suas et pascunt eum pulli sui, usque dum renovatur. Sic et nos per graciam sancti spiritus conburimur et arescunt vitia et peccata nostra interim, usque dum veniamus in futuro ad renovationem perpetuam." [David says in Psalm 102: Thy youth shall be renewed like the eagle's. The Physiologus says that the eagle is of such a nature that its wings grow heavy and its eyes are covered with darkness when it has grown old. Then, however, it looks for a spring of living water and, opposite the spring, flies high up to the fire of the sun, and there at the same time it kindles its wings and mends the darkness of its eyes. Breaking away at last from the beam of the sun, it sinks into the spring and immerses itself three times and is at once renewed. So it is with you also, man of God, whether you are Jew or Gentile, who have an old dress—and the eyes of your heart are darkened—according to the spiritual meaning of our Lord who said: If someone is not reborn out of the water and the Holy Spirit, he cannot enter the kingdom of God. If you are baptized with the water and the Holy Spirit, then your youth will be renewed as the eagle's. St Augustine, too, talked about the eagle, speaking thus: Now when the eagle has grown old, its upper beak—that is, its bill—grows, whereby it is then hindered from eating. But it goes to a rock and breaks it off and thus eats and lives, as long as God wishes it to. So we also are struck against the rock, that is, Christ. The beak is to be understood as the old dress, which we had from Adam. We are, however, renewed by baptism and afterwards we may eat the body of the Lord. Jerome also recounts that the eagle, when it grows old, seeks the upper regions of the sky—that is, as high up as the fire of the aether—and takes a little of that and burns its wings. And so it falls into its nest and wilts, as far as its feathers are concerned, and its offspring feeds it until it is renewed. Thus we also are burnt by the grace of the Holy Spirit and meanwhile our sins and offences wilt, until we reach an everlasting renewal in the future.]

According to Dietrich Schmidtke, *Geistliche Tierinterpretation in der deutschsprachigen Literatur des Mittelalters (1100–1500)* (Dissertation, University of Berlin, 1968), 570, n. 738, the rejuvenation of the eagle first makes its appearance in the version of the *Physiologus* known as *Dicta Chrysostomi* and goes back to Jerome. However, the relevant passages cited in Jerome do not agree with this quotation; cf. *PL* 24, col. 412A; *PL* 30, col. 187A (Pseudo-Jerome). Gudrun Schleusener-Eichholz, *Das Auge im Mittelalter*, 2 vols., Münstersche Mittelalter-Schriften 35/1.2 (Munich: Fink, 1985), vol. 1, 478f., only uses the vernacular adaptations and misses the fact that the Latin *Physiologus* offers two variants of the rejuvenation of the eagle.

45. *Theobaldi Physiologus*, ed. P.T. Eden, Mittellateinische Studien und Texte 6 (Leyden: E.J. Brill, 1972), 28–30. On the German prose version see Schmidtke (see note 12 above), 291–2.

46. *Novus Phisiologus. Nach der Hs. Darmstadt 2780*, ed. A.P. Orban, Mittellateinische Studien und Text 15 (Leyden: E.J. Brill, 1989), 42–4.

47. The quotation from the Bible (Ps. 102:5) introduces the final section of the chapter on the eagle. The text explains as follows: "Solet dici de aquila, dum senectute premitur, quod rostrum illius aduncetur, ita ut sumere cibum nequeat sed macie languescat. Veniens ad petram rostrum acuit, et cibum sic capiens, iterum iuvenescit.

Petra est Christus, aquila quilibet justus, qui a petram rostrum acuit, dum seipsum Christo per bonam operationem conformem reddit." [It is usually said about the eagle that when it is burdened by age, its beak becomes hooked, so that it is not able to eat, but becomes weak from thinness. Coming upon a rock, it sharpens its beak, and thus, eating again, it is rejuvenated. The rock is Christ, the eagle any righteous man who sharpens his beak on the rock while through good deeds he renders himself like unto Christ.] *The Medieval Book of Birds: Hugh of Fouilloy's Aviarium*, ed. and trans. Willene B. Clark (Binghamton, N.Y.: Medieval and Renaissance Texts and Studies, 1992), 254–5.

48. According to Traude-Marie Nischik, *Das volkssprachliche Naturbuch im späten Mittelalter. Sachkunde und Dinginterpretation bei Jacob van Maerlant und Konrad von Megenberg*, Hermaea 48 (Tübingen: Niemeyer, 1986), 30, n. 102, Adelinus is supposed to be identical with Aldhelm of Malmesbury. Aldhelm, however, writes little about the rejuvenation of the eagle in his *Aenigmata* (ed. Mario de Marco, CCSL 133 [Turnhout: Brepols, 1968], 450–1): "Corpora dum senio corrumpit fessa vetustas, / Fontibus in liquidis mergentis membra madescunt; / Post haec restauror praeclaro lumine Phoebi." [When weary age has bent my senile limbs, / In springs of limpid water then I plunge, / And, dripping, rise restored in Phoebus' light.]

49. Thomas Cantimpratensis, *Liber de natura rerum*, Part 1, ed. Helmut Boese (Berlin: de Gruyter, 1973), 178: "Aquila, sicut dicit Adelinus, cum senecta gravatur, fontem frigidissimum notans ibi decontra in sublime volat omnesque transcendit nubes. Ex calore autem propinqui solis oculorum eius caligo consumitur statimque in impetu cum ipsius caloris estu descendens aquis frigidissimis tertio immergitur, indeque resurgens statim nidum petit et inter pullos iam robustos ad predam inequalitate frigoris et caloris quasi quadam febre correpta sudore plumas exuit foveturque a pullis suis et pascitur, quoadusque plumas pennasque recuperans innovetur. Augustinus: Rostrum quoque, cui oboritur uncus immodice adeo, ut vix labore cibum capere possit, naturali modo petre allidit, allidensque uncum excutit et reparatur ad cibum." [As Adelinus says, the eagle, when it is oppressed by age, as soon as it sees a very cold spring, flies up high there opposite to it and soars above all the clouds. Now by the heat of the nearby sun, the darkening of its eyes is dispelled, and at once it hurls itself downwards filled with the intensity of that heat and immerses itself three times in those very cold waters. And when it rises up again out of them, it at once seeks its nest, and among its offspring who are already strong enough to hunt, it is overwhelmed by a fever, as it were, because of the great difference between that cold and that heat, and so in its sweat it loses its plumage. And it is warmed by its offspring and fed by them, until it is renewed, regaining its feathers and plumage. Augustine: It also hits its beak—which grows too hooked so that it can hardly feed itself by its labour—against a rock in a natural way and, by hitting, hammers the hook out of it and is again capable of feeding.]

For the encyclopaedia of Thomas Cantimpratensis, see Pierre Michaud-Quantin, "Les petites encyclopédies du XIIIe siècle," *Cahiers d'histoire mondiale* 9 (1966), 588–91; and Nischik, 28–36. The version of Thomas is also followed by Konrad of Megenberg, *Buch der Natur*, ed. Franz Pfeiffer (Stuttgart, Aue, 1861), 166. In contrast to the Latin original the German adaptation was printed several times; cf. Georg Steer, "Zur Nachwirkung des 'Buchs der Natur' Konrads von Megenberg im 16. Jahrhundert," in *Volkskultur und Geschichte, Festgabe für Josef Dünninger zum 65. Geb,* ed. Dieter Harmening (Berlin: Schmidt, 1970), 570–84.

50. For the encyclopaedia of Bartholomaeus Anglicus, see Michaud-Quantin, 584–8.

51. Bartholomaeus, 516: "Ad hac dicit Augustinus et Plinius, quod aquila in senectute patitur caliginem in oculis, et gravedinem in alis suis. Contra quod incommodum instruitur a natura, vt fontem aquae scaturientis quaerat, deinde ascendit, quantum potest, per aera, donec ex calore solis et labore volatus fortius incalescat, vnde tunc ex calore poris apertis et pennis relaxatis, subito descendens in fontem ruit, ibique mutatis plumis et purgata caligine in oculis, vires recipit et resumit. Super Psal. etiam dicit idem, quod cum senuerit, ita induratur et incuruatur eius rostrum, vt vix possit

sumere cibum suum, et contra hoc incommodum invenit remedium, quia petram sibi quaerit, contra quam fortius rostrum percutit et allidit, et sic deponit onus rostri, et cibum capiens, resumptis viribus, iuuenescit." [About this Augustine and Pliny say that the eagle suffers from blindness of its eyes in its old age and from a heaviness in its wings. As a measure against this ailment, it is instructed by Nature to seek a spring of bubbling water. Then it ascends into the air as far as it is able to, until by the heat of the sun and the effort of flying it becomes quite heated. Its pores being opened and its feathers loosened thereby, it descends very fast and plunges into the spring. And when its plumage has been changed and the darkening of the eyes washed away in it, it achieves and regains its strength. In his commentary on the Psalms he (Augustine) also says that its beak, when it grows old, grows so hard and crooked that it can hardly partake of its food. It finds a remedy against that trouble in the following way: it seeks a rock against which it knocks and hits its beak quite hard, and thus gets rid of the encumbrance of the beak and, feeding, regains its strength and thus grows young again.]

The passage from Bartholomaeus is also quoted almost literally, accompanied by a suitable interpretation, in the collection of exempla from natural history by Iohannes de San Geminiano, which was widely known and reprinted several times: *Summa de exemplis et rerum similitudinibus* (Venice, 1576), fol. 176v. This branch of the tradition is later followed by Petrus Berchorius (died 1362), *Reductorium morale* (Venice, 1583), 184 (VII, 2.14). On both authors see Schmidtke (see note 44 above), 96–7.

52. Vincentius Bellovacensis, col. 1179 (XVI, 36). For Vincent's encyclopaedia, see Michel Lemoine, "L'oeuvre encyclopédique de Vincent de Beauvais," *Cahiers d'histoire mondiale* 9 (1966), 571–9.

53. Iorach is already quoted by Arnoldus Saxo, who gives an extremely abbreviated version: "In libro de animalibus Iorach: Quando penne aquillarum senescunt et ebetatur visus eius, ter supernum ascendens se mergit in fonte semoch, et rostrum suum ad petram acuit. Sic tribus vicibus redit visus eius et plume et rostrum. Et cum quarto hoc atemptaverit, tunc moritur." [Iorach in his Book on Animals: When the feathers of eagles grow old and its [the eagle's] sight less keen, it rises up high three times, plunges into the spring Semoch, and sharpens its beak on a rock. Thus three times its sight and feathers and beak are restored. And when it attempts to do that for the fourth time, it dies.] *Die Encyklopädie des Arnoldus Saxo*, ed. Emil Stange (Programm Erfurt, 1905–6), 61 (II, 6). For this writer see F.J. Worstbrock, "Arnoldus Saxo," in *Die deutsche Literatur des Mittelalters. Verfasserlexikon*, 2nd ed., vol. 1 (Berlin: de Gruyter, 1978), cols. 485–8.

54. Albertus Magnus, *De animalibus libri XXVI*, ed. Hermann Stadler, 2 vols. (Münster: Aschendorff, 1916–1920), especially vol. 2, 1434 (XXIII, 10). Equally critical, Albertus also tests the account that the eagle whets its beak (cf. loc. cit., 1435).

55. Conrad Gesner, *Historiae animalium liber III, qui est de avium natura* (Zurich, 1555), 167: "Rabi Sahadias, ut testatur R. Dauid (in commentario in caput Esaiae 40 ni fallor) ait aquilam ante omnes aues esse maximus uolatus, & quolibet decennio donec ac[?] centum annos perveniat, petere ignem elementarem, atque eius calore supra modum accensam in mare se praecipitem dare, & sic renouari, plumasque ei nouas repullulare: at cum centesimo anno id facere tentet, destitui uiribus, ita ut e mari cum se in illud praecipitauerit, resurgere nequeat, atque emori." [Rabi Sahadias, as R. David attests (in his commentary on the fourth chapter of Isaiah, if I do not err), says that the eagle is the greatest flier among all birds and that every ten years, until it reaches one hundred years, it seeks out the elementary fire and, ignited by its heat beyond measure, precipitates itself into the sea and is renewed in this way and grows new feathers again, but when it tries to do that in its one hundredth year, its strength fails so that when it has precipitated itself into the sea, it is not able to rise up again out of it and so dies.]

56. Conrad Gesner, *Thierbuch* (Zurich, 1563), 8.

57. Johann Heyden, *Caij Plinij Secundi / Des furtrefflichen Hochgelehrten Alten Philosophi / Bücher und schrifften / von der Natur / art und eigenschafft der Creaturen oder Geschöpffe Gottes* (Frankfurt am Main, 1565), 407 (kindly pointed out to me by Udo Friedrich, Munich).

Cf. Vincent of Beauvais (see note 10 above), p. 1179 (XVI, 36): "Ex Papia. Physiologus dicit aquilam hanc habere naturam, cum senuerit grauantur alae eius, & obducuntur caligine oculi eius, tunc quaerit fontem aquae viuae, & contra eum euolat in altum vsque ad aethera solis. Ibique alas suas incendit, simul & caliginem oculorum exurit de radijs eius. Tunc demum descendens in fontem se mergit, & statim tota renouatur, ita vt alarum vigore, & oculorum splendore, renouetur in melius. Iorath vbi sup. Aquila senescentibus pennis, & hebetato visu ter sursum ascendens, visum suum, & alas contra Solem acuit, totiensque descendens in fonte Semoth se mergit, ac rostrum suum ad petram acuit. Sicque tribus vicibus redit visus eius, & plumae ac ristrum[?]. Cum adhuc quarto attentauerit, tunc moritur. Ex libr. de natur. rer. Aquila est auis magna, & nobilissima, vtpote auium regina, quae cum senecta grauatur, super omnes nubes in sublime volat, & ex calore solis oculorum eius caligo consumitur, & mox impetu cum ipso caloris aestu descendens aquis frigidissimis tertio immergitur. Indeque resurgens statim nidum petit, & inter pullos iam robustos ad praedam in qualitate frigoris, & caloris quasi quadam febre correpta, quodam sudore plumas exuit, foueturque a pullis suis, & pascitur, donec pennas plumasque recuperans innouetur." [From Papias. The Physiologus says that the eagle has the following property by nature. When it grows old, its wings become heavy and its eyes are covered with darkness. Then it looks for a spring of living water and, opposite it, flies high up to the aether of the sun. And there it kindles its wings and, at the same time, lets the darkness of the eyes be burnt away in its rays. Then finally it lowers itself into the spring and immerses itself, and at once it is altogether renewed so that it recovers the strength of its wings and the shining of its eyes. Iorath, loc. cit. When the eagle's feathers grow old and its sight is dulled, it rises up high three times, sharpens its sight, and its wings are stimulated by the sun and it lowers itself many times and immerses itself in the spring Semoth and whets its beak on a rock. And so three times its sight and feathers and beak are recovered. When it tries that again for the fourth time, it dies. From the *Liber de natura rerum*: The eagle is a big and very noble bird, for it is the ruler of birds. When it is weighed down by old age, it flies up high above all clouds and the darkness of its eyes is consumed by the heat of the sun. And at once it precipitates itself downwards, still glowing with that heat, and immerses itself three times in very cold water. As soon as it has risen from there, it seeks its nest among its young, who are by then already strong enough to hunt, it is seized by a kind of fever because of the nature of the coldness and the heat, and sweating in a certain manner, it sheds its feathers and is kept warm and fed by its young, until it is renewed and recovers its down and feathers.]

58. Heyden (see note 57 above), 409. I owe thanks to Udo Friedrich for pointing me to Fabri.

59. Pierius Valerianus, 193f.: "Diuus Hieronymus Aquilam ait, vbi consenuerit, pennis supra modum grauari, ideoque fontem ab ea quaeri, cuius aspergine pennas egerat, quibus leuata calorem intra se colligit, sanarique tum primum oculos, mox ab immersatione in iuuentam redire. Eucherius Aquilas ait vi nimiae senectae implumes fieri, et nido relatas a pullis suis vicissim ministrantibus pasci, donec deterso senij veterno, cum pennis volandi etam vsum recipiant. D. Augustinus Aquilam ait senio grauatam rostri immodice crescentis aduncitate eo redigi . . . , vt nec os aperire, nec cibum vllo pacto capere possit: impulsam itaque naturae vi, collidere rostrum ad petram, cuius attritu excussa ea parte quae redundabat, ad cibum redire, atque ita ex eo senio reparari, vt omnino iuuenescere videatur. Nostri petram loco hoc Christum intelligunt, proque rostro adunco, prauitatis peruersitatisque opera." [The Blessed Jerome says that the eagle, when it grows old, is weighed down too much by its feathers and therefore a spring is sought by it, in which it wets its feathers, on which it soars and thus collects heat within itself, and that then its eyes are healed first and, soon after, because of the immersion, it itself returns to youth. Eucherius says that eagles lose their feathers as an effect of extreme old age and are brought to their nests and fed there by their offspring, who each serve in their turn, until the lethargy of their

old age is wiped out and they gain the habit of flight together with their feathers. The Blessed Augustine says that when it [the eagle] is weighed down by old age, it is reduced to such a state because its beak is so hooked and grows too much, . . . that it can neither open its mouth nor consume food in any way: that impelled by the force of nature, it knocks its beak against the rock; and that it returns to its food, when it has ground it and knocked away the part that was too big; and that it thus is restored from its old age so that it positively seems to grow young again. Our people understand the rock in that passage to be Christ and interpret the hooked beak as the works of corruption and iniquity.]

60. Petrus Damianus, *PL* 145, col. 783f.: "Quis hoc medicinae genus aquilae tradidit, quae cum senuerit, et gravari coeperint alae ejus, atque oculi caligare, tunc quaerit fontem aquae, contra quem posita volat usque ad circulum solis, illicque in puriori aetheris vastitate librata, ad vaporem solis et alas incendit, et caliginem oculorum prorsus exurit, moxque descendens tribus in fontem vicibus mergitur, et sic alarum vigor et oculorum acies multo melius quam juventus attulerat renovatur?" [Who has told the story of that kind of medicine the eagle uses, which, when it grows old and its wings grow heavy and its eyes are darkened, then seeks a spring of water, positions itself opposite to it, flies up to the circle of the sun, and there—floating in the vast and purer aether—kindles its wings at the vapour of the sun, and the eagle burns away the darkness of its eyes completely, at once descends and immerses itself three times in the spring—and thus the strength of its wings and the sharpness of its eyes are renewed, much better than such as youth had gifted it with?]

61. Hieronymus Lauretus in his allegorical dictionary, which sums up known exegetical literature, does not know anything of the burning of the feathers either; cf. *Silva Allegoriarum totius Sacrae Scripturae* (1570); photomechanical reprint, ed. Friedrich Ohly (Munich: Fink, 1971), 125f.

62. Perhaps, the influence of the pictorial cosmos of alchemy cannot be excluded completely either.

63. Other motifs could have been transmitted by the printed editions of the encyclopaedia of Bartholomaeus Anglicus. As far as motifs that do not exclusively derive from the *Physiologus* are concerned, there are other possibilities as well.

64. Zincgref, no. 80.

PART 3
NEITHER MAN NOR BEAST

The Werewolf as *Eiron*

Freedom and Comedy in

William of Palerne

Norman Hinton

William of Palerne is a long alliterative poem; it may be the earliest, or the earliest survivor, of the fourteenth-century literary phenomenon known as the Alliterative Revival. It seems to be adapted from a somewhat older French poem in eight-syllable couplets, *Guillaume de Palerne*, though the English author has added a great deal of material which changes attitudes and plot elements.

The story of the poem is somewhat tangled, but it can be summarized fairly simply. The opening lines of the poem are missing in the sole manuscript, but assuming the plot is the same as that of *Guillaume de Palerne*, William, the son of the king of Sicily, is seized by a werewolf, who carries him off to the woods, swims the Straits of Messina with the child in its mouth, and settles near Rome. (The English manuscript begins at this point.) Sometime later, a cowherd finds William and takes him home, leaving the werewolf alone. When the Roman emperor rides by on a hunt, the wolf leads him to the cowherd's hut, where he finds the boy and takes him to his palace. William grows up there, fights in the emperor's wars, and falls in love with the emperor's daughter Meliors.

Because they cannot marry, William and Meliors don animal skins (at the behest of her servant Alisaundrine) and escape into the woods. There they are aided by the werewolf, who helps them evade the emperor's search parties and leads them to Sicily.

In Sicily, we learn that the werewolf is Alphouns, son of the king of Spain, who has been enchanted by his wicked stepmother so that her own son could inherit the throne. Alphouns is returned to human form by the repentant stepmother, and goes off to fight for Spain in its wars and to become its king. William similarly helps his father restore the kingdom of Sicily, and becomes king in turn. He and Meliors marry, rule the kingdom justly and fairly for the rest of their lives, take over the Roman Empire when her father the emperor dies, and have two sons, one of whom becomes emperor and the other becomes king of Sicily in his turn.

Perhaps *William of Palerne* would not be unthinkable without the werewolf: a werewolf-less plot would sound like a fairly standard romance narrative of loss and reinstatement. Without Alphouns the werewolf, the poem would very likely be unbearable with its stiff figures, almost frozen into conventional attitudes, sometimes devoid of interest or narrative subtlety. But with the werewolf, these aspects of the story take on a different coloration, as foils to the "witty werewolf" who rules the plot for so long.

Indeed, it has been argued by Tibbals[1] and Hibbard[2] that the werewolf is the central figure, even the hero, of the poem. A simple recital of the plot will show this is wrong: the narrative focus remains on William and Meliors throughout, and the werewolf's role is always supportive. (This and other refutations of Hibbard and Tibbals are found in McKeehan.[3]) But Tibbals and Hibbard are reacting to the intensity and vivacity of the werewolf and to the lack of those characteristics in William and Meliors.

Indeed, without the werewolf (and, as we shall see, his analog Alisaundrine), William seems almost frozen into painful inaction except on the battlefield (where his actions are reported but rarely displayed). He can neither resist nor surrender to the fires of love, but presents a figure beside whom Chaucer's Troilus seems a paragon of decision:

> Ac William to the window witterli might sene
> yif Meliors with hire maydenes in meleng there sete.
> Whan William under that trie tre hadde taken his place,
> he set his sight sadly to the windowe evene,
> bout flecchinge of feyntise, from morwe til eve,
> . . . .
> Siche a sorwe he suffred a sevennight fulle,
> that never mannes mete ne might in his bodi sinke,
> but held him finliche ifed his fille to loke
> on the mayde Meliors chaumbre. (*WP* 759–63, 766–9)[4]

> [William truly could see, at the window,
> If Meliors and her maidens sat there talking.
> When William had taken his place under the tree,
> He steadfastly set his sight on the window,
> Without wavering or faintness, from morning til night ,
> . . . .
> He suffered such sorrows a full week,

And no food entered his body,
But he took his fill completely by looking
At maid Meliors's chamber.]

Even his triumphs in battle seem somehow perfunctory:

And sothli forto seie, withinne a schort while
William with his owne hond so wightliche pleide,
that he slewe six of the grettest, soth forto telle. (WP 1195–7)

[And truth to tell, in a short while,
William, by his own hand, fought so manfully
That he slew six of the greatest warriors, to tell the truth.]

Heroic society is so stylized and incapable in this poem that characters simply die on cue, with no apparent reason or from shame:

the doughty duk of Saxonye, the duel that he made,
for his peple was slayn and to prison take,
and wist than he hade wrongly wrought thurgth his pride;
and swich duel drow to hert for his dedus ille,
that he deide on the fifte day, to talke the sothe. (WP 1318–22)

[The doughty Duke of Saxony had such suffering
because his people were slain and were put in prison,
and he thought that he had done badly because of his pride
so he died on the fifth day, to tell the truth.]

The author's insistence that he is reporting the truth may be as much a function of trying to create a sense of motivation for these cardboard figures as
it is a traditional oral formula.

Compared to these people, constricted by attitudes and postures, the werewolf is free: much of the time we see him rushing by on an errand, one that
usually serves also to further the plot's movement. (It is true that when the emperor of Rome goes hunting and is led to William, it is "a werewolf" that rushes
by [WP 214–5], but unless we assume that the woods near Rome are werewolf-
intensive, it seems likely that it is "our" werewolf that is moving the plot along.)

In *The Anatomy of Criticism* Northrop Frye distinguishes the groups
of characters found in classic comedy: the most famous of these groups are
the *alazons* ("imposters" or "blocking characters") and *eirons* ("self-

deprecators").[5] His Glossary defines *eiron* as "usually an agent of the happy ending."[6] He also connects the *eiron* figure to the "tricky slave" of Roman comedy and the "scheming valet" of Renaissance comedy: such characters include *Don Giovanni*'s Leporello, *Volpone*'s Mosca, and "the admirable Crichton." For Frye, the *eiron*s help to move the situation from wrong to right, from "opinion" to "knowledge."[7]

This is the movement of *William of Palerne* which, like many comedies, also moves from depredation to festivities and marriage (though like many romances, it devotes several hundred lines to the lives of the protagonists before the tale is ended).

This presentation of the werewolf as *dolosus servus*, or tricky servant, does not seem to be merely an accident of general resemblance: the English text of *William of Palerne* differs in many ways from the French *Guillaume de Palerne*.[8] While the numerous differences between the French and English texts cannot be readily classified, some of them are far more than simple variations. And while several critics have investigated these differences, none has focussed on the werewolf and his role.[9]

When William is removed from the werewolf's den by the cowherd, in the French text the werewolf behaves like a beast: he raves, howls, eats dirt, twists his feet together ("Et les piés ensamble detorde" [*GP* 236]), falls down, gets up, writhes, and so forth. In *William of Palerne* the werewolf "rore and rente al his hide / And fret oft of the erthe and fel doun on swowe / and made the most dool that man might divise" [roared and tore his skin / And ate the earth, and fell in a swoon / and made the most dole that one might devise] (*WP* 87–9), but he displays less than half of the French *loupgarou*'s melodramatic and frightful animal behaviors. Instead, after a few lines of manlike "dool," he follows the trail to the cowherd's house, and after spying through a peephole, he "thonked God mani thousand sithes, / and siththen went on is way" [thanked God many thousand times, / And then went on his way] (*WP* 103–4), acting rather like a 1930's B-movie mother whose lost child has been taken in by people better able to care for it. The French wolf makes a similar reconnaissance, but he does not, possibly cannot, thank God. The ability of *William of Palerne*'s werewolf to invoke God is just the first of many traits that set him apart from other medieval werewolves.

A much clearer change that speaks directly to the *eiron/dolosus servus* theme occurs when William and Meliors, disguised in bearskins, have reached the forest. In the French version (*GP* 3026–3235, passim), William speaks about their need for food and drink; the werewolf then obediently goes off and plays a trick on a passerby to obtain these. In *William of Palerne*, William makes no such analysis; instead, Meliors says that the lovers can live "bi frut

. . . that we finde in wodes as we wende aboute" [on fruit . . . that we find in the woods as we wander about] (*WP* 1831–2). The romance could have ended right here with the lovers' death by starvation, given William's and Meliors's ability to help themselves. However, the "witty werewolf" knows what they need: "the werewolf, as God wold, wist alle here happes" [the werewolf, as God willed, knew all their troubles] (*WP* 1840). After he "wist wher thei wolde rest" [learned where they should rest] (*WP* 1844) and "herd how hard for hunger thei him pleyned" [heard how hard they complained of hunger] (*WP* 1845), he sets out to do something about relieving their complaints. Ironically, though the royal lovers are disguised in bearskins, they have less than an animal instinct for survival in the forest. It is their animal companion the werewolf that assumes the human role of servant in order to save them.

The next section of the poem belongs entirely to the werewolf. Presumably William and Meliors would wander about the forest in their bearskins, living on nuts and berries, until they were found by her father or some other chance befell them. But the werewolf—who, like a good servant— knows everything, herds them toward Sicily where William can resume his place in society, supplies them with food, arranges for their sea passage, and generally creates the situations that allow the poem to move towards its conclusion, by playing a series of tricks on travellers, peasants, noblemen, and sailors. The tricks may not seem particularly complex, but they form a long set of variations on the general technique of "scream, leap, and run."

First the werewolf finds a peasant on the road:

> the werwolf ful wightli went to him evene
> with a rude roring, as he him rende wold,
> and braid him doun be the brest bolstraught to the erthe. (*WP* 1850–2)

> [the wolf went up to him full manly,
> with a rude roaring, as if he would tear the man to pieces,
> and pushed the man down by his breast bolt flat on the earth.]

It is hardly surprising that the peasant jumps up, runs off, and leaves his bags of food behind. Notice how the werewolf uses typical threatening animal behavior, such as roaring and springing to accomplish his "human" role as tricky servant. Now for drink:

> . . . a clerk of the cuntre com toward Rome
> with two flaketes ful of fine wynes,
> . . . .

the werwolf him awayted and went to him evene,
bellying as a bole that burnes wold spille. (*WP* 1887–8; 1890–1)

[A clerk of that country went toward Rome
with two flasks full of fine wine,

. . . .

the werewolf lay in wait for him and went straight to him,
roaring like a bull who wanted to kill folks.]

Comic clerks are notoriously cowardly: the sturdy peasant needs a good thumping, but a roar or two will do for the "clerk of the cuntre."

William and Meliors receive the provisions with a sense of wonder: "loo, whiche a grace God hath us schewed! . . . he sendeth us his sond to succor us atte nede"[10] [Lo, what grace God has shown us! He sends his messenger to help us in our need] (*WP* 1870–1), and they "make merie" with no thought of what to do next. They wander aimlessly through the woods in their bearskins, going nowhere in particular ("cairende over cuntres as here cas ferde" [wandering over countries as chance occurred] (*WP* 1922), but followed "wightly" by the werewolf. Every time they stop for the night, the werewolf, like a good servant, brings them "al maner thing that hem neded" [everything that they needed] (*WP* 1919).

Now the emperor sets greyhounds on their track, but this is a natural situation for the werewolf. As the hounds draw within bowshot of the lovers, the wolf, deciding to stake his life to save them (*WP* 2184), cries loudly and leads the dogs "over mountaynes and mires" (*WP* 2191), running so fast that "horse ne hounde for non hast ne might him oftake" [neither horse nor hound at any speed was able to overtake him] (*WP* 2198). What seems like a natural situation—hounds pursuing a wolf—takes on additional implications with the deliberate motivations of this particular wolf. Again, the werewolf successfully uses natural animal behavior to perform his "human" role as tricky servant.

William and Meliors, unwittingly led by the wolf ("that witty werewolf the wayes hem kenned" [*WP* 2212]), find themselves on the outskirts of Apulia, still wearing those bearskins. As they draw near Benevento, they are consumed with fear but do not (of course) know what to do. The provost and a large crowd come out to catch the bears. This calls for sterner measures; screaming and leaping, knocking people down and running off, may do for cleric, peasant, and hound, but the werewolf needs bolder measures in this situation. He "bethout how best the beress to save" [thought how best to save the bears] (*WP* 2370), and reverts to the werewolf behavior that opened the poem, at least in the French version ("devant le roi demainement / Son fils travers sa goule prent" [right in front of the King, / He seized his son by the throat] (*GP* 89–90):

[The werewolf] wightly as a wode best went hem ayens,
gapand ful grimli, and goth thanne ful evene
to the semli provost sone, and swithe him up caught
be the middel in his mouthe, that muche was and large,
and ran forth for al that route. (WP 2371–5)

(The wolf,) just like a mad beast, confronted them,
(his mouth) gaping very grimly, and goes right up
to the provost's seemly son, and quickly caught him up
by the waist in his large mouth,
and ran away before all that company.]

He runs for half a mile, stops to let the pursuers come near, then runs
again; he repeats this "alle the longe daie," then sets the child down and
"went wightly aweie." While the werewolf seems not even winded by this,
the excitement exhausts Meliors (who has gone nowhere) so much that they
spend two days recovering. But the bear disguises are well known: appropriately, the wolf brings the hunted lovers the skins of a hart and a hind to
wear instead (WP 2604–10).

The trio resumes its journey, but now instead of the lovers' aimless
wandering followed by the werewolf, he directs the noble couple to Sicily:

... here semli werewolf sewed fast after
that wittily taught hem the weies whider thei wende scholde
sechande towards Cisile the sotilest weyes.
. . . .
thei went fast on here way: the werewolf hem ladde. (WP 2601–3; 2618)

[... their handsome werewolf followed fast after them,
who, through his wits, showed them the routes they should go
seeking towards Sicily by the subtlest ways.
. . . .
they went quickly on their way: the werewolf led them.]

William, Meliors, and the werewolf come to the Straits of Messina,
where they wait until the guards are asleep and the sailors have gone on
liberty (WP 2736–7), then sneak on board a ship to hide amidst the cargo.
The werewolf has to play decoy one last time, and again the animal skin
disguises prove problematic to the lovers, who are now pursued as hind
and hart. Meliors almost does not escape:

the werewolf was wily, and went so soft,
the schipmen wend wel at wille him take,
and him all seweden that to the schip longed,
but a barlegged bold boie that to the barge yemed
· ·
and bethought him there the bestes for to quelle.
And happili to the hinde he hit thanne formest,
and set hire a sad stroke so sore in the necke,
that sche top over tail tombled over the hacches. (*WP* 2764–7, 2773–6)

[The werewolf was wily, and moved so slowly,
that the sailors thought they could take him at will,
and all those in the ship followed him,
except a bare-legged boy that belonged to the barge
· ·
who thought that he would kill the beasts.
And luckily then, he hit the hind first,
and set her a sad stroke so hard in the neck
that she tumbled top over tail among the hatches.]

This time William must actually bestir himself and catch Meliors before she falls into the sea. The werewolf's last trick exhausts his repertoire
and almost fails. This does not lower William's opinion of his wolf, however: "God mowe we thonk / and oure worthi werewolf" [God must we
thank / and our worthy werewolf] (*WP* 2795–6). The werewolf has one
last task: he leads William and Meliors to the castle of Palerne where these
two ornamental creatures appropriately take their place in the castle's pleasure park:

and ever as the witty werwolf wold hem lede,
he brought hem to a borwgh that bold was and riche,
and fairest of all fason for eny riche holde
that ever man upon molde might on loke.
Perles was the paleis, and Palerne it hight.
· ·
A pris place was under the paleys, a park as it were,
· ·
the hert and the hind there thanne hem hed sone,
as the werwolf hem wissed, that ay was here gye.
(*WP* 2834–8, 2845, 2848–9)

[and always the witty werewolf led them,
and he came to a city that was mighty and rich,
and fairest among any kind of rich keep:
that ever man on earth might see.
that palace was peerless: it was called Palerne.

. . . .

There was a fine place next to the palace, like a park,

. . . .

the hart and the hind hid there at once,
as the werewolf suggested, who was always their guide.]

The werewolf's task is accomplished: it has occupied almost half of the poem. The dolosus servus's antics have been carefully orchestrated and kept largely within the bounds of animal behavior (roaring, threatening, pouncing, and running) and they are not subtle. But no one claimed that physical comedy in the Middle Ages had to be subtle and complex to be successful.

This center of the poem presents the werewolf in a guise that is closest to Frye's tricky servant. He anticipates or outdoes the lovers' desires; he guides them when they do not know where they want to go or even that going is necessary; he manages to get them across the Straits of Messina; and he brings them exactly to where they need to be to start the plot on its way to resolution.

The werewolf even learns sign language and communicates it to William and Meliors, not so that they can tell him what to do, but so that *he* can tell *them* what to do: "bi certeyn signes sone he hem taught; / and thei folowed him fayre, fayn for that grace" [he soon taught them using certain signs; / and they followed him, desirous of that grace] (*WP* 2740–1). Note who is teaching whom: in this situation, we not only ask who is really master and who servant, but also ask which is the greater intelligence, human or animal? The werewolf is described as "witty" over and over again (e.g., lines 145, 158, 2204, 2212, 2403, 2448), but this epithet is used only twice to describe people (4134, 5493), one of whom is the werewolf's wicked stepmother.

"Wit," of course, does not mean "humor" but a kind of outgrowth of indwelling intelligence (and possibly sometimes grace). William and Meliors display very little of either quality, nor do the other humans come off much better: the emperor stares blankly at Meliors's empty bedroom, from which she has obviously fled; peasants walk through forests trying not to find wolves and then flee in terror when they do; everyone, it seems, runs after the wolf whenever he wants them to. Frye has noted how often, in comedies with tricky servants, the servants seem to be the central characters *except* when one relates the plot, so that *A Night at the Opera*, for instance, is a tale of young lovers overcoming adversity—if you just forget about the Marx Brothers.

From this point on, the tone of the poem alters. As the werewolf comes closer to returning to human form as Alphouns of Spain, he begins to act like other werewolves of medieval fiction: when he is brought into the presence of his wicked stepmother, for example, his behavior has reminded many readers of the betrayed shape-shifter of Marie de France's *Bisclaveret*, attacking the queen as Marie's wolf attacks his wife, who has deserted him and left him in his wolf aspect.[11]

This reversion to "werewolf mode" poses one of the difficult questions about Alphouns: when he was a werewolf, what did he retain of his humanity? The Hollywood notion of "human by day, wolf by night" does not apply here (nor was Alphouns bitten by some other werewolf, nor is there even a trace of wolfbane). This behavior, brought in from other werewolf texts (and the first such behavior since the wolf's fit of anger and sorrow when the cowherd takes the child William from his den, which is also borrowed from the French text), may mark a return to the normal world of romance and its rules. Certainly Alphouns has more intelligence than an animal, but nothing in his behavior seems to indicate to William and Meliors that he is more than a wolf: indeed, when the wolf once again becomes Alphouns, William is puzzled and asks who this naked man might be (*WP* 4505ff.). He is, they finally learn, the son of the king of Spain.

This high position raises a prickly question that modern readers may not immediately grasp: if Alphouns is a prince of Spain, does he not outrank William, who is merely prince of Palerne? How can he have been William's servant, even though he was not human at the time? The queen of Palerne recognizes the possible social predicament:

> "Swete sire, saie me now, so you Crist help,
> what gom wol ye that you give your garnemens nouthe?
> ye ne tok never, as I trowe, of knighthod the hordere;
> forthi thow telle me of whom ye take it thenk." (*WP* 4459–62)

> ["Sweet sir, tell me now, as Christ is your help,
> what man will you pick to give your (knightly) equipment now?
> So far as I know, you never took the order of knighthood:
> tell me from whom you intend to take it."]

So Alphouns has not been a higher-ranking nobleman while serving as *eiron* to William, and all the social niceties have been preserved! This nice distinction may well seem more comic to us than it did to the poem's audience, but it does in fact mark the end of Alphouns's service to William, as well as the end of the comic strain in the poem. As he loses his animal form and regains his human guise, Alphouns too becomes trapped in the conventional attitudes and postures that have stultified the human characters throughout the poem.

The rest of the work is situated steadfastly in the world of the aristocratic romance: the plot is concerned with marriages, military operations, and the tying-up of loose ends in the background plot, which deals with lands laid waste by war and with the required restoration of order and peace.

As the loose ends of the plot are tied up, Meliors's confidante Alisaundrine reappears: she has been absent from the story for almost 3,500 lines. Alisaundrine plays a sort of female version or equivalent of Alphouns: she directs William's and Meliors's love-longing to its fulfillment by means of herbs and dreams, and finally brings the lovers together much as Pandarus with Troilus and Criseyde. Like Alphouns, she is sensible and active, while William and Meliors are ineffective if not downright mopey. She not only brings the love story to its required end but, like Alphouns, she plays a role in deceiving the emperor so that the lovers can escape. It is she who suggests that the lovers put on bearskins, a device that has brought occasional snorts of disgust from critics who seem to want the poem to be "realistic," but one that is very much in keeping with the *eiron* world of disguise and trickery.

While the werewolf as tricky servant is only part of *William of Palerne*, it is the longest and the most memorable part, and it gives the poem a tone often lacking in romance: a tone of comedy, of good common sense as expressed by *eirons* from Sancho Panza to Molière's comic maids, a sense that if the plot were left to the nobles, it would never get done. *William of Palerne* is remarkable in this, and quite rewarding to read because of it, though critics who apparently have not noticed this aspect tend to be annoyed with the poem, if not downright severe.[12]

As a means of judging how remarkable *William of Palerne*'s *eiron* werewolf is, let us take a quick look at another werewolf, who may be more typical of contemporary thought about lycanthropy. This one appears in "Of men who become wolves" from the *Otia Imperialia* of Gervaise of Tilbury:

> The question is often put forth among the learned, of whether Nabuchodonosar, in the time of punishment set for him, was truly changed into an ox by divine power. . . . I know of one case . . . in which a man was changed by madness into a wolf.
>
> For we know . . . of a nobleman in Alvernia . . . strenuous in the arts of war and the exercise of arms. He became a wanderer and a

fugitive, and alone, like a wild animal, wandered in lonely places: one night, perturbed by too much fear, with his mind alienated, he turned into a wolf. . . . In wolf's form he devoured infants, but he tore old people into wild beast's morsels. He was gravely wounded by a wood-cutter, when a blow of an ax cut off one of his feet, at which time he immediately resumed human form.[13]

This story is so unlike *William of Palerne*'s werewolf that we can perhaps see the other boundary of high medieval werewolf stories. The unfortunate Alvernian knight has been disinherited (*exhaeredasse*) and, in a state of lonely and nervous alienation, goes mad and becomes a wolf. His behavior is that of the "textbook" werewolf, his ravenousness truly and mercilessly animal in nature as he preys on the young and the old in their helplessness. Alphouns also seizes children, not to devour them (though he probably hopes that the provost and his army will fear this) but to carry them off to a place of safety. His animal behavior serves a humane and human purpose in his role as tricky servant. Moreover, Alphouns's wolf form is a result of enchantment; in a sense, he is a Sleeping Beauty figure though not at all in repose, a positive figure who is identified with God and grace throughout the poem, a figure who probably would have outwitted the peasant woodcutter who may very well have cut off his own foot if he'd been a character in *William of Palerne* instead of the *Otia Imperialia*.

Thus we see that these typical werewolf motifs, like the pseudo-transformation of the lovers into bears and then deer, are transmuted in *William of Palerne* into something far more fascinating than simple tales about ferocious wolves. *William of Palerne* resonates with many other medieval works while resembling none of them: it is not like *Troilus and Criseyde* or *Bisclaveret* or *Lai de Melion* or *Roman de Renart Contrefait* or any of the other works cited occasionally by scholars. *William of Palerne*'s wolf has been cited (by Dunn[14]) as Stith Thompson's Helpful Animal, but his submerged humanity carries him far beyond the various helpful birds and animals from Celtic folklore and elsewhere that form the ten entries in the *Motif-Index* (all referenced in Dunn).

There is no poem like *William of Palerne*, not even, as we have seen, *Guillaume de Palerne*. No one could argue that the poet knew the New Comedy whose *eirons* Frye describes, and indeed, a full-blown tricky slave from New Comedy could hardly avoid turning to us on occasion to denounce the shallow, static society to which Alphouns so eagerly returns. It is not a matter of influence or derivation, any more than the appearance of braggarts or dupes in Chaucer means that he read Aristophanes. But approaching *William of Palerne* by way of its werewolf shows us a delightful and memorable character, a Mosca out of his time, a Brainworm without humours. Perhaps medieval culture was not devoid of such characters, as Feste suggested to Malvolio:

> "I'll be with you again,
>> In a trice,
> Like to the old Vice,
>> Your need to sustain." (*Twelfth Night*, IV: ii, 131–5)

NOTES

1. Kate Watkins Tibbals, "Elements of Magic in the Romance of *William of Palerne*," *Modern Philology* 1 (1903–4), 355–71, passim.

2. Laura Hibbard, *Mediaeval Romance in England: A Study of the Sources and Analogues of the Non-Cycle Romances* (Oxford: Oxford University Press, 1924), 217.

3. Irene McKeehan, "*Guillaume de Palerne*, A Medieval 'Best Seller,'" *Publications of the Modern Language Association* 41 (1926), 785–809.

4. G.H.V. Bunt, ed., *William of Palerne: An alliterative romance* (Groningen: Bouma's Buikhuis, 1985). I have also made use of, though there are no direct quotes from, N.T. Simms, *William of Palerne* (Norwood, Pa.: Norwood Press, variously dated 1973 and 1977). The section rather obscurely titled "Notes on Translation" (269–324) compares the English text of *William of Palerne* to the French text of *Guillaume de Palerne* (see note 8 below for reference) on a line-by-line basis. This section has been very helpful to me, though I have not used any of Simms's conclusions about the literary effect of the differences between texts.

5. Northrop Frye, *Anatomy of Criticism: Four Essays* (Princeton: Princeton Univ. Press, 1957), especially 170–8.

6. Frye, 345.

7. In Frye's terms, from *pistis* to *gnosis*.

8. Alexandre Micha, ed., *Guillaume de Palerne, Roman du xiiie Siècle*, Textes Littéraires Français (Geneva: Droz, 1990).

9. See, e.g., Dieter Mehl, *Die mittelenglischen Romanzen des 13. und 14. Jahrhunderts*, Anglistische Forschungen 47 (Heidelberg, 1968); Max Kaluzá, "Das mittelenglischen Gedicht *William of Palerne* und seine franzische Quelle," *Englische Studien* 4 (1881), 266ff.; John Finlayson, "Definitions of Middle English Romance," *Chaucer Review* 15 (1980), 171.

10. "Sond" here can mean "message," "grace," or "disposition": in any case, it refers to the wolf.

11. For comparisons of *William of Palerne* to *Bisclaveret* and to almost every other medieval werewolf story, cf. C.W. Dunn, *The Foundling and the Werewolf: A Literary History of Guillaume de Palerne*, University of Toronto Department of English Studies and Texts 8 (Toronto: University of Toronto Press, 1980).

12. George Kane has been particularly harsh toward *William of Palerne*'s plot while praising its characters in *Middle English Literature: A Critical Study of the Romances, the Religious Lyrics, Piers Plowman* (London: Methuen, 1951), 51–2.

13. Felix Liebrecht, *Des Gervasius von Tilbury Otia Imperialia* (Hanover: C. Rumpler, 1856), 51, my translation. The Latin text of "Tertia Decisio. CXX De Hominibus, qui fuerunt lupi" is as follows:

> Saepe apud doctores quaestio movetur, si Nabuchodonosar per injunctum tempus poenitentiae in bovem verum sit divina virtute mutatus. . . . Unus scio

... quidam per lunationes mutantur in lupos. Scimus enim ... in Alvernia ... militem strenuissimus et in armis excertitatum.

Hic vagus factus et profugus ... cum solus more ferino devia lustraret et saltus, una nocte nimio timore turbatus, cum mentis alienatione in lupum versus. ... Infantas in forma lupina devoravit; sed et grandaevos ferinis morsibus lacerabat. Tandem a fabro quodam lignario graviter attentatus, ictu securis alterum pedem perdidit, sicque specie resumta hominem induit.

14. Lists of various Stith Thompson folk motifs may be found in Dunn, passim.

Gargoyles

Animal Imagery and Artistic Individuality in Medieval Art

Janetta Rebold Benton

Animal imagery appears frequently in the art of medieval western Europe. Animals, like so many other subjects in the art of the Middle Ages, were often used as didactic devices in the teaching of Christianity. Widespread illiteracy encouraged use of imagery that was easily understood, visually striking, and memorable. The need for readily intelligible imagery fostered, understandably, conformity and convention rather than individuality and invention—open expression of personal artistic style cannot be considered a characteristic of medieval art. Rather, a medieval artist was an artisan, working anonymously within the guild system. Careful craftsmanship was desired; deviation from standard representation was not.

Figure 1. Gargoyle showing trough along back, courtyard, Hotel of the Catholic Kings, Santiago de Compostela.

Figure 2. *Monk pouring water from barrel, gargoyle, cloister, former cathedral of Saint-Etienne, Toul.*

Figure 3. *"Vomiting" gargoyle holding abdomen, west facade, church of Notre-Dame, Semur-en-Auxois.*

But ego, and the need for its visual assertion, seem to be innate components of the *human* animal. Certain types of animal imagery offered medieval artists rare opportunities for individual expression—opportunities that seem to have been seized and relished. This essay is not concerned with readily recognizable animals that play well-understood and conspicuous roles in Christian art, such as the lion, lamb, or fish. Rather, the focus is on the unusual or imaginary animals that play questionable roles, often in inconspicuous locations, specifically, as gargoyles.

Gargoyles are a characteristic feature of medieval architecture, in particular, of that created during the Gothic era in western Europe. The English term *gargoyle* may be translated into Italian as *grónda sporgente*, an architecturally descriptive phrase meaning "protruding gutter." The German *wasserspeier* describes what the gargoyle appears to do; he is a "water spitter." But the French *gargouille*, connected with the verb *gargariser* (to gargle), is surely the most evocative of these terms.

The true gargoyle is an elaborate waterspout, an architectural necessity turned into ornament, a functional fantasy. A trough runs along the back of the creature, as demonstrated in figure 1 by a view looking down on a gargoyle in one of the four courtyards of the Hotel of the Catholic Kings in Santiago de Compostela. Rainwater, rather than running down the masonry walls and eroding the mortar between the stones, is thrown clear of the wall as it pours from the creature's mouth. The many gargoyles on medieval buildings serve a practical role. Thus, on a sunny day, the gargoyles may glower down at you, but on a rainy day they spit.

In spite of the fact that the functional role of a water spout would be served quite as well by a simple half-cylinder, gargoyles became an area of artistic focus. The concentration of creativity on waterspouts, demonstrated by gargoyles, could be argued to be impractical for reasons beyond the usual concerns for economy of time and money. For although some gargoyles are located within easy viewing distance, a great many more are positioned so that they appear to peer down from the highest rooflines and pinnacles. The twentieth-century viewer may benefit from the illusion of proximity produced by field glasses. The armchair traveler studying gargoyles via illustrations in books and journals is served by the capabilities of the photographers' telephoto lens. But the ordinary earthbound visitors of the Middle Ages, few of whom even had eyeglasses, would have had little visual access to many of the gargoyles.

Gargoyles constitute a particularly puzzling category of the art of the Middle Ages—an era replete with artistic peculiarities. Several questions are discussed in the following pages: Which images were used for gargoyles—

and which were not? What was the meaning of gargoyles to the people of the Middle Ages? Finally, for whom were gargoyles intended?

This essay will not address the issue of restoration or replacement of specific gargoyles. It is understandable, and unfortunate, that gargoyles, because of their exterior location and projecting shape, are especially vulnerable to erosion and other forms of damage. Thus, while not all gargoyles on medieval buildings are medieval in manufacture, and much restoration work has been done in the nineteenth century, it may be hoped that the later carvers worked in the spirit of their medieval predecessors.[1]

WHICH IMAGES WERE USED FOR GARGOYLES—AND WHICH WERE NOT

Gargoyles routinely take the form of animals—real and imaginary, human and otherwise. Some types were rarely used while others appear with significant frequency.

Only occasionally were gargoyles carved in the form of real people. Religious personages seem not to have been represented, nor is there firm evidence that specific secular individuals were portrayed. When people are shown, they

Figure 4. "Defecating" gargoyle, south side, cathedral of Saint-Lazare, Autun.

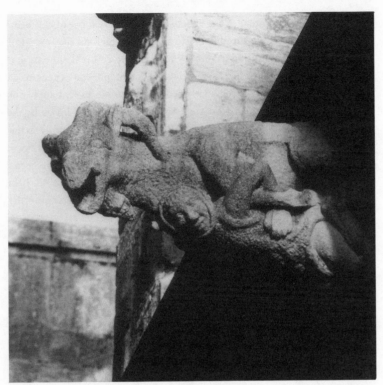

Figure 5. Smiling woman and goat, gargoyle, north side, church of Notre-Dame-des-Marais, Villefranche-sur-Saône.

are more often bizarre than beautiful, their behavior more likely laughable than laudable. Indeed, in view of their location on churches and cathedrals, their behavior is striking—in some cases bordering on the bawdy, in others going far beyond. Some stone people seem intent on attacking the real people, as in the cloister beside the former cathedral of Saint-Etienne in Toul, where gargoyles are poised to pour their water from barrels onto the unwary below (figure 2). In other cases, there is a strong implication that something other than rainwater spews forth: some gargoyles grasp their abdomens or throats as if vomiting, as on the facade of the church of Notre-Dame in Semur-en-Auxois (figure 3), while an extraordinary gargoyle in the form of a nude man on the south side of the cathedral of Saint-Lazare in Autun appears to defecate (figure 4).

Humans and animals may appear together, as evidenced by the antics of a woman and a goat, both smiling as they emerge from the shadows on the north side of Notre-Dame-des-Marais in Villefranche-sur-Saône (figure 5). During the Middle Ages, artists depicted the devil in, among other forms, that of a goat, an animal associated with lechery and license.

Realistic renderings of actual animals, like those of real people, were not often used as gargoyles. The stone bulls high on the towers of the cathedral of Laon provide a noteworthy example of real animals in medieval architectural sculpture. These, however, do not function as genuine gargoyles, and their presence here is explained by circumstances that apply only to this specific monument. Laon's towers, long touted, were drawn by the master mason Villard de Honnecourt while he was traveling in France in the 1230s.[2] Attributed to Villard is the statement of praise, "J'ai été en beaucoup de terres, nulle part n'ai vu plus belles tours qu'a Laon" [I have been in many lands, nowhere have I seen more beautiful towers than at Laon]. Laon's laudable bovine bounty is actually a public display of gratitude on the part of the people of this city. The materials used in the construction of the cathedral had been hauled by bulls to the top of the ridge on which the cathedral was built. It was not uncommon in the Middle Ages to honor saints by putting their images along the roofline of the church; at Laon, the bulls were elevated to a similarly prestigious position.[3]

Real animals may be used as gargoyles, but differing from Laon's bulls, they appear singly rather than as a group of the same animal—gargoyles are characteristically individual and unique in form. Remaining at Laon cathedral, an airborne boar (figure 6) demonstrates the use of a real animal as a gargoyle. The wild and domesticated animals used as gargoyles provide a permanent and indisputable inventory of the animals familiar to the people of the Middle Ages.

Animals that were *not* familiar to western Europe in the Middle Ages also serve as gargoyles. The appearance of a specific exotic animal, like the specific domestic animal (Laon's bulls), may have a specific explanation. Thus, the presence of the monkey gargoyle in the courtyard of Jacques Coeur's house in Bourges (figure 7), like the exotic trees carved in relief there, may be presumed to refer to the extensive travels undertaken by the owner.

However, the frequent use of lions and lionlike animals as gargoyles—as at the church of Thaxted, England (figure 8)—would appear to be due to the general popularity of lions in medieval art; among the many images of animals created during the Middle Ages, the lion was portrayed with the greatest frequency. The distinguishing feature of the lion, to artists who had little possibility of firsthand contact with lions, was the mane, used on lions as well as lionesses.[4] The lion's popularity goes back to antiquity, when he was already referred to as the "king of beasts" and lion heads were already used as waterspouts. The lion of antiquity was adopted into Christian iconography, and his characteristics adapted to Christian teachings. The

Figure 6. Boar, gargoyle, north side, cathedral of Notre-Dame, Laon.

Figure 7. Monkey, gargoyle, courtyard, house of Jacques Coeur, Bourges.

Figure 8. Lion, gargoyle, north side, church of Thaxted, England.

lion became a symbol of Christ: the Lion of the Tribe of Judah. The medieval lion's characteristics were linked to (or invented to correspond with) those of Christ. Thus, the lion was said to erase his tracks with his tail, and this "fact" connected with Christ's ability to elude the devil. The lion was said to sleep with his eyes open, and was therefore an emblem of vigilance. For this reason, images of lions serve as guardians at the entryway to churches and at tombs. The lioness supposedly gives birth to dead cubs, which are resurrected three days later by the father lion—a parallel to the resurrection of Christ by His Father. The lion is faithful to his spouse and to humans and others who have helped him. He does not become angry unless wounded, spares the fallen, and does not overeat—he is a model for human behavior. The lion's regal bearing and power in combat made him a favorite heraldic emblem. Only infrequently was the lion shown in an unfavorable light in medieval art.[5]

Rarely, if ever, used as gargoyles, in spite of their popularity for other uses in medieval art, were the so-called monstrous races of mankind. Inventions of antiquity, the monstrous races were created in various ways. Parts of the human body could be replaced with animal parts. The *cynocephali*, for example, are dog-headed people who communicate by barking. Alternatively, the size of parts of the body could be changed. Thus, the *panotii* are Dumbo-like people with ears so enormous that they can be used to fly away when the owner is frightened or as a blanket when the owner is cold. The *sciopods* have a single enormous foot, serviceable as an umbrella when the owner lies on his back and raises the foot aloft. A number of these amaz-

Figure 9. Harpy/siren, gargoyle, north side, church of Saint-Etienne, Cahors.

Figure 10. Composite monster, gargoyle, west facade, cathedral of Saint-Pierre, Poitiers.

ing anatomical anomalies achieved by unnatural amalgamation are carved on the celebrated twelfth-century tympanum in the narthex of the church of Sainte-Madeleine in Vézelay. The subject here, the Mission of the Apostles (Acts 11:9–11), required a portrayal of Christ instructing His apostles to spread His word to all the different peoples believed to live on the distant parts of the earth.[6]

Certain types of composite creatures were, like the monstrous races, also of antique origin and also not typically used as gargoyles. These include such creatures as the siren/harpy (human plus bird), centaur (human plus horse), satyr (human plus goat), and triton/mermaid (human plus fish). Although each has the head and torso of a human, these were regarded as animals and were distinguished from the monstrous races of mankind. The physiognomies and personalities of the antique hybrids became standardized by centuries of use as they produced significant medieval progeny in sculpture, wall painting, manuscript illumination, metal and enamel work, tapestry, and stained glass.[7] A rare example of such a creature as a gargoyle is the harpy/siren on the north side of Saint-Etienne in Cahors (figure 9).

Most gargoyles are in the form of completely bizarre beasts—unknown, unnamed, unspecified species. Indeed, gargoyles provide some of the most splendid specimens of fantastic fauna fabricated in the Middle Ages, an era known for multitudes of monsters. These gargoyles cannot be construed as misunderstood versions of actual animals that artists working in medieval western Europe had little opportunity to observe directly. Instead, these implausible animal amalgamations were created by disassembling the parts of known animals and reassembling them in ways *un*known to Mother Nature. This method of expanding Nature's repertoire was noted above to have been employed in antiquity, but reached its peak of popularity in the Middle Ages. Some of these composite creatures are witty, amusing, and clever; others, frightening or unnerving; and many are ugly—art was not always in the service of beauty in the Middle Ages.[8]

Nor was art necessarily in the service of nature. It is certain that artists did not view animal imagery as an obligation for realistic imitation of actual creatures. Rather, much like the artist's model book, nature was a source of inspiration. Just as any motif found in the model book could be copied in isolation, any part of an actual animal—beak, wings, claws, tail—could be used without the rest of that animal.

Gargoyles represent a realm into which composite creatures were welcomed. Among the most implausible assemblages of unrelated animals' parts is that demonstrated by a gargoyle on the cathedral of Saint-Pierre in Poitiers (figure 10). With the mane and claws of a lion, the wings of a bird, and the head of a human, he might claim a lineage that descends from the majestic sphinx of antiquity, were it not for his open mouth, fangs flashing, and his mouth-pulling companion below. The conception of such as creature is possible only within the extremely fertile human imagination. The medieval sculptor seems to display his dissatisfaction with the limitation of Mother Nature's already abundant inventions.

Because gargoyles are common adornments on churches but do not represent obviously religious subjects, their meaning has long been a subject of debate. The eminent iconographer Emile Mâle questioned the meaning of gargoyles, determining "that conceptions of this kind are of essentially popular origin. The gargoyles . . . came from the depths of people's consciousness, and had grown out of their ancient fireside tales . . . memories of their forefathers, echoes of a vanished world."[9] Images of monsters carried in street processions on feast days, as well as grotesque figures used in the mystery plays and in holiday celebrations such as the Feast of Fools, have been suggested as sources for gargoyle imagery. Gargoyles have been linked to passages in the Bible, to excavations of prehistoric animals, and even to the constellations.[10] It has been argued that gargoyles were meant to scare evils away from the church, to be symbolic of sins forbidden from entering the church, or to represent devils overcome by the church and now made to serve the church as waterspouts.[11] This is the position taken by, among others, Abbé Charles Auguste Auber in the later nineteenth century.[12] But Ronald Sheridan and Anne Ross argue against the idea that gargoyles symbolize evil outside the church from which worshippers were safe on the inside, correctly noting that horrifying figures appear inside the church, too, although they are fewer in number and more discrete in location. Grotesques as a whole, suggest Sheridan and Ross, are pagan survivors.[13] Michael Camille says, "The gargoyle is all body and no soul—a pure projector of filth. . . ."[14] But this view causes one to wonder why, then, do some gargoyles direct their water into the cloister (as at Toul)? And why would rainwater, coming from heaven, be regarded as filth? Water cleanses. Water is used in baptism. Luckily, however, both points of view can be satisfied by a description found in the *Roman d'Abladane*[15] of two "gargoules" on the gateway of Amiens that are said to be able to evaluate the motivation of each person who came into the city. Upon those who came with bad intentions, the gargoyles spit a venom so horrible that anyone covered with it died. But when the lord of the city came, one of the gargoyles threw down gold and the other silver.[16]

No matter what substance they are assumed to spew, it is certain that a great many medieval gargoyles bear a mean and menacingly monstrous mein. It therefore seems justifiable to suggest that in some cases, the grotesque physiognomy of the gargoyles was intended to intimidate or frighten. The preoccupation of medieval Christianity with sin and the eternal fate of one's soul, coupled with the general absence of literacy among the populace and the consequent emphasis on the didactic use of visual imagery, resulted in the creation of many monsters in medieval art.

Animal imagery that was certainly meant to frighten appears in forms other than gargoyles. For example, representation of the Mouth of Hell gave medieval artists the opportunity to create some of their most horrifying images. At Sainte-Foy in Conques, the depiction of the Last Judgment on the tympanum includes a vicious wolflike Mouth of Hell in which the feet of one victim are still visible as the next enters, head first. In the equivalent position on the facade of Bourges Cathedral, sinners simmer in a cauldron heated by the flames rising from the Mouth of Hell. The visitor to Bourges Cathedral was repeatedly reminded of the horrors of hell, since once one was inside the cathedral, the same imagery was encountered at the opposite end in stained glass, where brightly colored devils delight in assisting the descent of the damned.[17] The Hellmouth on a double capital from Saint-Guilhem-le-Desert (now in The Cloisters, New York) is a monstrous animal devouring the damned with wall-to-wall teeth as his fiery breath—the flames of hell—singes the sinner.[18] In the *Psalter of Henry of Blois*, now in the British Museum, an angel uses a key to lock the damned into an extraordinary double Mouth of Hell, which has tiny monsters in place of horns—and in many other places (MS. Cotton Nero CIV, fol. 39r). The illuminator of the *Cloisters Apocalypse*, in The Cloisters collection, depicted the dragon and the beasts of the Apocalypse in the tearing teeth of several hairy Hellmouths, one of whom flashes an evil grin (68.174, fol. 35r).[19]

The Mouth of Hell was certainly not the only example of a menacing monster in medieval art. Fantastic animals viciously attack their human victims on the facades of the churches of Notre-Dame in Neufchatel-en-Bray and Saint-Pierre in Beaulieu[20] and on many other medieval monuments, leaving little doubt as to the meaning intended by the medieval artist.

Demons were frequently shown as monstrous combinations of animals. For example, a demon in the Combat of Demons on a nave capital at the church of Sainte-Madeleine in Vézelay is compiled from the mane and claws of a lion, the wings of a bird, the face of a walrus, and the tail of a serpent.[21]

Evil may be portrayed by a person who is deformed in some way as to appear hideous or repulsive. On a nave capital at Autun Cathedral, the devil of Simon Magus is shown to be a horned and homely humanoid with clawed feet.[22] John's Revelation (16:13–14) says, "And I saw three unclean spirits like frogs come out of the mouth of the dragon, and out of the mouth of the beast, and out of the mouth of the false prophet. For they are the spirits of devils." Thus the relief of a frog with a woman's head, carved in the cloister of the cathedral of Le Puy, would seem to illustrate the medieval belief that women led men into sin. The extensive relief frieze in the Le Puy clois-

Figure 11. Hairy human with animal head, gargoyle, cathedral of Burgos, Spain.

ter depicts many creatures, including a human with a cat's head and tail that is bitten by a dog, in response to which the cat shrieks in pain. Sinful people who succumb to temptation are shown to be transformed into animals—lower forms of beings.[23]

Perhaps it is for this reason that the monstrous gargoyles, although compiled mostly of animals parts, will often retain something human.[24] Examples are offered by a hairy human with animal feet and head at Burgos cathedral (figure 11) and by a human who is literally "pig-headed" in the cloister beside the former cathedral of Saint-Etienne in Toul (figure 12).

Carefully crafting in a variety of media, the artists of the Middle Ages made permanent images of the inhabitants of our nightmares—those imagined horrors we hope will vanish upon waking. This fascination with the frightful was due in part to the fact that the "job description" of the medieval artist included correcting public behavior through visual intimidation. The physical deformations and torments in hell that were the result of sin were depicted as clearly as possible, the artist sparing no effort to maximize the didactic impact of his images. The viewer was strongly encouraged to think twice about the ramifications of his or her behavior, for as was noted in the Middle Ages, if love of God were insufficient as a deterrent to sin, perhaps fear of hell would be more effective. The similarity between the examples of monstrous creatures noted here to represent hell (the devil, or evil in general) and the monstrous gargoyles suggests that these gargoyles may have played similar roles.

Yet the impression conveyed was certainly not the same for all gargoyles. Those that appear to vomit or defecate (figures 3 and 4) may produce a sense of fear in the viewer, but it is not the viewer's eternal soul that is being threatened. A response very different from fear is elicited by certain gargoyles that must have appeared as delightfully entertaining in the Middle Ages as they do today. For example, the gargoyles that surround the cloister at Toul are positioned so they appear to eavesdrop on the monks chatting in the cloister below, or to read over their shoulders. A stone monk here empties the contents of his barrel onto his fellow monks (figure 2).[25] The pig-headed man here has been muzzled (figure 12). And surely the "spitting images," such as the enthusiastic creature from Thaxted seen in figure 8, were as amusing when it rained in medieval England as they are today under the same weather conditions. Further arguing against an exclusively religious interpretation for all gargoyles is the simple fact that they were used not only on religious architecture but also on homes, such as that of Jacques Coeur in Bourges (figure 7).

It becomes apparent that the gargoyles are not consistent in symbolic or emotional connotation. Instead, gargoyles were intentionally and unusually varied in form and meaning. Indeed, current questions about the meaning of the gargoyles may be regarded as a perpetuation of the medieval acceptance of, if not preference for, layered meaning. The medieval affection for ambiguity of interpretation allowed for a multiplicity of meanings that are neither black nor white; gray was enjoyed also, if not more so. Further, it is not unlikely that the gargoyles were interpreted differently at different times, and perhaps also by different people living at the same time. It is probable, however, that gargoyles have been, are, and will be appreciated by all people at all times as a most intriguing type of architectural embellishment. This leads to the third question.

For Whom Were Gargoyles Intended?

Taken as a whole, gargoyles do not seem to have been intended to contribute to the education of the medieval populace in Christian beliefs. Visual imagery, though a universal language, must be readily intelligible if it is to function didactically. This necessity is the mother not of *invention* but of *convention*; repetition enhances familiarity, which enhances recognition. The fact that the gargoyles are so very varied in form argues against their use as instructive devices. Although a caption would serve to explain the meaning

of a unique image to the literate, the written word was unintelligible to the majority of people living in medieval western Europe, as well as to a portion of the clergy. Further eliminating the possibility that the role of gargoyles was the edification of the general public are their often visually obscure or even visually inaccessible locations.

It is also improbable that gargoyles, as a whole, were intended solely for a select educated group within the church hierarchy. The use of gargoyles was not restricted to religious edifices: gargoyles were noted above to have been used also on domestic architecture, and the gargoyles on the church were no more accessible to the eyes of the clergy than to the eyes of the laity.

Gargoyles are among the types of art to receive recent attention by scholars as "marginal art." Gargoyles—along with figures on corbels, on misericords, in manuscript margins, and in other "fringe" art forms that differ from official church art—have been discussed in terms of central and peripheral, high and low, elite and minority, pious and grotesque, sacred and profane, spiritual and worldly art.[26] To suggest, however, that gargoyles, as "marginal" art, were created without the knowledge or supervision of ecclesiastics and patrons of the church[27] seems to be a facile explanation based upon traditional conceptions of medieval religious iconography. Most of the actual carving of the gargoyles would not have been done up on the roofline of the church but down at ground level, along with the other sculptures for the church, and therefore, they were easily accessible to the eyes of the sculptors' patrons: it cannot be imagined that the members of the clergy were unaware of the art they funded. Further, if these images were considered objectionable by the church, they would have been removed from the church. Instead, they are found on a great many medieval churches and cathedrals. A sort of compromise explanation is offered by Sheridan and Ross, for they explain grotesqueries in medieval art (which include gargoyles) as stemming "directly from earlier pagan beliefs," and note "that the representations are pagan deities dear to the people which the Church was unable to eradicate and therefore allowed to subsist side-by-side with the objects of Christian orthodoxy."[28]

Although much of the animal imagery in medieval art was symbolic in content, it seems gargoyles often were not. Only a relatively small percentage of the animals used as gargoyles are found on the folios of the *Physiologus* and the bestiary, prime repositories of medieval animal symbolism. Differentiated in this respect from the usual use of animals by the artists of the Middle Ages, gargoyles may be regarded as "marginal."

Perhaps, however, what is called "popular culture" was not as distinctly divided from "religious culture" in the Middle Ages as is currently assumed. It may be suggested that the Church recognized the ability of these queer creatures in the form of gargoyles to attract attention—and attendance! The innate appeal of gargoyles is their fantastic nature. The medieval preference for the impossible creature dominates the comparatively few realistic depictions of actual animals or humans. But we humans seem to be attracted to the monstrous; drawn to things we have never seen before; lured by the new, the novel, the unknown, and even the nasty—we are intrigued by images of what the mind knows (or hopes) does not exist.[29]

How did the sculptors who created the gargoyles regard their work? Much of medieval sculpture was produced by artisans working within rigid rules—guidelines established by the apprenticeship system of training, by the sculptor's patron, his guild, the dominantly religious subject matter, and medieval traditions of representation. Customarily, a medieval artist was told what he was to depict and how it was to be depicted. One artist routinely copied the work of another—without the negative connotation of plagiarism. Use of model books was standard and accepted artistic practice.

The modern belief that novelty and artistic invention are innately desirable was quite unfamiliar to medieval artistic practice. Gargoyles, however, represent one of the few areas of medieval art in which the artist's "artistic license" was not severely restricted. Their sculptors—working beyond the bounds, carving creatures that were to be placed out-of-doors in ancillary areas of the church—seem to have been freed from the usual restraints imposed upon more prominently placed sculptures.

In this, comparison might be made to the multitude of minute monstrosities that meander in the margins of medieval manuscripts, their behavior rarely more refined than their physiognomy.[30] As the illuminator doodled with brush or pen in the margins of the manuscript folios, the sculptor did the same with chisel and mallet in the margins of the church. For illuminator and sculptor, analogous artistic liberties were allowed at "the edges." Peculiarities were permitted to proliferate at the peripheries—of the page and of the church. Once outside the main scene or outside the confines of the church, literally and figuratively, illuminator and sculptor could work outside the normally restrictive rules.

Like gargoyles and manuscript marginalia, medieval misericords were a breeding ground for fantastic animal imagery. The Latin *misericordia* means "pity" or "mercy." A misericord is a "mercy seat," a small bench used by members of the clergy during the long medieval services. The seat consists of a little ledge with a carved corbel on the underside, which is out of sight until the hinged seat is needed by the clergyman and is tipped up. Although some of the subject matter is traditional and pious in intent, some misericords record behavior that can only be described as rude, while others are openly crude, and animal grotesques abound.[31]

It may be proposed that the gargoyles on the roofline of the church—like those creatures that cavort in the margins of the manuscripts, under the seats of the clergy on the misericords, on corbels, and on vault bosses, or in other locations at a distance from the focal points of the medieval church—were a form of embellishment made largely for the satisfaction of the artist and his fellow workers—in the case of gargoyles, the sculptor and other people actually involved in the construction of the building on which the gargoyles were to be installed.

Perhaps it may even be suggested that sculptors used the gargoyle as a sort of signature on their work. Personal ego is not a recent invention; the individuality of gargoyles may have been a way of personalizing one's work in an era before an artist, no matter the medium in which he worked, was likely to actually add his name to the image he created. Gargoyles offered the sculptor a rare opportunity to create something profoundly personal and outside of the rules of medieval art and the anonymity of the medieval guild system.

NOTES

1. Perhaps the most famous and frequently photographed examples of this are the so-called gargoyles on the balustrade of the cathedral of Notre-Dame in Paris, which do not function as waterspouts and are the creation of the nineteenth-century master restorer Eugene Viollet-le-Duc, based upon examples at Reims Cathedral. The

gargoyles at Sainte-Chapelle in Paris are a nineteenth-century restoration. The splendid winged rhinoceros and winged hippopotamus on the facade of Laon Cathedral were restored in the nineteenth century. Rhinos and hippos were unknown in medieval western Europe; Dürer's woodcut of the rhinoceros, regarded as a curiosity when the animal arrived in Lisbon, was made in 1515. Although the modern date of these examples may be suspected from the smoothness of their surfaces, it is often difficult to determine just when a gargoyle was carved. The historian of Autun Cathedral, Denis Grivot, told me that he is unable to distinguish with certainty the medieval gargoyles from their nineteenth-century copies at Autun. Lester Burbank Bridaham, *Gargoyles, Chimeres, and the Grotesque in French Gothic Sculpture* (New York: Da Capo Press, 1930; 2nd edition revised and enlarged, 1969), deals with this dating dilemma.

2. Illustrated in Janetta Rebold Benton, *The Medieval Menagerie: Animals in the Art of the Middle Ages* (New York: Abbeville Press, 1992), figs. 143, 144. The sketchbook kept by Villard de Honnecourt is in the Bibliothèque Nationale, Paris, MS. Fr. 19093; the drawing of Laon's tower is on plate XIX.

3. The example of Laon's bulls seems indicative of the medieval approach to animals in general, and of the place of animals in medieval thought. The bulls received a level of appreciation and affection unlikely to be bestowed today upon the medieval bull's modern equivalent, the tractor.

4. The sexes of the lions and lionesses on the trumeau of the narthex at Saint-Pierre in Moissac are clearly differentiated, yet both are maned.

5. On the various roles of the lion in medieval art, see Benton, 112–29, 142.

6. See John Block Friedman, *The Monstrous Races in Medieval Art and Thought* (Cambridge, Mass.: Harvard University Press, 1981); *Monsters and Demons in the Ancient and Medieval Worlds, Papers Presented in Honor of Edith Porada*, ed. Ann E. Farkas, Prudence O. Harper, and Evelyn B. Harrison (Mainz on Rhine: Verlag Philipp von Zabern, 1987).

7. See Benton, 19–64.

8. As such, these gargoyles may be described as grotesques. See Geoffrey Galt Harpham, *On the Grotesque: Strategies of Contradiction in Art and Literature* (Princeton: Princeton University Press, 1982), especially 81–6 on the meaning of gargoyles; T. Tindall Wildridge, *The Grotesque in Church Art* (London: Andrews, 1899).

9. Emile Mâle, *The Gothic Image: Religious Art in France of the Thirteenth Century* (New York: Harper & Row, 1984), 58–9.

10. See Bridaham, x–xiv.

11. The sinister nature of the creatures along the balustrade of Notre-Dame in Paris has been linked to this interpretation, and would provide strong supporting evidence, were they actually gargoyles in function and were they actually medieval in date. See note 1.

12. Abbé Auber, *Histoire et théorie du symbolisme réligieux* (Paris: A. Franck, 1870–1).

13. Ronald Sheridan and Anne Ross, *Gargoyles and Grotesques, Paganism in the Medieval Church* (Boston: New York Graphic Society, 1975), 12.

14. Michael Camille, *Image on the Edge: The Margins of Medieval Art* (Cambridge, Mass.: Harvard University Press, 1992), 78; see also 78–84.

15. The *Roman d'Abladane*, now known only in later copies, was perhaps written by Richard de Fournival, bishop of Amiens (1236–47), chancellor of the chapter of Amiens (1240–60), and author of the celebrated *Bestiaire d'Amour*.

16. These gargoyles are described as made of copper and may have been automated. See T. Link, "Der Roman d'Abladane," *Zeitschrift für Romanische Philologie* 17 (1893), 215–32, especially 222, ll. 9–88; L.-F. Flutre, "Le Roman d'Abladane," *Romania* 92 (1971), 458–506, especially 478, ll. 82–91. The *Gesta Romanorum*, a storybook popular among the monks of the Middle Ages, contains the tale of a similarly judgmental statue created by Virgil that told the Emperor Titus about people who committed crimes in Rome. *Gesta Romanorum*, ed. Charles Swann and Wynnard

Hooper (New York: Dover Publications, 1959), tale LVII, 96–9; Camille, *Image on the Edge*, 78; Michael Camille, *The Gothic Idol: Ideology and Image-Making in the Middle Ages* (Cambridge: Cambridge University Press, 1989), 251.

17. Illustrated in Benton, figs. 58, 95, 57 respectively.

18. Illustrated in Bonnie Young, *A Walk Through the Cloisters*, The Metropolitan Museum of Art (New York: Harry N. Abrams, 1988), 26.

19. See Benton, figs. 59, 60.

20. Benton, figs. 54, 55.

21. Benton, fig. 52.

22. Illustrated in Jean Baudry et al., *Bourgogne Romane* (Paris: Zodiaque, La Nuit des Temps, 1956), fig. 12 on p. 185.

23. See Benton, 111, figs. 96, 147, 83.

24. See the discussion in Harpham, 83.

25. Similar barrel-bearing gargoyles are seen at Wells Cathedral.

26. See Camille, *Image on the Edge*, and his useful bibliography; the review of Camille's book by Jeffrey F. Hamburger, *Art Bulletin* 75 (1993), 319–27; and Nurith Kenaan-Kedar, "The Margins of Society in Marginal Romanesque Sculpture," *Gesta* 31 (1992), 15–24.

27. Camille, *Image on the Edge*, 69; and Harpham, 82.

28. Sheridan and Ross, 8.

29. Comparison might be made to the art of other eras—such as twentieth-century Surrealism, exemplified by the enigmatic and unnerving paintings of Salvador Dali—or to modern horror fantasy literature and cinema, such as that of Stephen King.

30. For a wealth of examples see Lilian M.C. Randall, *Images in the Margins of Gothic Manuscripts* (Berkeley: University of California Press, 1966).

31. See Anthony Weir and James Jerman, *Images of Lust: Sexual Carvings on Medieval Churches* (London: B.T. Batsford, 1986); Claude Gaignebet and J. Dominique Lajoux, *Art profane and religion populaire au moyen âge* (Paris: Presses Universitaires de France, 1985); Dr. O.D. Johnton (Henry Joanneton), *Gargouilles* (Troyes: Imprimerie de G. Frémont, 1910); Jurgis Baltrusaitis, *Réveils et prodigues, le gothique fantastique* (Paris: Armand Colin, 1960).

"EFFIGIES AMICITIAE ... VERITAS INIMICITIAE"

ANTIFEMINISM IN THE ICONOGRAPHY OF THE WOMAN-HEADED SERPENT IN MEDIEVAL AND RENAISSANCE ART AND LITERATURE

Nona C. Flores

> Now the serpent was more subtil than any beast of the field which the Lord God had made. And he said unto the woman, Yea, hath God said, Ye shall not eat of every tree of the garden? And the woman said unto the serpent, We may eat of the fruit of the trees of the garden: But of the fruit of the tree which is in the midst of the garden, God hath said, Ye shall not eat of it, neither shall ye touch it, lest ye die. And the serpent said unto the woman, Ye shall not surely die. For God doth know that in the day ye eat thereof, then your eyes shall be opened, and ye shall be as gods, knowing good and evil. And when the woman saw that the tree was good for food, and that it was pleasant to the eyes . . . she took of the fruit thereof, and did eat, and gave also unto her husband with her, and he did eat. (Genesis 3: 1–6)

In its opening verses, the third chapter of Genesis provides the bare scenario for one of the key episodes of Christian history: the Fall of Man. For centuries, its basic elements—a man, a woman, a tree and a snake—have provided the foci for religious commentators and the identifying characteristics for visual representations. Though "more subtil than any beast of the field," the tempter serpent of Genesis 3 is an animal acting on its own initiative, a clever reptile with an unusual ability for speech but, nevertheless, just a snake. Consequently, throughout the first eleven centuries of Christianity, the tempter serpent of Eden—whether working on its own initiative or as an agent of the devil—was generally understood by both commentators and artists to be a zoomorphic creature, usually a simple snake but occasionally a composite animal figure.[1] With the appearance of Peter Comestor's *Historia Scholastica* in the last half of the twelfth century, a major shift in the representation of the serpent begins, one that would find repetitions and revisions as well as repercussions during the next five centuries.

In his commentary on Genesis 3:1. Comestor discusses why Lucifer chose the serpent as his tool:

> Timens vero deprehendi a viro, mulierem minus providam et certam [*sic*; *lege* ceream] in vitium flecti aggressus est, et hoc per serpentem, quia tunc serpens erectus est ut homo, quia in maledictione prostratus est, et adhuc, ut tradunt, phareas erectus incedit. *Elegit etiam quoddam genus serpentis, ut ait Beda, virgineum vultum habens, quia similia similibus applaudant,* et movit ad loquendum linguam ejus, tamen nescientes sicut et per fanaticos et energumenos loquitur.

> [Because [Lucifer] was afraid of being found out by the man, he approached the woman, who had less foresight and was "wax to be twisted into vice" and this by means of the serpent; for the serpent at that time was erect like a man, since it was laid prostrate when it was cursed; and even now the pareas is said to be erect when it moves. *He also chose a certain kind of serpent, as Bede says, which had the countenance of a virgin, because like favors like;* and he moved its tongue to speak, though it knew nothing itself, just as he speaks through the frenzied and possessed.][2]

Comestor incorporates Jewish legends, describing a serpent erect like a reed, but also adds a new attribute whose origin he ascribes to Bede: this species of snake has a virgin's face, since similar things attract one another. Presumably the reasoning behind the concept is that Satan chose a beast whose physical appearance would attract Eve by its similarity to her own. Comestor's virgin-faced serpent became a familiar figure in subsequent biblical commentary, in popular typological manuals such as the *Speculum Humanae Salvationis*, and even in natural history encyclopedias where it is called a dracontopede, or virgin-faced dragon. Consequently, artists from the thirteenth to the seventeenth centuries often depicted the Edenic tempter as having a woman's face and torso attached to a serpent's tail, the body of a winged dragon, or a salamander-like body.

Readers of this essay will perhaps be familiar with the woman-headed serpent in its incarnations as Spenser's dragon Errour in Book I of *The Faerie Queen* or Milton's figure Sin in *Paradise Lost*, since interest in this biform creature largely derives from its relationship to these later literary creations. Rarely has the woman-headed serpent been the central concern of a study. J.K. Bonnell's 1917 article, though still valuable today, is primarily a handlist of examples in art and mystery plays; H.A. Kelly's more recent work (1971) discusses the possible sources and the occurrences of the woman-headed serpent in medieval literature, but concludes by dismissing the figure as fundamentally absurd.[3]

In this essay I will examine the use of the Edenic dracontopede in a small number of the many extant examples available in medieval and Renaissance art and literature. My interest is an iconographic one: I have tried to elicit the significance of an image that is largely unsupported by authority but that was developed so creatively by artists and writers for over 400 years. I have further limited my focus to the dracontopede of Genesis 3 and analogous biform creatures associated with this figure. Thus I do not discuss the woman-serpents of folklore and romance; though fascinating, these come from a tradition separate from Christian patristics. Finally, I have chosen examples in which the depiction of the woman-headed snake underlines the sins ascribed to Eve at the Fall—primarily lust, pride, and fraud—all of which provided a basis for centuries of antifeminist moralizing.

Called "one of the most famous books of the Middle Ages" and even "the most famous book of the Middle Ages" by modern scholars,[4] the *Historia Scholastica* was an immediate popular success. Covering the Bible from Genesis through the Gospels (though omitting certain of the prophets), the *Historia* was designed to supersede the *Glossa Ordinaria* as a compendium of biblical commentary. The text's comprehensiveness made it a university "setbook" (hence *Scholastica*), and it was included as one of the three required texts, along with the glossed Bible and the *Sentences* of Peter Lombard, for theological study by the Paris General Chapter in 1228. Outside of the schools, both clergy and laity used the text; its popularity is attested to by the many citations in medieval wills as well as by the many extant manuscripts listed in Stegmüller's *Repertorium Biblicum Medii Aevii*.[5] By the late thirteenth century, versification and translation into various vernaculars further spread the *Historia*'s content throughout western Christianity.

Why would Peter Comestor so readily accept such a strange biform creature as the demonic tempter of Eve? Both divine and demonic figures in many cultures have been visualized in such hybrid half-human, half-bestial representations as a way of indicating the superhuman characteristics of such beings. Christian art is especially given to a mixed visual representation of the devil. As R.M. Frye points out:

> Satan is essentially a perversion and distortion of created good, and therefore should be understood as a distortion of created beauty. In the Christian understanding of this tension, the demonic is essentially hideous and destructive, but perennially appeals to man under appearances which are both attractive and tempting.[6]

Although "the devil hath power / t'assume a pleasing shape,"[7] many are the repulsive representations of Satan in Christian art. As Daniel Defoe wryly comments in his *History of the Devil*, "Really, it were enough to fright the Devil himself to meet himself in the dark, dressed up in the several figures which imagination has formed for him in the minds of men."[8]

Such hideous images of the devil are not reasonable, as Maximilian Rudwin explains, when his function is to tempt man to sin, since his effectiveness would be seriously hampered by his frightening appearance. Rather, "he might be expected to approach his intended victim in the most fascinating form he could command."[9] Such an attraction to beauty would explain Eve's seduction by a serpent whose attractive and innocent (note that Comestor uses *virgineum* rather than the more general *femineum*) face gives visual reassurance to the lying words and simultaneously distracts from the serpentine tail, a widely recognized attribute of the demonic. St. Bonaventure, in the mid-thirteenth century, interprets the function of Comestor's hybrid serpent in just this way:

> Verum est enim, quod si fuisset in effigie humana, affabilior fuisset; sed divina providentia non debuit hoc permittere, sed cautelam diaboli debuit temperare; et idea concessum est sibi corpus serpentis, quod tamen habebat faciem virginis, sicut dicit Beda, et reliquam corpus erat serpentis, ut sic ex parte posset latere, ex altera deprehendi.

> [Thus it is true, that if he had been in human form, it would have been easier to talk [to Eve], but divine providence did not permit this, but also allowed the devil's caution to rule in due proportion; and the body of a serpent was allowed him; that had, however, the face of a virgin, as Bede said, and the rest of the body was that of a serpent, so that from one end he could be concealed, from the other discovered.]

St. Bonaventure continues, in his next point, by explaining the psychology behind this physical duality: "Quia sic debuit permitte ostendi *effigies amicitiae*, ut posset deprehendi *veritas inimicitiae*." [Although the serpent was thus allowed to have displayed the appearance of friendship, she could have perceived the truth of its enmity.][10]

William Jordan incorporated the idea of the deceptive maiden's face in his Cornish mystery play *Gweans an Bys* or *The Creation of the World* (1611), where the stage direction calls for "A fine serpent with a virgin face and yellow hair upon her head."[11] Satan seeks this creature out "in spite to her face" (l. 519) and, in a well-conceived scene, negotiates with the reluctant serpent, saying:

Allow me to enter thee
For thou wilt not be feared
    Because thou art so fair.
Thou shalt be entertained
And by Eve surely believed
    Thy visage will please her. (ll. 523–7)

Obviously Satan's plan is a success, since Eve later tells the serpent, "There is no fear in me of thee, / Because thy face is so fair" (ll. 562–3). Similarly, Lucifer in the *Mistère du Viel Testament* urges his minion Satan to use a false semblance to deceive man.[12] Satan chooses a serpent whose form exploits the biformity of the dracontopede as described by St. Bonaventure:

J'aray visage de pucelle
Pour demonstret toute doulceur
Mais ma queue poignante et mortelle
Lui brassera autre saveur. (ll. 4069–72)

[I will put on the face of a maiden
In order to show all sweetness
But my tail sharp and deadly
Shall brew for him another taste.]

The many possible sources for, and analogues to, Comestor's striking physical characterization of the Edenic serpent have been examined more fully elsewhere,[13] and I will limit my discussion here to three analogous forms that share the deceptive physical biformity discussed above, and that also derive from the "animal" kingdom: the viper, the scorpion, and the siren. Christian moralizations of these biform creatures are closely related to the iconographic interpretations of the dracontopede, and often bear an anti-feminist bias.

Latin versions of the *Physiologus* describe the male viper as having "the face of a man, while the female has the form of a woman down to her navel, but from her navel down to her tail she has the form of a crocodile."[14] In the oldest extant illustrated Latin *Physiologus*, a ninth-century Carolingian manuscript now in the Stadtbibliothek in Bern, the artist has drawn the viper with a limbless serpentine lower body rather than the crocodilian extremity;[15] this increases the viper's physical likeness to Comestor's Edenic tempter. The viper is actually described in the eighth-century *Liber Monstrorum* as a serpent that is human to the waist.[16] Furthermore, the viper is one of the serpent species mentioned when commentators sought to identify the kind of serpent that tempted Eve.[17] In the bestiary, the female viper's unfriendly habit of literally biting her husband's head off is also linked to Eve's deception of Adam.[18]

Similarly, the scorpion, not a serpent proper but classified with the *vermis*, was sometimes conceived of as having a human face. This representation was influenced in part by the hellish locusts of Revelations 9, which look like horses having human faces, long hair like a woman's, lion teeth, and golden crowns. The human-faced scorpion also derived from a misreading of Solinus, who described the female of the species as "subtiliora sunt capita femina" [those with a feminine head are more subtle].[19] There is also an early representation of the zodiacal sign of Scorpio that has a woman's face and long hair as well as a double-barbed tail.[20] A third-century Greek horoscope for those born under the sign of Scorpio ascribes "a virginal face" among other physical characteristics, and describes Scorpios as "deceivers, cunning, liars, they confide in no one, dissimulators, evil-doers, inclined to adultery, of good health, apt to learn, and incapable of friendship."[21] Luigi Aurigemma argues that this premier physical characteristic, the virginal face, is the earliest evidence of what was to become the essential element in Christian symbolism of the scorpion: its apparently innocent appearance that hypocritically disguises its aggressive intentions. Furthermore, the character reading reflects the overwhelmingly negative response to the scorpion shared with Christian moral tradition,[22] emphasizing its lack of trustworthiness and its evil-minded disposition.

Like Comestor's virgin-faced serpent, the woman-headed scorpion uses its fair face to allay suspicion while its stinging tail indicates its true vicious nature. Such behavior marked the scorpion as a symbol of falsehood, hypocrisy, and treachery. For Gregory the Great, scorpions represented those who "blandi et innoxii in facie videntur, sed post dorsum portant unde venenum fundant" [23] [are charming and innocent by appearance, but they carry behind their back venom which they secure]. The scorpion therefore became an emblem for anything treacherous or deceptive. Chaucer compared Fortune, for example, to the fraudulent scorpion that can "peynte" with its face while preparing to sting with its deadly tail.[24]

The scorpion is made an even stronger analogue by certain associations given to it by the Fathers. Rabanus Maurus, in his chapter on serpents in *De Universo,* follows Isidore's definition of the scorpion as a kind of terrestrial worm that wounds with the poisonous sting in its tail, but then adds that "scorpio diabolum significat vel ministros"[25] [the scorpion signifies the devil or his ministers].

In addition to being a "feminine" astrological sign, the scorpion has other associations with women. In Ecclesiasticus 26:10, we are warned that "a wicked woman is like a loose ox-yoke; he who holds her is like one who seizes a scorpion." The *Ancrene Riwle*, a twelfth-century manual for nuns, described the scorpion as an adder that has a woman's face and a stinging tail, using the scorpion as a symbol of lechery.[26] Also, the scorpion's special animosity was thought to be directed towards women, especially virgins, an idea deriving from Pliny and reappearing in such medieval encyclopedias as the *De Proprietatibus Rerum* of Bartholomaeus Anglicus.[27]

In classical antiquity, sirens were understood to be biform creatures with a woman's head, arms, and torso connected to a lower body composed of a bird's legs, wings, and tail.[28] In the *Liber Monstrorum*, the avian half becomes a fish's tail so that the siren becomes identified with the mermaid.[29] On some representations, the scaly fishtail looks suspiciously like a scaly serpent's tail except for the fin at the end, and even Romanesque bird sirens (generally identified as harpies) often bore a serpent's tail. This is a significant addition to their iconographic anatomy, according to Denise Jalabert, since a serpent's tail associates a creature with not only the serpent but also Satan and all his connotations: evil, death, and sin. Sculptors would further compound the serpent-tailed siren's satanic associations by placing it in the company of a serpent or dragon.[30]

In all its physical permutations, the siren remains a hybrid, a "natura biforma" that was allegorized in the *Physiologus* of Theobaldus to mean human duplicity of character, smooth speech, and injurious action.[31] Thus the physical similarity and its moral implications link the medieval siren with the Edenic tempter serpent. The association is clearly drawn in an early fourteenth-century marble statue now in the Louvre but originally from the Ile-de-France, whose creator actually replaces the traditional serpent beneath the Virgin's feet with a fish-tailed siren.[32]

Moralized interpretations of the siren's song strengthen this association. In both the eastern and western branches of the Church, the Fathers understood the sirens to be symbols of both deadly lust and deadly knowledge.[33] Like the scorpion, the siren was seen as a symbol of Satan and his ministers. Clement of Alexandria in the *Exhortation to the Heathen* explicitly states that the siren's song is only an imitation of man's first deception by the devil.[34]

Furthermore, the sirens were not just agents of deadly temptation but, specifically, seducers to lust. Maximus, Bishop of Turin, for example, compares Ulysses to Christ, his ship to the Church, and the sirens to the carnal pleasures of the world.[35] Comestor's own exegesis of the consequences of the Fall in the *Historia* describes the loss of sexual innocence due to the Fall:

Et sicut inobedientes fuerunt suo superioro, sic et membra coeperunt moveri contra suum superius, id est rationem. Et primum motum concupiscentiae contrarium rationi sensurunt in genitalibus . . . erubuerunt.[36]

[And just as they were disobedient to the superior one, so also their members conspired to be moved against their rightful superior, which is reason. As they felt the first movement of desire, which is contrary to reason, in their genitals . . . they blushed.]

This rather gentle description was considerably heightened by later writers, possibly influenced by interpretations of the siren. As we shall see below, Adam and Eve's temptation and consequent loss of sexual innocence was interpreted, especially during the Renaissance, as a seduction and succumbing to lust and carnality.

According to other writers, the sirens were thought to tempt men with the promise of worldly possessions. In the twelfth-century bestiary of Philippe de Thaün, the siren is symbolic of the world's riches and the evils arising from them.[37] Although Comestor does not develop this concept, certain contemporary writers saw the temptation of Eve as an exhortation to embrace earthly possessions. The mid-twelfth-century Anglo-Norman *Mystère d'Adam*, as we shall see below, has Satan encourage Eve to become queen of the world and mistress of all worldly goods.

Thus the maiden-faced viper, scorpion, and siren all share with the dracontopede an innate ability for fraud merely because of their dual form. Physical biformity becomes a sign of moral duplicity. However, we shall see that in the case of the woman-headed serpent, this deceitfulness is seen as a woman's sin in particular, one made even more heinous by the fact that it is directed against a man.

The description of the woman-headed serpent in Eden was dispersed through western Christianity by citation in such authoritative texts as the *Historia Scholastica*, popular typological manuals, and natural history encyclopedias. A more wide-ranging means of popularizing the image, however, was religious art. The appearance of the human-headed serpent in visual representations of the Fall of Man became commonplace from the thirteenth to the seventeenth century, along with a simultaneous tradition using a naturalistic serpent. By the end of the seventeenth century, the zoomorphic snake had become the dominant form, reflecting the shift from the medieval interest in nature as a source for moral allegory and symbol to the modern concern with nature as an exact science.

Figure 1. The Fall of Man. Paris, Notre-Dame (1220; restored nineteenth century).

The remainder of this essay will examine how artists and writers varied or emphasized different aspects of the Fall in order to elaborate on Comestor's original idea of "similia similibus applaudant." Artists in particular were able to imply certain relationships between Adam, Eve, and the serpent by the way they visually depicted the figures' glances, gestures, and appearances. Not only is the viewer's understanding of the psychological drama of the Fall thus enriched, but certain theological interpretations of the Fall can also be emphasized by changing details within the traditional tableau.

Although restored in the nineteenth century, the sculpture of the Fall of Man decorating the base of a statue of the Virgin at Notre-Dame Cathedral in Paris (1220) is still instructive in the art of making "sermons in stone." Three scenes (the Creation of Eve, the Fall of Man, and the Expulsion from Paradise) are carved beneath a statue of Mary holding the infant Christ. In the central scene, the Fall, the serpent has not only the head but also the naked breasts and shoulders of a beautiful woman (figure 1). The body, wound around the Tree, tapers into a scaly snake's tail that is much like the fishtail of a mermaid in texture. From her superior height in the tree, the serpent dominates the scene, smiling down on Eve, who eats one apple while handing another to Adam. Neither human registers any emotion at this important moment of man's spiritual history, but the tempter's smile indicates its pleasure. Satan was commonly thought to have tempted man out of envy; the apocryphal Wisdom of Solomon 2:24, for example, reads "through envy of the devil came death into the world." Both the smile and the sideward glance of the serpent become important in light of this. Chaucer warned of the "smiler with the knife under his cloak,"[38] as an example of treacherous deceit. The Dreamer in the *Roman de la Rose* describes a personification of Envy itself as having "a sidewise glance, / And never gaze direct";[39] her greatest pleasure derives from the fall (or Fall, in this case) of someone of high lineage to shameful depths.[40] The *Ancrene Riwle*, the first English work to associate the vices with animals, refers generally to the serpent of envy, and this association is made in several later English works, sometimes identifying the serpent specifically as an adder or asp of envy.[41]

Both humans look passive and accepting as well as innocent: Eve's bent arm hides a rather flat chest, and leaves from the Tree sprout at opportune places to shield both Adam's and Eve's genitals. In contrast to this modesty are the voluptuous breasts of the serpent, jutting toward Adam. The snake's duplicity is further suggested by the position of its body, the head turned to look over one shoulder, the torso thrust in the opposite direction. Closer examination confirms the deceptive physical appearance of this agent of sin. Though the initial impression is one of beauty, the voluptuous shoulders hide deformed arms which end in claws, and a pair of wings issue from its back. The scene as a whole suggests both the primacy of *luxuria* in the Fall and the two-faced nature of sin, with its initial attractiveness and its ugly consequences. Not to be ignored, however, is the context of this sculpture. Both typology (Eve/Mary) and God's curse on the serpent (Genesis 3:15: "I will put enmity between thee and the woman, and between thy seed and her seed; it shall bruise thy head, and thou shalt bruise his heel") come into play in the larger context, for one of Mary's feet rests on the head of the gloating serpent. The redemptive message of the New Testament is the overall meaning of the entire sculpture.

The *Speculum Humanae Salvationis*, a popular typological poem written around 1324, survives in some 250 manuscripts, many in Latin, but there are also translations into contemporary German, Dutch, French, English, and even Czech. Many of these are illustrated and served as model books for artisans working on stained glass windows or wall-paintings in churches.[42] The text of the poem (quoted here from a Middle English translation)[43] dealing with the Temptation and Fall heavily underlines woman's culpability in the Temptation and Fall of Man. The serpent approaches Eve, rather than Adam, because he considers the man "more warre, more wyse, more avyse" [more wary, more wise, more prudent] (l. 324). Already we sense a bias similar to Comestor's opinion of Eve, who had "less foresight and was 'wax to be twisted into vice.'" According to the *Speculum* author, Eve's first sin was pride:

> The woman therefore sinned more than the man
> Because she thought herself capable of being made like God. (ll. 351–2)

Adam, however, only ate the apple for love of his wife: "he ne hoped neuere the more to be like God olyve" [he never ever hoped to be like the living God] (l. 350). Eve's sin is made the more heinous because it shows her ingratitude to both God and man. God honored woman by making her from man's flesh and bone rather than from earth's slime; He made her from man's side so she would be his companion, rather than from his foot (so that he would not despise her), or from his head, to keep her pride from "overrise" (l. 338). Thus woman is rightfully punished by man for her failure to keep her place in the cosmic order:

> And if this honour [yet] sho had kept in swete mekeness
> Thare shuld neuer man o lyve hafe done woman distresse;
> Bot for, trowing the devel, sho wald be like to God,
> Sho has descerved forthi to soeffre of manes rod . . . (ll. 341–4)

> [And if she had maintained this honor in sweet meekness
> No man alive should ever have done distress to a woman;
> But because she believed the devil, and wanted to be like God,
> She has therefore deserved to suffer man's rod . . .]

Nor is this condemnation directed only towards Eve, whose name is used only a few times in the text. Otherwise the author inveighs against the *woman* who believed the devil instead of her husband, the *woman* who urged man to sin, the *woman* who condemned man and all her seed: in short, an antifeminist tirade. Second, Eve—and all womankind—are condemned for "glosing," smooth talk or deceptive flattery. In this case, not only Eve but also the women who deceived Samson, Solomon, and David are all condemned for their ability for verbal deceit:

O man, be warre of wikked wommans glosing,

. . . .

Sen thus strong men and wise eschaped nought wommans arte,

Figure 2. The temptation of Eve. Speculum Humanae Salvationis, *London, British Library, MS. Harley 4996, fol. 4v (detail). (Reprinted by permission of the British Library.)*

If thov be nothing swilk, in tyme ware at thi parte. (ll. 359, 363–4)

[O man, beware of wicked woman's flattery,

. . . .

Since men both strong and wise were not able to escape woman's art,
If you would not be of their number, always, for your part, be wary.]

Woman's responsibility for man's expulsion from Eden is further emphasized by the manner in which the serpent's temptation of Eve is often portrayed in the accompanying illustrations. Figure 2 is an illustration from a fourteenth-century *Speculum Humanae Salvationis* manuscript (London, B.L. MS. Harley 4996, fol. 4v) that depicts what appears to be a rather cordial conversation between Eve and an attractive virgin-faced tempter dracontopede standing upright on its tail. This serpent lacks a human torso and arms, thus accomplishing its task solely by the "verba deceptoria" [deceptive words] specified in the original Latin poem[44] and written beside the beautiful blue-banded temptress: "Nequaquam moriemini. Sed eritis sicut dii, scientes bona et mala." [By no means shall you die. But you will be like gods, knowing good and evil."]. The femininization of the serpent through its hairstyle doubles the virulence of the antifeminist sentiments of the text because the illustration virtually shows *two* women sharing the responsibility for man's fall. However, unlike many depictions, in which the virgin-faced serpent and Eve are virtually doppelgängers, these two figures look very different from one another. While Eve's hair flows in luxurious and innocent abandon, the serpent wears the demure but intricate fillet and braid of an aristocratic maiden, emphasizing the tempter's attractiveness and femininity. The hairstyle also indicates a higher level of sophistication, that urge to rise above the level of existence intended by God. In other examples, the serpent's femininity is further emphasized by giving the figure an even more elaborate hairstyle (such as a crown of braids), a headdress (such as a wimple), or an elaborate hat as well as a feminine torso.[45]

The ultimate earthly headdress is, of course, a crown, and royal regalia were common attributes given to both literary and visual personifications of pride, "the sin of exaggerated individualism."[46] Such signs of personal grandeur are appropriate, since pride is defined, by Augustine, as "perversae celsitudinis appetitus"[47] [a desire for unnatural eminence]. An early fifteenth-century window by Hans Acker in the Besserer Chapel of Ulm Cathedral reflects how the dracontopede is often incorporated into this tradition (figure 3). The serpent, which has Eve's face and long hair,

Figure 3. *The Fall of Man. Stained glass window by Hans Acker, Besserer Chapel, Ulm Cathedral (early fifteenth century). (Reprinted by permission of Reed International Books Ltd/Sonia Halliday.)*

is wearing a crown. This appearance of royalty is a "visual counterpart to the exalted image of Eve" that the serpent was thought to have instilled in her by flattery.[48] In the twelfth-century Anglo-Norman *Le Mystère d'Adam* (in which Satan ingeniously manipulates a mechanical naturalistic snake), Satan tries twice to tempt Adam to eat the forbidden fruit by telling him that he will become his own master and God's equal by doing so. Adam angrily sends the devil away. But then Satan approaches the more susceptible Eve, saying

> A ton bel cors, a ta figure,
> Bien covendreit tel aventure
> Que tu fusses dame del mond,
> Del soverain e del parfont.
> E seüses quanque est a estre
> Que de tuit fusses bone maistre.[49]

> [With your beautiful body, with your figure,
> You deserve such a chance
> To be queen of the world,
> Of heaven and of the earth beneath.
> Knowing all that is to be,
> Being mistress of it all.]

Not only does Satan raise Eve's own expectations of herself, he also becomes abusive about Adam, reducing man to a servile position to woman, and commiserating with woman for this mismatch made by God. Finally he urges her, "Del ciel avrez sempres corone" [Have always the crown of heaven] (l. 264): eat of the fruit and become God's equal. In the Ulm window, Eve must look up and reach up for the forbidden fruit because of the crowned serpent's superior height in the tree. Adam, on the other hand, keeps his eyes cast toward the ground and his hand below shoulder level. In the upper third of the window are two angels kneeling on either side of the image of God: with heads bowed in prayer, their humble posture of submission to the deity also contrasts with the woman's lack of humility.

When, as is often the case, the woman-headed serpent is twin to Eve in face and features, she functions as a mirror whose message is made explicit by its ability to speak enticements to sin. Lydgate's personification of Pride in *The Pilgrimage of the Life of Man* looks at herself in a mirror held by Flattery and preens herself:

> I wex swollë with ther bost
> And thynke my place and my degre
> Must gretly enhaunsyd be,
> And thynke yt sytteth wel to me
> Tave a cheyre off dygnity
> Lyk as I were a gret pryncesse,

A lady, or A gret duchesse,
Worthy for to were A crowne.[50]

[I grow swollen with their flattery
And think my place and my degree
Must be greatly enhanced.
And I think that it well befits me
To have a chair of honor
As if I were a great princess,
A lady, or a great duchess,
Worthy of wearing a crown.]

Such are the thoughts urged on Eve by the devil's flattery as seen in dialogue from mystery plays of the Fall, which, as Rosemary Woolf points out, demonstrate that "Eve's initial response springs from awakening of feminine self-esteem."[51] Clearly, part of Eve's pride is excessive (and very) feminine vanity. In a *Speculum Humanae Salvationis* printed in 1473 by Günther Zainer,[52] the serpent looks like a royal queen wearing robes and a crown while she offers Eve the apple; only the spotted bat's wings behind her back and the serpent's tail winding out from beneath her skirts make her something more than a noble queen of courtly romance (figure 4). In this woodcut, Eve eagerly stretches both hands out for the forbidden fruit while stepping toward the serpent: she looks

Figure 4. The Temptation of Eve. Speculum Humanae Salvationis, der Spiegel menschlicher Behaltniss, *Augsburg, Günther Zainer, 1473.*

Figure 5. The Story of Adam and Eve. Pol de Limbourg, Les Très Riches Heures du Jean, Duc de Berry, *Chantilly, Musée Condé, MS. 65, fol. 25v. (Reprinted by permission of Giraudon/Art Resource, New York.)*

as desirous of grasping this exalted image of femininity as the apple itself.

Woman's pride is an antifeminist commonplace in literature, so that the clown Launce in Shakespeare's *Two Gentlemen of Verona* can excuse his sweetheart's pride by saying, "It was Eve's legacy and cannot be ta'en from her" (III, i, 139). Eve's *superbia* can be visually represented in other ways. In the famous miniature of the Fall by the brothers Limbourg done for the *Très Riches Heures* of Jean, Duc de Berry (Chantilly, Musée Condé MS. 65, fol. 25v; figure 5), the artists have followed Comestor's "similia similibus applaudant" in their depiction of this beautiful dracontopede: her human upper half is visually divided from the twisting serpentine body and lizard hind legs by the tree trunk, so that she is, in effect, a mirror image of Eve. Eve herself is portrayed as a contemporary ideal of beauty: fair, blonde, and high bosomed, with a thin waist and slightly protruding stomach. When the first

Figure 6. The Fall of Man. Hans Holbein the Younger, Historiarum Veteris Testamenti Icones, *Lyons, Trechsel and Frellon, 1543. Original size: 6.5 cm. × 4.95 cm. (Reprinted by permission of the British Library.)*

woman reaches up to accept the fruit from her other self high in the tree, she "enacts the fall of Narcissus who tried to grasp his reflected image."[53] The reflective face of the dracontopede serves the same role as the Mirror Perilous, "where proud / Narcissus saw his face and his grey eyes, / Because of which he soon lay on his bier."[54] Both serpent and pool reflect the self-love of the gazer and lead to his destruction.

Narcissus served as an example of self-love and selfish desire in medieval mythographic tradition.[55] In the *Ovidius Moralizatus* of Petrus Berchorius, for example, the story is explained thus:

[I]t often happens that some who have great beauty see that they have great beauty of body, of soul, and of fortune when they consider their form, their knowledge or their wealth. So they are raised up in pride and despise all others. . . . It is certain that when they see the reflection of worldly prosperity which, in the worlds of Wisdom 5:9, will "all pass away like a shadow," they will love it madly and glorify themselves in it so that, as a result, they lose the life of the soul.[56]

In the Limbourg brothers' illumination, Eve's pride and her resultant disregard of God's appointed hierarchy are apparent in her posture. She stretches up to the dracontopede for the fruit which is beyond her grasp. She then stands over her husband, whose awkward and servile position puts him in a place subordinate to hers. Eve's activity and prominence throughout the miniature's scenes emphasize her dominance and the responsibility placed on her actions. Only when she is chastised by God, on the right side of the picture, does she remember her place in the universal hierarchy, finally casting her eyes down in shame.

What is perhaps most striking in the miniature is what Marcel Thomas calls "a discreet but powerful eroticism" with which the Limbourgs endowed Eve's nudity.[57] The serpent has borrowed Eve's own physical charms to seduce her with self-love; Adam is led astray by those same charms, embodied in the sexual appeal of his mate. That Adam's genitals are not concealed is due not only to possible classical models[58] but also to the narrative and theological content of the miniature. Again, we are reminded that Comestor in the *Historia Scholastica* explains the consequences of the Fall largely in sexual terms.

Perhaps the most famous of all Renaissance Bible illustrations are those of Hans Holbein the Younger, which were both popular and highly influential, going through ten editions in Latin with French, Spanish, and English translations between 1538 and 1551. The same woodcut of the Fall of Man (figure 6) is commonly used in both Holbein's *Historiarum Veteris Testamenti Icones* and the popular Dance of Death series.[59] Immediately noticeable is the shift in responsibility: here Adam is the active member of the pair, straining to grasp the fruit high up in the tree. Also unusual are the downward-hanging position of the snake and the lazy half-sitting, half-lying position of Eve. More traditional are the intricate coils of the serpent around the branches, its careful coiffure, and the narrow fillet suggesting a crown. Both Eve and the serpent have assumed unusually languid poses, reflected in the rather rubbery quality of their musculature.

Holbein presents the Temptation as a decision to follow the voluptuous life of inglorious ease rather than the active life of virtuous deeds, a popular Renaissance opposition. Frequently in literature, vice is presented as a deceptive but beautiful enchantress, while the life of pleasure is figured as a false paradise of sensual delights, such as Acrasia'a Bower of Bliss in Book II of

The Faerie Queene and Alcina's island in *Orlando Furioso*, cantos VI–VII. Spenser describes Acrasia's bower as a *locus amoenus* constructed by Art in despite of Nature, more pleasant than "Eden selfe, if aught with Eden mote compayre."[60] Acrasia's knightly lover sleeps beside the enchantress:

> His warlike armes, the ydle instruments
> Of sleeping praise, were hong upon a tree
> . . . .
> Ne for them, ne for honor, cared hee,
> Ne ought that did to his advauncement tend,
> But in lewd loves, and wastfull luxuree,
> His dayes, his goods, his bodie he did spend . . . (II, xii, lxxx)

Similarly, Rogero in Ariosto's poem falls victim to the sorceress Alcina because "He thought no fraud, no treason, nor no guile / Could be accompanied with so sweet a smile."[61] (Ariosto also spends several stanzas describing more sensuous parts of Alcina's anatomy.) Rogero becomes completely engrossed in the pursuits of love:

> And so while sensual life doth bear the sway,
> All discipline is trodden into dust.
> This while Rogero here his time misspends,
> He quite forgets his duty and his friends. (canto 7, p. 159)

In Holbein's woodcut, the devil presents his deceptive face through the beautiful virgin-faced serpent, making sin a seemingly pleasurable experience. Both the serpent and Eve play the role of the deceitful enchantress. The naked reclining Eve is even posed in the same fashion as Spenser's Acrasia (II, xii, lxxvii–lxxviii).

In Ariosto, the fraud is revealed when Rogero puts on a ring that nullifies all enchantments: he sees Alcina as she really is, a hideous and deformed old hag. In Holbein's series, Adam and Eve learn of the devil's deceit too late: a grinning skeletal death plucks at a mandolin as the couple flee the avenging angel posted at the gates of Eden. Adam "quite forgets his duty and his friends" by forgetting God's interdiction, which is printed above (in Latin) and below (in French) the woodcut: "Dieu leur deffend que l'arbe de vie / Ne mangent fruict, sur peine de la Mort" [God forbid that they eat the fruit of the tree of life, on pain of death]. Thus Adam loses the true Paradise by seeking a false "Paradiso uoluptatis" in which he is like God. His submission to sin leads to terror and despair rather than pleasure, and is portrayed as such in Holbein's subsequent woodcuts of the Expulsion from Eden and of Adam and Eve at toil.

Sexual temptation is thus apparent in the poses of Eve and the serpent. It also figures in the choice of animals surrounding Eve, many of them emblems of sensuality and deceit. In medieval thought, the ape was associated almost entirely with feminine qualities, especially those that Eve employed to beguile Adam: wiliness, sensuality, and uncertain temperament.[62] Here it is apparent in a supportive (and possibly an imitative) position behind Eve. Lasciviousness is the consistent note in descriptions of the he-goat: "Hyrcus, the He-Goat, is a lascivious and butting animal who is always burning for coition. His eyes are transverse slits because he is so randy."[63] Sheep are generally known for their character *in bono*, but Martin Luther refers to a little-known tradition that the devil can take two forms for disguise—the serpent when he wishes to kill or frighten, or the sheep when he wants to lie or deceive—making the sheep's position directly beneath the serpent's head significant.[64] Behind Adam stands the stag: in heat the animal was known for its lechery, while its horns made it an apt symbol for cuckoldry.[65] Also present is the rabbit, with its many sexual associations.[66]

Centered in the woodcut are the serpent's feminine head and that of a horse, which is not cropping grass or standing still like so many of the other beasts, but running wildly, its mane flying and its mouth open like that of the triumphant snake. The horse is the central symbol of the Fall in this picture, for it clearly represents the passions of man, unbridled and uncontrolled by the rider Reason, an equivalence seen so often in medieval and Renaissance works. For the medieval world the idea stemmed from the Pauline idea of the *homo duplex* or double nature of man,[67] whose passionate, sinful side was compared to a spirited horse, and whose rational side was compared to the rider who should exert his control over his mount. As mentioned above, the Fall of Man is similarly interpreted by many as the triumph of the carnal side of man, represented by Eve, over his spiritual side, represented by Adam.

Again, the loss of reason is another component in the thematic choice between inglorious ease and virtuous deeds. Ariosto's Rogero becomes imprisoned by love: his fetters and chains are a jewelled collar and golden bracelets. His hair is curled and perfumed so that he assumes "wanton *womanish* behavior":

> So changed in speech, in manners, and in favor
> So from himself *beyond all reason led*
> By the enchantments of this amorous dame
> He was himself in nothing but in name. (canto 7, p. 163; my italics)

The fay Alcina actually transforms her ex-lovers into beasts, rocks, and trees. This metamorphosis, notes Sir John Harington, the Elizabethan translator of Ariosto's poem, shows "how men given over to sensuality, leese in the end the very form of men (which is reason)" (canto 6, p. 149, 7n.).

In fact, sexuality was an increasingly important concept in sixteenth-century representations of the Fall, especially in the work of northern artists.[68] This is sometimes made apparent in the way the nude figures of Adam, Eve, and even the serpent are depicted. Albrecht Dürer's 1510 drawing (now in the Albertina Museum, Vienna)[69] differs significantly from his earlier representations of the Fall, which showed Adam and Eve as figures of ideal beauty and proportion.[70] The figures in a 1504 engraving of Adam and Eve standing on opposite sides of the Tree derive from the Apollo Belvedere and Venus.[71] In the 1504 engraving the delicately delineated figures, their genitalia hidden by foliage, neither touch nor look at one another, but concentrate their attention on the apple in the crowned serpent's mouth. In the 1510 drawing, the muscular physicality of the couple is strongly apparent: in particular, Eve's buttocks and thighs are grossly emphasized, the curve of her body suggesting a prominent belly as well. Similarly, the female-headed serpent, which looks down on the couple from above in the tree, has a crown and long hair, as well as breasts almost as large as its head. Moreover, the human couple now stand on the same side of the tree and embrace closely, seeming to kiss (his arm around her waist, hers about his neck), while their free hands jointly hold the forbidden fruit, indicating a shared responsibility for their fall.

A 1522 woodcut by Lucas Cranach the Elder (figure 7) shows Eve tempted by a mirror image of herself, an upright dracontopede that actually separates Eve from Adam physically. Thomas Milles gives the following allegorical reading of the serpent-tempter as carnal appetite or sensuality; the reading is taken from Leo Hebraeus' *Philosophy of Loue* and provides an enlightening commentary on this woodcut. The serpent

> inciteth and first deceiveth the corporall Feminine part. It is called Corporal, when it is found any way divided from the intellect, which is tearmed the Husband, resisting against his strict and severe Lawes, to acquaint her selfe with carnall Delectations, and darken her Native splendor, with acquisitions of superfluous and abounding riches or treasure.[72]

This dracontopede is unusual in the extent of its femininity, having a human body virtually to the knee, though it lacks arms and hands. Unlike other limbless serpents, this one is not stymied into passivity by its physical limi-

Figure 7. The Temptation of Eve and the Fall of Man. Lucas Cranach the Elder, 1522 (multiple sources).

tations. In contrast to Adam's modesty, visually conveyed by the branch covering his genitals, the serpent presses suggestively against Eve while appearing to whisper deceptive blandishments and promises of self-enrichment into Eve's ear; the two feminine nudes are realized in voluptuous detail. An iconographic variant is seen in the representation of the archangel at the left as a rather surly foot soldier brandishing a whip rather than the customary fiery sword. The central positioning of the female doppelgängers separates

Adam from the archangel, a personification of God's verbal prohibition, a second example of passion isolating man from reason within the picture.

The artistic shift toward the naturalistic snake had already begun when the scientific minds of a more rational age turned to the same question. In the *Pseudodoxia Epidemica* (1645), Sir Thomas Browne deals with the question of the Edenic tempter in his fifth book, "Of many things questionable as they are commonly described in Pictures." He admits that the woman-headed serpent in Eden is "not a mere pictorial contrivance or mere invention of the picturer, but an auncient tradition and conceived reality" supported by Bede and other authors of antiquity. It is, however, "a conceit not to be admitted."[73] But let us end with the thoughts of Edward Topsell, as expressed in his *History of Serpents* (1608) in the section on the dracontopede, described as a virgin-faced dragon of the type that is said to have tempted Adam and Eve in the Garden of Eden:

> [T]his is a fable not worthy to be refuted, because the Scripture itself doth directly gainsay every part of it. For first of all, it is called a serpent, and if it had been a dragon, Moses would have said so.[74]

NOTES

1. Rabbinical commentary and pseudepigraphic literature often gave the serpent feet or even legs, since God's curse, "Upon thy belly shalt thou go" (Gen. 3:14), implied that the creature had a vertical stance. Rabbi Hoshaya the Elder in the *Midrash Rabbah*, for example, describes the serpent as being erect like a reed and having feet: *Bereshith Rabbah* 19:1, in *Midrash Rabbah: Genesis*, trans. H. Freedman (London: Soncino Press, 1939), 149. This upright serpent, usually balanced on its tail rather than on feet, is preserved in Christian art in such diverse examples as the judgement of Adam, Eve, and the serpent in the eleventh-century Anglo-Saxon *Genesis B* (Oxford, Bodleian Library, MS. Junius 11, 41) and the Fall of Man as represented on the Medici Tapestries, a mid-sixteenth-century series of Flemish wall hangings now in the Accademia in Florence.

2. *PL* 198, 1072 (my italics); translation by Henry Ansgar Kelly, "The Metamorphoses of the Eden Serpent During the Middle Ages and Renaissance," *Viator* 2 (1971), 308.

3. J.K. Bonnell, "The Serpent with a Human Head in Art and Mystery Play," *Journal of the Archeological Institute of America* 21 (1917), 255–91; Kelly, 301–29. See also Hugo Schmerber, *Die Schlange des Paradies* (Strassburg: J.H. Ed. Heitz, 1905); and Alice Kemp-Welch, "The Woman-headed Serpent in Art," *The Nineteenth Century and After* 52 (Dec. 1902), 983–91.

4. Beryl Smalley, *The Study of the Bible in the Middle Ages* (Oxford: Basil Blackwell, 1952), 178; E. Shereshevsky, "Hebrew Traditions in Peter Comestor's *Historia Scholastica*. I. Genesis," *Jewish Quarterly Review* 59 (1968–9), 268.

5. F. Stegmüller, *Repertorium Biblicum Medii Aevi*, IV (Madrid: Francisco Suarez, 1954), 280–300; see also Smalley, 179.

6. Roland Mushat Frye, *Milton's Imagery and the Visual Arts: Iconographic Tradition in the Epic Poems* (Princeton: Princeton University Press, 1978), 65.

7. William Shakespeare, *Hamlet* II, ii, 599–600.

8. Daniel Defoe, *The History of the Devil, Ancient and Modern* (London: A. Law, W. Millar and R. Cater, 1793), 1.

9. Maximilian Rudwin, *The Devil in Legend and Literature* (Chicago: Open Court Publishing Company, 1931), 38.

10. Sententiarum, II, Dist. XXI, Art. I, Quaes. ii, in *Opera Omnia*, ed. Studio et Curia PP. Collegii A. S. Bonaventure II (Quarrachi: Collegii S. Bonaventura, 1885), 495 (my italics). I would like to thank Richard Mitchell of the University of Illinois for reviewing my translation of this passage.

11. William Jordan, *The Creation of the World*, ed. and trans. Whitley Stokes (London: Williams and Norgate, 1864), 35.

12. This scene is missing in the printed editions of the work, but is conserved in a manuscript at Troyes and reprinted in the introduction to the *Transgression d'Adam et d'Eve* in *Le Mystère du Viel Testament*, ed. James de Rothschild, Société des Anciens Textes Français 15 (Paris: Firmin-Didot, 1878), I, li–lv.

13. See above, note 3. For the association of the woman-headed serpent and the demon Lilith see Gershom Sholem, "Lilith," *Encyclopedia Judaica* (New York: MacMillan, 1971), II, 245–50; and Jeffrey Hoffeld, "Adam's Two Wives," *Bulletin of the Metropolitan Museum of Art* 26 (1967–8), 430–40.

14. *Physiologus*, trans. Michael J. Curley (Austin, Tex.: University of Texas Press, 1979), 15.

15. *Physiologus bernensis: Voll-Faksimile-Ausgabe des Codex Bongarsianus 318*, ed. Christoph Steiger and Otto Hamburger (Basel: Alkuin-Verlag, 1964), 111.

16. *Liber Monstrorum de Diversis Generibus*, ed. Corrado Bologna (Milan: V. Bompiani, 1977), III, 18, p. 148. Albertus Magnus, on the other hand, dismisses this idea as false: "Some authors claim the viper in the foreportion of its body is like a human, and its posterior degenerates into a serpent. But this is sheer nonsense and can only be taken as the fabulous imaginings of poets who cloak their meaning in metaphors." Albert the Great, *Man and the Beasts. De Animalibus (Books 22–25)*, trans. James J. Scanlan (Binghamton, N.Y.: Medieval and Renaissance Texts and Studies, 1987), XXV, 61, p. 418.

17. Alexander Neckham protests against the identification of the viper or the pareas as the Eden serpent in *De Naturis Rerum*, II, 105, ed. Thomas Wright, *Rerum Brittanicarum Medii Aevi Scriptores* 34 (London: Longman, Green, Longman, Roberts, and Green, 1863), 138.

18. T.H. White, ed. and trans., *The Bestiary: A Book of Beasts* (New York: G.P. Putnam's Sons, 1960), 170.

19. For the locusts of Revelations 9, see Kelly, 312; human-faced locusts can be seen in many illustrated Apocalypse manuscripts, such as the one at Oxford, Bodl. Lib., MS. Tanner 184, fol. 56, reproduced in Frye, pl. 12. For scorpions in Solinus, see *Collectanea Rerum Memorabilia*, ed. T. Mommsen (Berlin: Weidmannsche Verlagbuchandlung, 1958), 123; John Block Friedman, "Antichrist and the Iconography of Dante's Geryon," *J. Warburg and Courtauld Institutes* 35 (1972), 113n., suggests that Solinus is the ultimate source for the woman-headed scorpion.

20. See figure 7 in Luigi Aurigemma, *Le Signe zodiacal du Scorpion dan les Traditions occidentales de l'Anquité gréco-latine à la Renaissance* (Paris: Mouton, 1976).

21. Hippolytus, *Refutatio Omnium Haeresum*, IV, 22, in *Werke*, ed. Paul Wendland, III (Leipzig: J.C. Hinreichs, 1916), 52.

22. Aurigemma, 38.

23. Gregory the Great, *Homiliarum in Ezechielem Prophetam Libri duo*, I, 9, 21; *PL* 76, 879.

24. *The Merchant's Tale*, ll. 2062–4, in *The Riverside Chaucer*, ed. Larry D. Benson, 3rd ed. (Boston: Houghton Mifflin, 1987). All Chaucer quotations are from this text. See also George B. Pace, "The Scorpion of Chaucer's *The Merchant's Tale*," *Modern Language Quarterly* (1965), 369–74.

25. *PL* 111, 232; Isidore of Seville, *Etymologiae* XII, 5, 4.

26. *The Ancrene Riwle*, ed. Mabel Day, Early English Text Society, o.s. 225 (London: Oxford University Press, 1952), 91.

27. Pliny, XI, xxx; *On the Properties of Things. John Trevisa's Translation of Bartholomaeus Anglicus' De Proprietatibus Rerum: Critical Text*, M.C. Seymour, gen. ed. (Oxford: Clarendon Press, 1975), XVIII, lxxxx, viii.

28. Edmond Faral, "La Queue de Poisson des Sirènes," *Romania* 74 (1953), 433–506, esp. 439–40.

29. *Liber Monstrorum* I, 6, p. 42; Faral, 44.

30. Denise Jalabert, "De l'Art oriental antique à l'art roman: Recherches sur la Faune et la Flore romans. II. Les Sirènes," *Bull. Monumentale*, 95 (1936), 433–71, esp. 454–7.

31. *Theobaldi Physiologus*, ed. and trans. P.T. Eden, Mittellateinische Studien und Texte 6 (Leiden: E.J. Brill, 1972), 62. For hybrid forms as a contradiction or debasement of nature, see Conrad Rudolph, "Bernard of Clairvaux's *Apologia* as a Description of Cluny, and the Controversy over Monastic Art," *Gesta* (1988), 127–8.

32. Reproduced in Ernst Guldan, *Eva und Maria: Eine Antithesis als Bildmotiv* (Graz: Verlag Hermann Böhlaus, 1966), pl. 109.

33. For a summary of Hellenistic and Christian interpretations of the siren, see Hugo Rahner, *Greek Myths and Christian Mysteries*, trans. Brian Battershaw (London: Burns and Oates, 1963), 353–71.

34. *Exhortation*, 12; *ANF* 2, 205.

35. *Homilia*, 49; *PL* 57, 340.

36. *PL* 198, 1072–3.

37. Philippe de Thaün, *Le bestiare*, ed. Emmanuel Walberg (1900; rpt. Geneva: Slatkine Reprints, 1970), ll. 1383–8.

38. *The Knight's Tale*, l. 1999.

39. Guillaume de Lorris and Jean de Meun, *The Romance of the Rose*, trans. Harry W. Robbins (New York: E.P. Dutton, 1962), 2, ll. 101–2.

40. Guillaume de Lorris and Jean de Meun, *Le Roman de la Rose*, ed. Ernst Langlois, SATF 113 (Paris: Firmin-Didot, 1920), ll. 240–7:

> Nule rien ne li puet tant plaire
> Con fait maus e mesaventure.
> Quant el voit grant desconfiture
> Sor aucun prodome cheoir,
> Ice li plaist mout a veoir.
> Ele est trop liee en son courage
> Quant el voit aucun grant lignage
> Decheoir ou aler a honte.

41. *Ancrene Riwle*, trans. M.B. Salu (Notre Dame, Ind.: University of Notre Dame Press, 1956), 88–9. Wycliff, attacking the sins of the cloistered life, refers to the adder or asp of envy; *Tractatus de Civilii Domino*, III, 2, ed. Reginald Lane Poole and Johann Loserth, III (London: Trübner for the Wycliff Society, 1903), 15–6. Morton Bloomfield, *The Seven Deadly Sins* (East Lansing, Mich.: Michigan State University Press, 1952) lists several other literary references associating the snake with envy in appendix I.

42. *Speculum Humanae Salvationis: Texte critique. Traduction inédite de Jean Mielot (1448)*, ed. J. Lutz and Paul Perdrizet (Mulhouse: E. Meiningen, 1907–10), I, 287–98; and M.D. Anderson, *The Imagery of British Churches* (London: John Murray, 1955), 22, 76.

43. *The Mirour of Mans Saluacioune*, ed. Avril Henry (Philadelphia: University of Pennsylvania Press, 1987).

44. *Speculum*, I, chap. I, ll. 15–6:

In hunc fradulosus deceptor mille artifex intrabat,
Et per os ejus loquens, verba deceptoria mulieri enarrabat.

45. For examples of the woman-headed serpent with a crown of braids see Augustine, *City of God*, London, British Library, MS. Add. 15245, fol. 57v, where both Eve and a delicate harpy-like serpent wear the same elaborately braided hairstyle; and London, British Library, MS. Add. 11639, fol. 520v, a late thirteenth-century Hebrew Bible and prayerbook whose depiction of the woman-headed serpent is apparently influenced by contemporary Christian iconography.

For the wimpled woman-headed serpent see Jacobus, *Omne Bonum*, where the serpent is a small monkey-like hausfrau with a long tail; London, British Library, MS. Royal 6.E.VI, fol. 46v. More typical is just the wimpled human head, the only indication of the creature's sex, attached to a long serpentine tail, as in the Tickhill Psalter, New York Public Library, Spencer Coll., MS. 26, fol. 5.

Serpents with more elaborate headdresses include one in a Flemish Book of Hours from around 1500, which has a netted headdress with jewels and is human to the waist except for her reptilian arms; Oxford, Bodleian Library, MS. Douce 112, fol. 36. The serpent in the Fall of Man portrayed on the Great East Window of York Cathedral (1405–8) has a frill or lace headdress, as well as an elaborately patterned "skin" held up by a visible shoulder strap; the depiction, which also includes patterned wings, is probably influenced by costumes in local portrayals of the mystery plays.

An exceptionally elegantly coiffed and curled human-headed serpent who mirrors Eve's face and hairstyle appears quite late in the tradition (mid-sixteenth century) in a painting sometimes attributed to Bronzino now in the National Galleries of Scotland (Coll. of Earl Crawford and Balcanes); reproduced in J.B. Trapp, "The Iconography of the Fall of Man," in *Approaches to Paradise Lost*, ed. C.A. Patrides (London: Edward Arnold, 1968), pl. 27. Trapp, however, feels the serpent "has the face of one of the painter's handsome young men" (263).

46. Bloomfield, 75. Samuel Chew, *The Pilgrimage of Life* (New Haven: Yale University Press, 1962), 339, 1n., lists several examples in art. Spenser's Lucifera is described as a crowned queen in *The Faerie Queene* I, iv, 12; in the eleventh-century Anglo-Saxon *Genesis B* (Oxford, Bodleian Library, MS. Junius 11, 3) the upper zone of the picture shows Satan about to mount the throne of God, holding a scepter in his left hand while other rebel angels honor him: four bear crowns to represent his presumption upon deity; reproduced in Frye, pl. 33.

47. *De Civitate Dei*, XIV, xiii; *CSEL* 40, I, 31.

48. Albert C. Labriola, "The Aesthetics of Self-Diminution: Christian Iconography and *Paradise Lost*," *Milton Studies*, 7 (1975), 299; Labriola also refers to the Bamberg *Biblia Pauperum* of 1471, in which the serpent has a woman's face, long hair, and a crown. Similar crowned human-headed serpents appear in the *Passional of Abbess Cunegunda*, Prague University Library, XVI.A.17, fol 4v; in a *Biblia Pauperum* done in Austria about 1330, Budapest, Museum of Fine Art, fol. 5v, reproduced in Gerhard Schmidt, *Des Armenbibeln des XIV Jahrhunderts* (Graz: Böhlaus, 1959), pl. 11a; and in a fifteenth-century engraving of the Fall of Man by the Master of the Power of Women, reproduced in Max Lehrs, *Late Gothic Engravings of Germany and the Netherlands* (New York: Dover, 1969), pl. 55.

A rather stiff woodcut of the Fall attributed to Hans Holbein and printed in the Luther Bible (Lyons, 1544) shows an erect carrotlike serpent with a crowned female head, whose expression—like Queen Victoria's—is definitely not amused; reproduced in Frye, pl. 190.

49. *Le Mystère d'Adam*, ed. Paul Studer (1918; rpt. Manchester: Manchester University Press, 1949), ll. 253–8.

50. John Lydgate, *The Pilgrimage of the Life of Man*, ed. F. J. Furnivall, EETS, e.s. 77, 83, 92 (London: Kegan Paul, Trench, Trübner and Company, 1899–1904), ll. 14144–51.

51. Rosemary Woolf, *The English Mystery Plays* (Berkeley: University of California Press, 1972), 118.

52. This book has been called one of the most beautiful of the incunabula created in Western Europe by virtue of the unity of character between Zainer's type and the woodcuts; Alan G. Thomas, *Great Books and Book Collectors* (London: Weidenfeld and Nicolson, 1975), 49. See also Adrian Wilson and Joyce Lancaster Wilson, *A Medieval Mirror: Speculum humanae salvationis 1324–1500* (Berkeley: University of California Press, 1984), 207–8. I would like to thank Professor Alfred Young of Northern Illinois University for his assistance in unraveling my bibliographic confusion about Zainer's edition.

53. Labriola, 299.

54. *Romance of the Rose*, 6, ll. 102–3; see also *Roman de la Rose*, ll. 1571–4.

55. See Rosamund Tuve, *Allegorical Imagery* (Princeton: Princeton University Press, 1966), 36, for Narcissus and the mythographic tradition.

56. William Donald Reynolds, "The *Ovidius Moralizatus* of Petrus Berchorius: An Introduction and Translation" (Diss., University of Illinois, 1971), 195–6.

57. Marcel Thomas, *The Golden Age: Manuscript Painting at the Time of Jean, Duke of Berry* (New York: George Braziller, 1979), 93.

58. Paul Durrieu, *Les Très Riches Heures du Jean de France, Duc de Berry* (Paris: Plon-Nourrit, 1904), 38–9; and M. Thomas, 22 and pl. VI.

59. The entire series as printed in the 1543 edition by Trechsel and Frellon of Lyons is conveniently reprinted in *Images from the Old Testament: Historiarum Veteris Testamenti Icones by Hans Holbein*, intro. Michael Marquise (New York: Paddington Press, 1976). The four Adam and Eve scenes can also be found reprinted in J.M. Clark, *The Dance of Death by Hans Holbein* (London: Phaidon, 1947).

60. *The Faerie Queen*, Book II, canto xii, stanza lii. All references to *The Faerie Queene* are from *The Complete Poetical Works of Edmund Spenser* (Boston: Houghton Mifflin, 1908).

61. *Ariosto's Orlando Furioso: Selections from the Translation of Sir John Harington*, ed. Rudolf Gottfried (Bloomington, Ind.: Indiana University Press, 1963), canto 7, p. 156.

62. See the chapter on the ape and the Fall of Man in H.W. Janson, *Apes and Ape Lore* (London: The Warburg Institute, 1952), 107–36.

63. White, 74.

64. *The Table Talk of Martin Luther*, trans. and ed. William Hazlitt (London: George Bell and Sons, 1902), DCVIII, p. 264.

65. For the characteristics of the stag's rutting see *On the Nature of Things*, XVIII, xxx; and Edward Topsell, *The History of Four-footed Beasts* (1658; rpt. New York: Da Capo Press, 1967), 101. Bloomfield gives literary references and one pictorial reference associating the stag with lechery.

66. For more on the rabbit as a sexual symbol, particularly in Old French literature, see Claude K. Abraham, "Myth and Symbol: The Rabbit in Medieval France," *Studies in Philology*, 60 (1963), 584–97. For folk and mythological lore on the rabbit, see George Ewart Evans and David Thomson, *The Leaping Hare* (London: Faber and Faber, 1972).

67. See *Liber de Spiritu et Anima*, PL 40, 819–20. This work was formerly attributed to Augustine but is now thought to be the work of Alcher of Claivaux.

68. Trapp, 251–2.

69. Reproduced in Erwin Panofsky, *The Life and Art of Albrecht Dürer* (Princeton: Princeton University Press, 1955), fig. 195.

70. See H.T. Musper, *Albrecht Dürer*, trans. Robert Erich Wolf (New York: H.N. Abrams, 1962), 104, on a pair of panels painted in 1507.

71. Reproduced in *The Complete Engravings, Etchings and Drypoints of Albrecht Dürer*, ed. Walter L. Strauss (New York: Dover Publications, 1972), fig. 42.

72. Pedro Mexio, *The Treasvrie of Avncient and Moderne Times*, trans. Thomas Milles (London: W. Iaggard, 1613), I, 28.

73. *Pseudodoxia Epidemica*, V, iv, in *The Works of Sir Thomas Browne*, ed. Geoffrey Keynes (Chicago: University of Chicago Press, 1964), II, 344.

74. Edward Topsell, *The History of Serpents* (1608, 1658; rpt. New York: Da Capo, 1967), 711.

CONTRIBUTORS

JANETTA REBOLD BENTON is Professor of Art History at Pace University, Pleasantville, New York, and Lecturer at the Metropolitan Museum of Art in New York. Dr. Benton is the author of *The Medieval Menagerie: Animals in the Art of the Middle Ages* (French edition, *Bestiaire Médiéval*) (New York, 1992) and guest curator and catalogue author for the exhibition *Medieval Monsters: Dragons and Fantastic Creatures*, Katonah Museum of Art, Katonah, New York, 1995. Articles by Dr. Benton appear in *Zeitschrift für Kunstgeschichte*, *Artibus et Historiae*, *Arte Medievale*, and elsewhere. She is co-author of *The Humanities*, a major text on global cultures, forthcoming from Prentice-Hall.

NONA C. FLORES is a graduate of Harvard University and completed her Ph.D. in English at the University of Illinois at Urbana-Champaign. Her research interests include medieval and Renaissance iconography as well as the use of animals in medieval literature and art.

STEPHEN O. GLOSECKI was educated at Beloit College, the University of California at Davis, and Oxford University. He is currently Associate Professor of English at the University of Alabama at Birmingham. An Anglo-Saxonist, he is primarily interested in Old English poetry, particularly *Beowulf*, the elegies, and the charms. Also interested in Old Norse literature, Glosecki spent 1991–2 as Fulbright Professor at the University of Tromsø in Norway. The essay published here reflects his ongoing exploration of the overlap between early Germanic graphic and literary arts, especially as embodied in animal imagery. Accordingly, his work applies anthropological and archeological approaches to the study of classical Germanic literature.

NORMAN HINTON is Professor and Chair of English at Sangamon State University in Springfield, Illinois. His main research interests are in Middle English language and literature, as well as the history of the English langauge and modern popular fiction.

LESLEY KORDECKI is Associate Professor and Chairperson of English at Barat College in Lake Forest, Illinois. She has published a number of articles on how Middle English writers gloss animals in their texts, and is currently at work on a study of Chaucer's *Manciple's Tale*.

DIETMAR PEIL is Professor of German Language and Literature of the Middle Ages at Ludwig-Maximilians-University, Munich. He has published articles and books about Middle High German literature (*Die Gebärde bei Chrétien, Hartmann und Wolfram* [Munich, 1975]), emblematics (*Zur "angewandten Emblematik" in protestantischen Erbauungsbüchern* [Heidelberg, 1978]), historical metaphorology (*Untersuchungen zur Staats- und Herrschaftsmetaphorik in literarischen Zeugnissen von der Antike bis zur Gegenwarrt* [Munich, 1983]), and proverbs and fables (*Der Streit der Gleider mit dem Magen: Studien zur Fabel des Menemius Agrippa von der Antike bis ins 20 Jahrhundert* [Frankfurt, 1985]). He has edited the most compendious German beast epic (Georg Rollenhagen's *Froschmeuseler*, 1595 [Frankfurt, 1989]) and a religious emblem book (Dilherr/Harsdörffer, *Drei-ständige Sonn- und Festtag-Emblemata, oder Sinne-Bilder*, 1660 [rpt. Hildesheim, 1994]).

MARY E. ROBBINS directs the Office of Graduate Studies for the College of Arts and Sciences at Georgia State University and teaches in the Department of English. Her research is in Middle Scots literature.

JOYCE E. SALISBURY is Frankenthal Professor of History at the University of Wisconsin-Green Bay. Her most recent books include *The Beast Within: Animals and Bestiality in the Middle Ages, Church Fathers, Independent Virgins*, and *Medieval Sexuality: A Research Guide* and edited volumes on *The Medieval World of Nature* and *Sex in the Middle Ages*.

DAVID A. SPRUNGER is Assistant Professor of English and Discourse at Concordia College in Moorhead, Minnesota. His fields of specialization are folklore and Old and Middle English languages and literature. His research interests include medicine, madness, and wildness in medieval literature and art, and he is currently working on a study of the Perilous Bed.

General Index

cathedrals: Autun (St-Lazare), 151, 158;
Bourges, 158; Burgos, 159; Laon,
152; Le Puy, 37, 158–9;
Nürnberg, 43; Paris (Notre-
Dame), 175–6; Poitiers (St-Pierre),
156; Strasbourg, 43; Toul, 160,
(St-Etienne) 151, 159; Ulm
179–81
Caxton's Mirrour of the World, 35
Chaucer, Geoffrey, 144; *The Canterbury
Tales*, 87; *General Prologue*, 67,
69; *Knight's Tale*, 176; *Manciple's
Tale*, 87; *Merchant's Tale*, 172;
Nun's Priest's Tale, 78; *Parson's
Tale*, 87; *Wife of Bath's Tale*, 89;
House of Fame, 85; *Parlement of
Foules*, 86; *Troilus and Criseyde*,
134, 143, 144; Ellesmere Chaucer,
69, 71
Christ, 155; and Eucharist, 42; as a lion,
91–2, 94–5, 152, 154
churches: Beaulieu (St-Pierre), 158;
Cahors (St-Etienne), 156;
Conques (St-Foy), 158;
Eggenfelden (Pfarrkirche), 38;
Hall-in-Tyrol (Pfarrkirche),
38; Hylestad, 6, 7; Neufchatel-
en-Bray (Notre-Dame), 158;
Semur-en-Auxois (Notre-Dame),
151; Thaxted, 152, 160; Urnes,
4, 6, 15; Vegusdal, 6; Vézelay
(St-Madeleine), 155, 158;
Villefranche-sur-Saône (Notre-
Dame-des-Marais), 151
Cistercian order, 50, 62
Clement of Alexandria, *Exhortation to the
Heathen*, 173
Coeur, Jacques, 152, 160
comedy, 135–6, 141–2, 144
Comestor, Peter, *Historia Scholastica*,
167–8, 169, 170, 173–4, 177,
183, 185
Corpus Christi pageants, 41 (*see also*
mystery plays)
costume and clothing, 69–70, 72, 75,
182; crowns, 172, 179–80,
182, 185; hair and hairstyles,
172, 179, 185, 187; hats
and headdresses, 72, 179
(*see also* sumptuary laws)
court society, animals as mirrors of, 50, 52,
60–4
Cranach the Elder, Lucas, 188–90
Creation of Eve, 175

Damianus, Petrus, *De bono religiosi status*, 120
De bestiis et aliis rebus, 112, 121
death, 25, 30–1, 32, 41, 173
deceit/deceitful, 172, 174, 178, 179, 186,
187, 189
Defoe, Daniel, *History of the Devil*, 170
Deguileville, Guillaume de, *The Pilgrimage
of the Life of Man*, 36
devils and demons, 29, 31, 39, 41, 157, 158;
Combat of Demons, 158 (*see also*
Satan)
discourse, 87, 90, 91, 92, 95, 96, 99 (*see
also* speech)
doctors, 67–79; iconographic representations, 69–71, 75 (*see also* medicine,
practice of)
Dominican order, 76
Dürer, Albrecht, 188

eating/devouring, images of, xi–xii, 30, 31–
32, 34–42 (*see also* gluttony)
ecclesiastical society, animals as mirrors of,
50, 52, 60–4
eiron, xiv, 135–6, 142, 143, 144; as *servus
dolosus*, 136, 141; as tricky servant,
xiv, 136, 137, 138, 141–2, 143
Eleanor of Aquitaine, 50
Emblemata, 103, 104, 113, 121
emblems and emblem books, xiii, 30, 99,
103–22; death emblem, 30–1; early
Germanic battle emblems, 7–11,
16; heraldic emblems, 154
encyclopedias of natural history, 88, 94, 121,
168, 174 (*see also* natural history)
envy, 36, 176
epic literature, 11, 12
Epiphanius, St., *Physiologus*, 104–6, 108,
110–2, 113–5, 121
Eucherius of Lyon, St., 120
Eve/Mary typology, 176
exegesis, 89–92, 96, 103
exemplar literature, 33, 49
Expulsion from Paradise, 175, 179, 187

fable literature, 86, 88; classical, 50–1, 52;
socio-political conservatism of, 51–
2, 54–5, 57–60; used to reflect con-
temporary society, xii, 49–64
Fabri, Iohannes, 119
Fáfnismál, 9, 16
Fall of Man (*see* Temptation and Fall of Man)
Fasciculus Morum, 37–9
Feast of Fools, 157
flattery, 177, 182; Flattery, 181

Index of Animals and Creatures

mermaid, 156, 173, 176
monkey, 152
mouse, 59, 62, 63

nightingale, 85

onocentaur, 90, 98–9 (*see also* centaur)
owl, 26, 77–8, 85
ox, 52, 58, 67

panotii, 154
panther, 90, 96, 98, 112, 113
pelican, x, 105, 110–1
phoenix, x, 111–2, 121
predators, 52–4, 56
pygmies, 73

rabbit, 58, 67, 75–6, 187
rat, 62
raven, 4, 19, 59–60
reptiles, 33

salamander, 26, 168
satyr, 156
sciopods, 154
scorpion, 39, 171, 172–3, 174; as symbol of the devil 173; Scorpio 172
serpent, 4, 31, 90, 96–7, 158, 167, 176, 177, 179, 188; serpent's tail, 173, 182 (*see also* snake)

sheep, 55–6, 60, 61, 93, 187
siren, 90, 98–9, 156, 171, 173–4; as symbol of the devil, 173; siren's song, 173
snail, 67
snake, 29, 32, 33, 35, 39, 112, 176, 185, 187 (*see also* serpent)
sphinx, 156
spider, 31, 35–6, 90, 99
stag, 9, 90, 96, 99, 187
stork, 29, 59, 72, 73

toad, xi, 25–43, 63
tortoise, 59
triton, 156
turtledove, 90

unicorn, x

viper, 31, 105, 112, 171–2, 174

walrus, 158
water-lizards, 34
weevil, 39
werewolf, xiv, 133–45
whale, x, 98, 99
wolf, 9, 14, 19, 53, 54, 55–6, 61, 64, 73–5, 138, 142; Fenrir, 14; Geri and Freki, 14; Isegrim, 54
worm, 31, 34, 35, 37, 41; as *vermis* 172